DEEP TRUTH

ALSO BY ADRIAN HAVILL

The Last Mogul:
The Unauthorized Biography of Jack Kent Cooke

DEEP TRUTH

The Lives of Bob Woodward and Carl Bernstein

Adrian Havill

A Birch Lane Press Book

Published by Carol Publishing Group

Lines from "Meru" are reprinted with permission of Macmillan
Publishing Company from *The Poems of W.B. Yeats: A New Edition*,
edited by Richard J. Finneran. Copyright 1934 by Macmillan Publishing
Company, renewed 1962 by Bertha Georgie Yeats.

Excerpts from the transcript of "Larry King Live," March 30, 1989, are
used with permission.

A Birch Lane Press Book
Published by Carol Publishing Group
Birch Lane Press is a registered trademark of Carol Communications, Inc.
Editorial Offices: 600 Madison Avenue, New York, N.Y. 10022
Sales and Distribution Offices: 120 Enterprise Avenue, Secaucus, N.J.
    07094
In Canada: Canadian Manda Group, P.O. Box 920, Station U, Toronto,
    Ontario M8Z 5P9
Queries regarding rights and permissions should be addressed to
Carol Publishing Group, 600 Madison Avenue, New York, N.Y. 10022

Carol Publishing Group books are available at special discounts for bulk
purchases, for sales promotion, fund-raising, or educational purposes.
Special editions can be created to specifications. For details, contact: Special
Sales Department, Carol Publishing Group, 120 Enterprise Avenue,
Secaucus, N.J. 07094

Manufactured in the United States of America
10 9 8 7 6 5 4 3 2 1

Library of Congress Cataloging-in-Publication Data

Havill, Adrian.
    Deep truth : the lives of Bob Woodward and Carl Bernstein /
|by Adrian Havill.
        p.   cm.
    ISBN 1–55972–172–3
    1. Woodward, Bob. 2. Bernstein, Carol, 1944–   . 3. Journalists—
United States—20th century—Biography. I. Title.
PN4874.W6H38   1993
070'.92—dc20
[B]   92-35892
                                                              CIP

This book is for
A.D.H.
and especially
Georgiana

"I have a dark side which I conceal. . . . Everyone has to be interested in his or her own demons. I'm not sure what mine are."

—Bob Woodward, as quoted by
the *Wheaton* (Ill.) *Journal*, 1984

"It's now gotten to the point where sometimes I can't remember what happened in real life, what happens in the book and what happens in the movie."

—Carl Bernstein, as quoted by
Playboy magazine, 1986

"If somebody sets out to lie, you're dead. . . . Walter Lippmann said it all in 1910 . . . to make the truth emerge. You don't get it right the first time. You get a single small bite. . . . It takes years."

—Ben Bradlee to David Frost
on public television, 1991

CONTENTS

PREFACE

In December of 1990 I was finishing up a book on the life of the irascible, thrice-divorced, billionaire owner of the Washington Redskins, Jack Kent Cooke. When I called my literary agent, Jane Dystel, to tell her the book was complete, she urged me to begin another book "right away."

"Don't sit around until the book comes out," she told me. "Start another project now."

Jack Kent Cooke had been a challenge. His attorneys had threatened my publishers with legal action if any parts of the book were in error, they had subpoenaed me, and three of them put me through a three-hour interrogation. Cooke himself had unearthed old friends and employees and commanded them not to speak with his unwanted biographer.

So I decided to write about two of my heroes, Bob Woodward and Carl Bernstein. Bob and Carl had certainly seen their share of controversy, but as defenders of the First Amendment they would at least talk with me. And they certainly wouldn't try to prevent people from speaking to me.

I wrote to both Bob and Carl the day after the review of my book on Mr. Cooke appeared in the *Washington Post* (to avoid any question of conflict). They were asked for an interview, asked to give me names of people with whom they thought I should talk, and were offered fact-checking privileges. They never answered. Sources in New York told me Carl was "upset." I soon learned of Bob Woodward's views. After speaking with his second wife, Francie Barnard, by phone three times, I asked her for a face-to-face interview. She told me that it was "okay" with her, but she would have to "check with Bob." It wasn't okay with Bob. He told her, "Surely you have better things to do with your time."

Scott Armstrong, one of Bob's closest friends, was a similar story. When we first spoke, in March of 1992, he was pleasant and gave me some biographical facts, but he was "doing a conference"

and could I "call back next week." I called during the first week of
April, and Scott said he was busy. Still, I managed to glean more
information from him during our conversation. He asked me to
phone again during the third week of the month.

On the third Monday of April I called Scott. He was going to be
with lawyers on a Freedom of Information inquiry but "Thursday
looks good—call me then." I did. Now Scott said, "I talked to
Woodward. He doesn't think this is a good time for such a project."

I disagreed. I told Scott in the same words I had written to Bob
and Carl that 1992 was the twentieth anniversary of the Watergate
break-in, 1994 was the twentieth anniversary of Richard Nixon's
resignation, and between those two dates both Bob and Carl
would reach their fiftieth birthdays. In addition, I told Scott, there
was a long and varied body of work that could be examined.

But Scott was now "too busy." Suddenly, he wouldn't even
confirm his father's occupation. But Scott had a suggestion. Why
not mail him some chapters of the book and he would review
them and "attempt to help." I told him that I would have to check
that with my publisher, wondering at the same time what Scott's
reaction would have been if Richard Nixon had asked to read
some of the draft chapters of *The Final Days*. When I countered
with a suggestion that I submit written questions, Scott was again
"too busy."

Bob Woodward told the Canadian newsmagazine *Maclean's* in
1980 that he "believed in the First Amendment, with no footnotes
or exceptions, and if [his colleagues] wanted to spend the time,
they should go ahead and talk. I don't think people should be
afraid of their secrets." Bob Woodward has changed.

Perhaps the long buildup of controversy that presently surrounds him and Carl Bernstein has created a thin skin. In February
of 1992, Bob chastised a young reporter for the *New York Times* for
asking questions he thought were a little impertinent. Then he
telephoned the reporter's editor to further complain. He was also
reported to be "startled" when a *USA Today* reporter wrote that
the "nestlike" retreat near Annapolis, Maryland, in a spread in
House and Garden magazine was Bob's, even though he had allowed the pictorial. The place was described as belonging to
"prominent Washington journalists"—the other journalist being
Elsa Walsh, Bob's third wife. "Is there no privacy?" he said.

If *USA Today* was puzzled, it had every right. Just a few months earlier, Bob had willingly posed, snuggled up to Elsa Walsh, at his Washington home for *People* magazine in order to promote his new book, *The Commanders*. A year later he posed for *Esquire* for two pictures—one kissing his wife, the other with her sitting on his lap—while at the same time turning down as "inappropriate" a request to have his picture displayed on the wall of a Washington restaurant near a photo of his former editor Ben Bradlee.

Carl currently spends part of each interview he gives railing against celebrity journalism. In March of 1992, he told the CNBC cable television network, "When gossip columnists are accorded as much attention by their news organizations as we reporters, something is askew." That's interesting, considering that the biggest complaint by critics of one successful book he cowrote, *The Final Days*, was that it was "too gossipy." Carl was also not above revealing personal information about his parents in his last book, *Loyalties*, even after they begged him not to. In Carl's words, his father "wanted to register his disapproval in the strongest terms."

Carl, too, has seemed to want the line between privacy and a public life drawn by him alone. While complaining about the press and its intrusion into his private life, Carl was not reluctant to pose for *GQ*, a men's fashion magazine, in January of 1991 for a six-page spread in which he showed off his New York apartment's furnishings. The tour included photographs of his bathroom and bedroom and coy references to some of the women in his life. He described one brass lamp as belonging to close friend Kathleen Tynan and made sure the magazine's writer saw that his Rolodex was open to actress Elizabeth Taylor's numerous phone numbers. In June of 1992 he would pick a fight with Geraldo Rivera and Phil Donahue by calling their programs "freak shows." Rivera would respond by calling Carl a "failed TV journalist."

This book is not a "revisionist" Watergate book in the manner of *Silent Coup* or its predecessor, *Secret Agenda*. It is a biography, a presentation of two lives. I neither have a point of view nor claim any "conspiracy" theories. The revelations within evolved from simple curiosity and diligent fact-finding efforts over a two-year period.

I suspect Carl and Bob will have a lot to say after reading this book. So be it. It is an honest, balanced book with no ax to grind.

At the end, there is a list of people interviewed, a bibliography, and other source notes.

Adrian Havill
Reston, Virginia
March 1993

INTRODUCTION

T HE STENCH of the rotting, rancid flesh of animals had been with the writer for weeks. The stink permeated his clothing, seeping into the pores of his skin. It was with him wherever he went during the day and haunted his nights. The young novelist wondered if it was worth it. To live under such conditions was less than human, certainly not worth the $500 advance he had received from his publisher.

In six weeks' time he had witnessed horrors that, years later, would cause him to shudder when the subject was broached. There had been rats tossed in with beef and diseased pork, then ground together and liberally dosed with spices to make potted meats. He had seen it with his own eyes. He had witnessed goats being butchered and then displayed in butcher shops as fresh lamb. And he had been told of men who had fallen into the giant, boiling vats of the slaughterhouses and who were later reincarnated as hundreds of single-pound blocks labeled "pure lard."

Who would care? The young Upton Sinclair had already written five books that had gone largely unnoticed. The royalties from all five had yielded less than $1,000. Why should one think that the plight of these poor, this underclass of men and women who butchered diseased animals in the heart of Midwestern America, would raise the eyebrows of the populace, let alone the powerful?

But sweeping fundamental changes had taken place since the great Civil War. The first was education. Thirty years before the beginning of the twentieth century, 7 million students had been enrolled in public high schools. By 1900, that number had more than doubled to just under 16 million. Americans were becoming literate, great masses of them.

Reading matter, at least in terms of magazines, was changing as well. The snob and literary appeal of *Harper's*, *The Atlantic Monthly* and *Scribner's*, which all sold at an expensive thirty-five cents, was giving way to the appeal of a new breed of monthlies. These included *Cosmopolitan* and *Munsey's*, which were written for ordinary people. A new upstart, *McClure's*, was going in for sensational exposés. Aimed at the pocketbooks of the literate poor, these periodicals sold for just fifteen cents.

The more-than-half-price savings were made possible by a new type of paper and innovations in the printing process. Expensive rag papers were being replaced by glaze-coated stock made from wood pulp. New engraving methods made illustrations and photographs easy to place throughout the publications. A revolution in publishing had begun.

McClure's first edition, in 1895, had a pressrun of 120,000 copies. Ten years later, each edition would total nearly half a million. The magazine had something for everyone. There were fiction and nonfiction, debates between public figures, and, even more important, articles that pressed for social reform.

Price wars flared, as did a drive to see which magazine could produce the most sensational, hair-raising articles. *Cosmopolitan* went to twelve and half cents a copy, *Munsey's* to a dime, and then *Cosmopolitan* and *McClure's* matched the ten-cent price. A writer named Lincoln Steffens wrote a series of articles called "The Shame of the Cities" for *McClure's* in which he toured America, highlighting corruption in Minneapolis, Chicago, St. Louis, Pittsburgh, Philadelphia and New York. William Randolph Hearst's *Cosmopolitan* countered with such articles as "The Treason of the Senate."

It was "The Treason of the Senate" piece that prodded President Theodore Roosevelt to call the new journalists "muckrakers." The president, quoting from *Pilgrim's Progress* in a speech to the Gridiron Club in Washington, said that such a writer could "look no way but downward, with a muckrake in his hands, but who would neither look up nor regard the crown he was offered but continued to rake to himself, the filth of the floor."

In "The Treason of the Senate," journalist Charles Edward Russell observed that the elected senators were "well-fed and portly gentlemen" who served as "a chamber of butlers for industrialists and financiers." The article, written by David Graham Phillips, disclosed damning tidbits, such as that Sen. Chauncey Depew of New York served on the board of directors of seventy companies and received more than $50,000 a year for his services. Henry Cabot Lodge was described as "the familiar coarse type of machine politician disguised by the robe of 'gentleman scholar.' "

The series concluded, "A corrupt system explains a corrupt man; it does not excuse a corrupt man."

Roosevelt, in addition to condemning muckrakers, wrote a letter to the editor-in-chief of the *Saturday Evening Post* saying that Phillips's articles did not do "anything but harm. They contain so much more falsehood than truth that they give no accurate guide for those who are really anxious to war against corruption, and they do excite a hysterical and ignorant feeling against everything existing, good or bad."

Muckrakers—a new breed of writers who both exposed wrongs and pressed for social changes through their writings—were everywhere at the beginning of the twentieth century. Among them was Ida M. Tarbell, perhaps the "mother" of the muckraker movement. Her series on Standard Oil, which ran in *McClure's* beginning in 1902, fearlessly exposed a powerful John D. Rockefeller and his illegal dealings with railroads. Tarbell traced Rockefeller's wealth and his near-monopoly in petroleum to "rebates" he got from railroads in transporting oil from the source in Pennsylvania to the refineries of Cleveland.

Will Irwin wrote on graft in Chicago in a 1909 *Collier's* article. "I went to Chicago," he wrote, "and established that the collectors for the 1st Ward machine were shaking down the department stores, the office buildings, the saloons, the gamblers, the madams of the bawdy houses, even the small prostitutes of the cribs— everyone who needed influence or protection—from two to 500 tickets apiece."

Irwin was referring to a ward ball, funded by the criminal elements of the city for the benefit of a Chicago politician. Writing about it for *Collier's* in a deadpan manner, Irwin described those present as "women of the half-world and of no world, all in the cheapest, dirtiest and most abbreviated costumes, hired, for two dollars and deposit, from professional customers; scrubby little bags of the slums, patching out their Sunday clothes with five-cent masks that they might obey the rules of the floor; pickpockets, refraining, by the truce of the Devil which reigned that night, from plying their trade; scarlet women and the yellow men who live from and by them; bartenders; professional repeaters; small politicians; prosperous beggars; saloon bouncers; prizefight promoters; liquor salesmen; police captains; runners for gambling houses." After the piece was printed, no more ward balls were held.

Ida Tarbell, Lincoln Steffens, and Will Irwin were examples of a new breed of writer. They wrote to raise the conscience of a newly literate populace that could not only read, but vote.

America, in danger of being controlled by a few families, was in need of social reform. It could have gone the way of South American "democracies" without the changes wrought by the articles and the books of a wide-open press. In 1900, 10 percent of the population controlled 90 percent of the nation's wealth.

The new journalism at the beginning of the twentieth century may have prevented America from becoming the domain of a rich minority ruling a majority of citizens enslaved by poverty. The Standard Oil monopoly was broken up. The graft and bribes of city governments were diminished although not eradicated. The country was no longer apathetic nor as overly trusting of its elected leaders.

The muckraking movement thrived just over a decade before dying out. The public began to tire of an endless diet of articles on corruption and government injustices. Advertisers in the magazines began complaining of the environment in which they were forced to appear. The magazines began to get regular pressure from the corporations that paid the ad bills. The government began to reform itself, curbing its excesses. And the onset of World War I focused attention on international conflict and away from domestic problems.

A half century later, a new era of muckraking began. In its embryonic form, it could be said to have originated in the daily newspaper columns of Drew Pearson, who would later pass his torch to Jack Anderson. In the 1960s, when the lies about Vietnam gave false hope to so many Americans, there would be journalists such as Seymour M. Hersh, who would unearth the ugly realities of My Lai, secret bombings in Cambodia, and Henry Kissinger's electronic eavesdropping on his own staff assistants. Some would credit Hersh with being a singular force in turning the nation against the war in Southeast Asia.

But of all the investigative journalists of the last half of the century, two—Robert Upshur Woodward and Carl Milton Bernstein—would become, partly by accident but also through contacts, persistence, and hard work, more famous than all their peers combined. With the fame would come riches and strife. Together or separately, they would become better known than many of their subjects. The peak of their fame would arrive shortly after their emergence on the public stage. After that, there would be decades of controversy for Bob Woodward. His prolific output of books would bear severe scrutiny and expressed doubt. For Carl Bernstein there would be a series of public adventures that would result in a sharp, precipitous fall, transposing his reputation from that of a "character" to a caricature.

The works of Woodward and Bernstein, like those of Upton Sinclair, would lay bare and explain the inner workings of an institution or expose a political system gone wrong. Sinclair revealed corruption through novels based on fact and experience. "Woodstein," as they would come to be known in their early days, would write books of fact that read like novels. The two forms merged as one, the reader never being sure what was poetic enhancement, what was cold fact. Yet no matter how those books were scrutinized, they did result in political reforms.

Alistair Cooke, the sage of Public Broadcasting, summarized the new muckraking journalists shortly after the publication of Bob and Carl's first book, *All the President's Men*, by heralding "the great age of muckraking. Anything a public official does wrong will wind up on the front page."

The odor of decaying flesh stayed in Upton Sinclair's clothes for weeks after he returned to New Jersey. He isolated himself in an eight-by-ten-foot cabin on a hillside near Princeton and began writing. He finished the manuscript in nine months.

The magazine that serialized his book on unclean meat and the plight of the workers who slaughtered and processed the animals, *Appeal to Reason*, was a publication aimed at the working class. The issues containing Sinclair's episodes, now called *The Jungle*, sold out, and readers who couldn't find copies inundated the periodical's offices with mail orders for back issues.

Still, the writer couldn't find a book publisher, even though *Appeal to Reason* had twelve thousand orders for the story in a more permanent form. Five New York firms rejected the book as being too controversial.

Eventually, Doubleday, Page and Company told the young author that it would publish the book if its contents could be examined in a most unusual fashion. The publisher would send one of its editors to Chicago to interview sources and investigate the writer's charges. In essence, the Doubleday employee would be recreating the experiences by living in much the same manner.

This resulted in the editor's not only verifying Sinclair's charges but adding this postscript: "I prowled over its foul-smelling domain and I was able to see with my own eyes much that Sinclair had never even heard about."

When *The Jungle* was published by Doubleday in early 1906, it riveted public attention to the question of the purity of meat sold at retail in civilized nations worldwide. President Theodore Roosevelt, spotting a good and just cause, made political hay by inviting the writer to the White House and, in effect, giving the book his personal endorsement.

The meat-packing industry fought back, even to the extent of attacking Sinclair as being mentally unbalanced. It ran ads and placed articles by ghostwriters in popular magazines of the day. Nothing worked. An amendment to an agriculture appropriation bill extended government inspections to every meat-preparation process. The Pure Food and Drug Act was passed. The Beef Inspection Act was passed. All this took place within a year after *The Jungle* was published.

The Jungle was by far the most successful of Upton Sinclair's many books. His novels, which continued to preach social reform, eventually received nearly eight hundred translations in forty-seven different languages. Sinclair tried to join the system he had changed. The author would unsuccessfully run for a seat as a U.S. congressman, then senator, and would even come close to a victory in a race for the California governorship. But *The Jungle* would be the high point of his life, and he would always be remembered for it.

When Upton Sinclair neared his ninetieth birthday, he was invited to the White House again, this time by a beleaguered Lyndon Johnson, in December of 1967. The eighty-nine-year-old writer stood side by side with a new breed of muckraker, a thirty-three-year-old Ralph Nader, to witness the president's signing of yet another meat-inspection bill into law.

"This bill crowns the crusade you began sixty years ago," the *Washington Post* quoted Johnson as saying to Sinclair. And for Nader's benefit, the president added that the new law was "a landmark in consumer protection."

Just blocks away from the president, who would a year later give way to a resurrected Richard Nixon, Carl Bernstein hammered out yet another investigative piece on landlord violations at a once-elegant apartment building in Washington, Clifton Terrace.

Carl was already tired of his *Post* duties. He wanted to be a full-time critic—of rock-'n'-roll music—but the *Post* wouldn't give him that niche. Less than five years later, he would become involved in another muckraking crusade. It would catapult him and an earnest partner, Bob Woodward (in 1967 a naval officer at sea desperately seeking to avoid direct contact with the Vietnam conflict), to become a part of American history. Bob and Carl's assignment to the simple burglary that came to be known as Watergate would result in the resignation of the president of the United States.

DEEP TRUTH

1

[Bob, 1943–61]

Most Likely to Succeed

GENEVA, ILLINOIS, thirty-five miles west of Chicago, is, according to the local citizenry, where the commuter rail ends and the prairie begins. Geneva, the governmental seat of Kane County, is also the center of the Fox River Valley, a Brigadoon-like land where soy and corn crop futures are still discussed in the spring and accorded the same degree of importance as the annual prospects of the Cubs and White Sox.

The Fox originates far to the north in Wisconsin. It is a pleasant though shallow river with enough bass and catfish to keep a casual fisherman happy. It is wide enough to accommodate water-skiers and small boats in the summer. In the winter it is host to ice skaters and hockey games. The Fox runs south, eventually emptying into the Illinois River. That tributary carries the brown waters of the Fox to St. Louis, Missouri, where it becomes part of the Mississippi. The Illinois, Fox and hundreds of other smaller rivers and streams contribute to the width and might of the Mississippi, providing its majesty. The combined flow of water and silt travels more than a thousand miles south until it reaches New Orleans and empties into the Gulf of Mexico.

It was to Geneva, during the last week of March 1943, that Alfred Eno Woodward drove with his bride, Jane, to the Geneva Hospital for the birth of their first child. Al and Jane were from Wheaton, about fifteen miles away. There was no medical facility in Wheaton or in its surrounding county. Community Hospital in Geneva, a large, venerable old stone house built in Dutch colonial style, was the closest destination for a sterile birth.[1]

3

It had warmed that day to thirty-eight degrees in these communities west of Chicago, but it was a false spring. Patches of snow were still on the ground from the flurries that had fallen on March 21. The remaining drifts crunched underfoot, but were soft below the crust, like good bread. It would become colder again before the end of the month.

Births at the Geneva Hospital in 1943 were more primitive than today. The initial stages of labor were spent in a five-bed maternity ward. In the delivery room, a woman was generally "knocked out" with ether, the alternative being the injection of an anesthetic into the spinal column. But there was an additional reason for concern. The world then was in the midst of an epic struggle—a war to which more than half the nations of the world had committed both arms and men's lives. Al and Jane knew that soon after the birth of their child Al would leave their small house on East Wesley Street in Wheaton and be gone for the duration of the conflict. A naval commission as a communications officer, "radio electronics," awaited.

Jane gave birth to a boy on March 26, 1943. He weighed just over eight pounds and was named Robert Upshur Woodward. Upshur was Jane's maiden name, and Robert was the name of more than one of Al's ancestors. Al left for the war two and a half months after their son was brought home to Wheaton, in Du Page County, Illinois.

Al Woodward was from the southeast corner of De Kalb County, nearly halfway between Chicago and the Iowa border. The village in which he had grown up, Sandwich, contained just over three thousand people. His father had managed the John Deere plant in Dixon, 50 miles away, and the roots of the Woodward family can be traced back to the midnineteenth century in Illinois.

Al Woodward had been a small but wiry football star, just over 150 pounds, at tiny Oberlin College, just outside Cleveland, Ohio. As a senior, he had been the captain of the team. After graduation and upon receiving a law degree, Al and his older brother, John, also an attorney, apprenticed themselves to Bert and Bill Rathje, two dour Scandinavians who headed one of Wheaton's better-known law firms.[2] Bert's father had been a judge in Du Page County, as Bert himself would later become. Although interrupted by the war, the law firm of Rathje and Woodward was soon to become one of the most highly regarded in the far-west

Chicago suburbs. Al's specialty was trial law, and the hometown *Wheaton Journal* would later write that "he has one of the most brilliant legal minds in the county."

Rathje and Woodward's offices in the 1940s were at 123 Front Street in Wheaton, on the top floor of a two-story office building in the middle of a commercial block. Front Street, so called because it fronted the railroad tracks of the Chicago, Aurora, and Elgin line that ran through town, vibrated several times an hour with bustling commuter trains. Running parallel were groaning freight engines from the Chicago and Western Pacific railroad network pulling seemingly endless strings of open cars piled high with coal or cattle. Rathje and Woodward's offices—on the "right" rather than the "wrong" side of those tracks—looked out on the heart of Wheaton, the train depot itself. From those windows, they could observe the daily growth of the town, then a village of just under thirty thousand.[3] Today, a limited form of urban renewal has made its way to the center of the suburb, and the old station is flanked by trendy eating places and shops.

The Midwestern states of the United States—Ohio, Indiana, Illinois and Iowa—have always seemed to exemplify the very ideals of America. But these virtues of religion, hard work and family were even further distilled in Wheaton. Wheaton was not a microcosm of America but rather the essence of what many upright American citizens believed was a near-perfect place in which to live, a Norman Rockwell canvas. The town's utopian appearance was a natural result of being initially populated by hardy pioneers, who succeeded through tenacity and a devout dedication to Protestant principles. The fertile prairie embraced them and rewarded their hard work with productive lands, fueling the prevalent belief that all things were possible. The squalor of inner-city life were alien ideas given substance only by the intruding headlines from the major Chicago dailies.

Wheaton was founded by Warren and Jesse Wheaton, who claimed most of the land shortly after arriving in 1835 from Putnam, Connecticut. The two Wheaton brothers' stated mission was to form an "ideal" town, basing their concept on "hard work and Christian ethics." In 1848, they offered the city of Chicago free passage through their land in exchange for a railroad line the city was constructing. Chicago accepted, and after the tracks were laid, the Wheaton brothers built a depot with a plaque on it bearing their name. A few years later, they filed a twelve-block plat with Du Page County for the "City of Wheaton" and in 1859 incorporated the city. In 1860, the Wheaton brothers were persuaded by the village leaders to donate fifty acres of the town for the purpose of forming a Christian Bible college. In exchange they were promised by the founders that the school would be named for them. "This will save your heirs the expense of a good monument" was the promise made by one of the college's founders.

Wheaton College (motto: "Since 1860, for Christ and His Kingdom") is today still the backbone of the town. This is where William Franklin Graham, better known today as the evangelist Billy Graham, received his higher education. He would later fund the library and museum that bear his name.

David Halberstam, in *The Powers That Be*, his epic book on the American press, wrote about the baby-sitters who would come to the home of Al Woodward in Wheaton and in the course of an evening ask a young Bob, "Have you found Christ, Bob? Have you found Christ?" Young Robert Woodward would always answer in the affirmative. The smart alecks of the town would wisecrack back to the evangelists: "Why, is he lost again?" Bob never did.

But Wheaton would probably be a city of conservative Christian beliefs even without its college. According to a 1988 report by the City of Wheaton, there were thirty-five Protestant churches (many of them fundamental or evangelical) and three Catholic ones. A Protestant teen who even dated a Catholic during Bob Woodward's youth would have been "talked about." There were and still are no Jewish synagogues or "other" religious meeting places. The racial makeup in this WASP paradise, according to the same report, was 94.4 percent white, 2.6 percent black, and 3 percent "other." More than 40 percent of all adults had four or more years of college. The 1985 median income was nearly $37,000, a third higher than the national average. Republicans outnumbered Democrats on the voter rolls by nearly four to one—the highest GOP-to-Democrat majority in the country for incorporated municipalities. Unlike the rest of the nation, strong drink, as defined by liquor, beer or wine, was not sold in restaurants or stores in Wheaton until the late 1980s. A bizarre city statute said that alcoholic beverages were not allowed to be served even in the privacy of one's home. The beverage delivery vans from Chicago were stopped at the village borders and searched by police to insure the town's piety. And although there was little manufacturing of note, one of the few industries was the printing of Christian religious books and tracts.

Bob Woodward, in many ways, would come to typify the straight-arrow Calvinistic culture of Wheaton. It would be his strength in difficult times. The self-righteous ideals of the town would serve him well against sniping critics who would later question the ethics and veracity of his reporting. Honorable men, one might say, ignore such carping.

The memory dims when being asked to recall the place. "It was either in a basement on Cross Street in Wheaton or out behind the pony farm," Barbara Simpson remembered.⁴ "We were in the sixth grade, playing some sort of kissing game. I'm pretty sure it was Bob's first kiss."

It was the kind of event about which girls whisper at school the next day. Many others in the town of Wheaton were already murmuring in shocked tones, not about Bob, but the Woodward family. His mother, Jane, was having an affair with Robert Barnes. Extramarital activity was taboo in Wheaton, a straitlaced world with Peyton Place secrets.

"The Barnes affair was kept hush-hush," said Steven Matson, who lived across the street from Bob Woodward at the time. "Both families were prominent and divorce was a rarity." The 1955 separation and divorce took place just before Bob Woodward's thirteenth birthday.

Robert "Tom" Barnes, a Sears executive, was looser, more jovial than the hardworking Al Woodward. Bob's mother, after divorcing Al, moved away with her new husband to another western suburb, River Forest. Al Woodward got custody of the children.

Bob was now the eldest of three. Anne was four years younger, and David, born some ten years after Bob, was the "baby." After Hawthorne Elementary, Bob attended Wheaton Junior High School where he was named the "most outstanding boy" in the eighth grade. The Woodward divorce marked Bob's transition from intermediate to high school, and a noticeable change in his personality.

"Bob was more reserved in high school," a classmate remembered.

Another recalled, "He was considered a little stuck-up, always just outside the popular group."

Still, Bob showed himself to have a typically Midwestern work

ethic even though his family was affluent by Wheaton standards.
Teenage pocket money was picked up by caddying at the Glen
Oak golf course in nearby Glen Ellyn, where Al Woodward was a
member. Getting there meant catching a train on the Chicago,
Aurora, and Elgin rail line.[5] Bob also worked part-time in his
father's office for $11.75 a week. He soon learned about Wheaton's
secrets, and about those of his own family. Friends remember that
Bob's budding curiosity led him to rifle through law cases that
were casually stacked on the desks of Rathje and Woodward. One
contained the details of his father's divorce.

It was the announcement that the Soviets had launched Sputnik, *made
over the school intercom on October 4, 1957, that led Bob Woodward to
begin questioning adults. Until then, Bob had believed what all of Wheaton had believed—that America was superior to all other countries on the
face of God's earth.*

Bob felt betrayed. After Sputnik, *Bob began to ask hard questions of his
high school teachers and other Wheaton authority figures. When he got an
answer he didn't like or when the adult was evasive, Bob would follow
with an even harder question.*

*"What's the real issue there?" the teenage Bob Woodward liked to ask
the village elders.*

The Wheaton high school yearbook would attest to Bob's early
achievements by recording his "in" activities—football, track, student conference and student council. But there were other clubs
and endeavors in which Bob participated that might be considered
somewhat "nerdy." Bob Woodward was an avid ham-radio operator and part of the "pocket protector set" in junior high and
through his sophomore year. In his freshman term he belonged to
Wheaton High's radio club, which broadcast under the license of
K9TBM. What today would be "unhip" habits included member-
ships in the Latin club and the lighting crew. It was a serious
young Woodward who preferred bridge and chess to more frivo-
lous pursuits. He also stole into Chicago with best friend Paul
Chummers to attend Chicago Symphony concerts while other
Wheaton youths were spinning Elvis Presley 45-RPM vinyl discs
in their parents' dens. It was Al Woodward who fostered Bob's
love for serious music. Al, who had an impressive collection of
classical and jazz compositions, played music on a then-modern
hi-fi system. The sounds of Bach and Brubeck filled the house.

Bob went out for football hoping to emulate his father's gridiron achievements. At five feet ten inches and 170 pounds he was just an average size for his high school's pigskin wars. "He was a third-string running back on the football team," remembered Sonny "Atiba" Kee, a star halfback for the Wheaton Tigers.[6] "He was kind of slow."

Bob's lack of speed was also the reason why he lasted a single season on the track squad. Bob's teammates recall him as being a plodding but willing miler.

The eldest Woodward offspring soon discovered he was more suited to academics. In high school he always made the honor roll, and magazine profiles in the 1980s would say he was class valedictorian, which he was not. Bob's class ranking was far from the top among the 403 Wheaton High graduating seniors of 1961. Although he was one of four selected to speak at the graduation ceremonies, it had little to do with his class standing. He was voted the honor with three other classmates. His speech, "The Citizen and His Role in the Government," was right out of the Barry Goldwater wing of the Republican Party. The serious Bob Woodward was also voted "most likely to succeed."

"Bob was perceived as being arrogant, with a superior attitude," Steve Matson said. "He always had a political bent. He would be very nice to people if he was running for something."

Bob Woodward, who was elected class president in his sophomore year, seemed to fall from popularity among his peers as he advanced through high school. Running for president of student conference on a slate with Paul Chummers, Bob lost to a last-minute dark-horse candidate, Dave Pardonner. Bob was defeated easily. Pardonner, years later at a Wheaton high school reunion, said, "The only reason I ran was because there were so many people who didn't like Woodward."

A Wheaton High classmate and friend, Craig Simpson, who was Bob's campaign manager during his try for the student conference presidency, recalled, "He was a hard guy to package. He was always well-intended, but remote. In many ways, he was like Nixon."

High school nightlife in Wheaton, Illinois, during the late fifties could have been a model for the classic teen film *American Graffiti*. The increasingly introverted, classical-music-loving young Woodward had several requisites that ensured him a star role in Wheaton's Friday-night ritual of cars and burgers. Foremost was his access to his family's two-toned 1955 Chevrolet Bel Air convertible. Bob, the Chevy ragtop and friends were prominent among those making Friday-night cruises down the main avenues of Wheaton before heading over to nearby Glen Ellyn where one always made an obligatory circle of the A & W root-beer stand and McDonald's.[7] The young Woodward would wear the Wheaton youth uniform of the times—a checked cotton shirt exposing the white T-shirt underneath. Below that one wore jeans with the cuffs rolled up exactly twice.

Glen Ellyn was special. One necked and petted by the lake next to its high school. It was also in Glen Ellyn or Gee Eee, as it was called, just over the border from a dry and sober Wheaton, where Wheaton teens went to drink. "We all drank, of course," Craig Simpson remembered. "But Bob would never let completely loose. He never got drunk, never smoked."

Virtue notwithstanding, the teen-aged Bob Woodward forged a close relationship with neighbor Kathleen Middlekauff beginning in the ninth grade. Not a Wheaton native, Kathy had moved to the town with her parents when she was six from adjacent Cook County. Kathy Middlekauff was, according to several members of Bob's 1961 graduating class, beautiful, brilliant and popular. She was a cheerleader who, together with her best friend, Carolyn Billingsley, cavorted for the black and orange of the Fighting Tigers wearing a uniform consisting of a V-neck sweater over a turtle top and a short pleated plaid skirt. She was also on the school's honor roll. The daughter of an engineer, she had early aspirations to be a writer, long before the profession occurred to Bob Woodward himself.[8]

"I moved to New Jersey after my sophomore year," Kathy, who was a year behind Bob in high school, said. "We continued to write to one another and kept in touch by telephone. I also came back regularly to Wheaton to see my grandmother and Bob."

But the partial abandonment of both his steady girlfriend and his mother, compounded by Al Woodward's messy divorce followed by a subsequent remarriage three years later, may have contributed to Bob's dwindling popularity during his final high school years. Al Woodward's new wife, Alice, also had three children—she had previously been married to a Keebler Cookie executive. Al and his new wife then had a daughter, creating a his, hers and ours arrangement—a large household of seven children.

The more than doubling of family size led to a new home as well. The expanded but far from happy family moved from the modest New England–style clapboard house that featured two dormer windows (one of which provided a view from Bob's bedroom) on Cross Street. The more expansive white frame and brick rambler at 504 West Prairie was just south of Northside Park, Wheaton's main public recreational facility. Northside had a large public pool and a lagoon used for winter ice-skating. In the new house, Bob was given his own private phone, which included a separate listing in the Wheaton telephone book.

Bob viewed his new stepfamily with suspicion and jealousy. During one Christmas season the eldest son of Al Woodward looked up the prices of the gifts everyone had received and concluded that his stepbrothers and stepsister had gotten the most expensive presents. So distressed was the young Bob that he had a showdown with his father over it. "I confronted him," he told *Playboy* in 1989, "and showed him that the money he spent on them and on us was so dramatically out of balance . . . it was kind of sad, but the fact is that it's a very competitive world when two families are brought together that way." Bob disliked his new immaculately coiffed, frosted-blond stepmother. Years later he would accuse her of making "a mess of my little brother."

His new family was the main reason Bob's popularity declined all through high school. In his sophomore year, he was elected class president, Tiger Turnout chairman and, in all, compiled eleven listed clubs or credits. But by his senior year, he held no offices and the number of credits had been cut to five. Part of this demise could be chalked up to the departure of his steady girlfriend, Kathy Middlekauff, to New Jersey. His mother's affair, the subsequent remarriage of his father, the expansion of Al's children from three to seven seemingly overnight and the move to a new house, all within a five-year period, were tiny traumas that reshaped Bob Woodward. He evolved quickly and somewhat prematurely from a lively teen to an inward-looking young adult with a firstborn's classic determination to succeed.[9]

Bob's final high school yearbook photo was the most solemn on a page of ten seniors. His class quote, perhaps referring to his defeat for president of student conference, was, "Though I cannot out-vote them, I will out-argue them."

Bob Woodward wanted out of Wheaton. He became one of the few to head east for college and the only one of his graduating class to enroll at Yale University in New Haven, Connecticut. Part of the decision for attending the Ivy League school was to go away to college and be a thousand miles from a difficult family situation. Another was to be near Kathy Middlekauff, who had told him she planned to attend Smith College in nearby Northampton, Massachusetts. But Yale was expensive, even for a lawyer's son from Wheaton. The burgeoning Woodward family of seven left little room for frills. The issue of cost was eliminated when Bob applied for and received a naval ROTC scholarship that paid for his tuition, room and board. The U.S. Navy also presented him with a $50-per-month stipend during the school year. Bob would later say he chose the naval scholarship because there were lots of photos of his father in a Navy uniform around the house.

The passage from innocent Wheaton to prestigious Yale gave him a new, more sophisticated arena in which to continue questioning authority figures. It was this new academic world that would give him his first leg up when he began his unexpected career a decade later.

2

[Carl, 1944–61]

A Victory Baby

DOLORES MORAN stepped out of a life-size, heart-shaped card wearing a diaphanous gown. She carried a bow and arrow. This publicity photo ran in the *Washington Post* on February 14, 1944, with a headline over it: VALENTINE'S DAY, REMEMBER? Ms. Moran, a Hollywood starlet of the day, reminded everyone via the photo caption below her picture that she would soon be seen in *The Horn Blows at Midnight* with Jack Benny.

The news in the other pages of the *Washington Post* was not as pleasant. On a small piece of tropical land in the Bismarck Archipelago, just below the equator and bordering the U.S. Solomon Islands, the town of Rabaul had felt 134 tons of bombs rained upon it by U.S. forces. The "Japs" or the "Nips," as the *Washington Post* referred to the enemy in its pages, were getting a pounding.

The war news was good everywhere for the Allies according to the pages of the *Post* that day. The U.S. Flying Fortress was softening up northern France. The Russians were driving the Nazis out of Estonia. The British and Americans were closing in on Rome.

In the nation's capital, the weather was nasty—an unrelenting grimness kept people inside. A cold drizzle fell from gray skies—the temperature would only rise as high as thirty-four.

Sylvia Bernstein faced a problem shared by millions of American women that year. She was giving birth alone, at the age of twenty-nine and for the first time. Her husband, Alfred David Bernstein, whom she had married almost five years earlier, in June

13

of 1939, was at a military camp, preparing to go to Europe. He was one of what was probably only a handful of U.S. Army privates who were also members of the American Communist Party.

Sylvia Bernstein, with the help of her parents, Thomas and Mary Walker, brought her firstborn back to 1601 Argonne Place in northwest Washington.[1] She would live with her parents there until Pvt. Alfred Bernstein returned, nearly two years later, from the second great war of the century.[2]

Carl is sitting on a pony named Piccolo. He is nine. He is strumming his guitar and singing a song to Tricia and Julie Nixon. Playing the guitar is something he does regularly on The Pick Temple Show. *The program, a typical fifties kids' show on WTOP, Channel 9, in Washington, is broadcast daily, a mixture of cartoons, commercials and homilies. Piccolo is trucked to the studio each day from a farm on East-West Highway near Silver Spring, Maryland. Pick also brings his collie dog, Lady. Carl lives on Chesapeake Street, within walking distance of the studio in the northwest section of D.C. He is a student, a good one academically, at Janney Elementary. Carl has freckles now. His friends call him Howdy Doody, after the character on the popular national children's puppet show of the era. Carl doesn't mind. He enters Howdy Doody look-alike contests. And wins.*

Because Carl is sitting on Piccolo, he also has the honor of introducing Pick's Popeye cartoon. The Howdy Doody kid says, "Hocus pocus, start the show," and then Pick gently hits the pony on the side of its head with a soft loaf of Wonder bread.

After Popeye, Bluto and Olive Oyl finish their battling ménage à trois, Carl, Pick, Julie, Tricia and the rest of Pick's little "Rangers" recite the show's daily pledge: "I will live up to the creed of a Pick Temple Ranger and carry on the principles of good citizenship—to help the needy, aged and sick. To respect my parents and teachers. To love my neighbors, city and country. Don't put off until tomorrow what you can do today."[3]

Carl's father and mother joined the U.S. Communist Party in 1942. It was expected, the thing to do if you were a union leader. Al and Sylvia Bernstein signed on as members in San Francisco. They had moved there when Al had been hired as an executive with the United Federal Workers of America, becoming its chief organizer for California.

Carl was ten when his mother was ordered to appear before Republican congressman Harold Velde of Illinois with five other

Washington residents. All were asked questions about their past Communist activities. Sylvia Bernstein was described as a "thirty-eight-year-old housewife of 4230 Chesapeake Street, N.W." The *Washington Post* ran her picture next to a caption that said: RED PARTY HARD CORE IN CAPITAL.

Bob Woodward had been upset by his mother's affair and then by seeing his father awarded custody of him and his siblings. That it happened in a straitlaced, uptight, Republican town didn't help. Carl's boyhood, too, was branded by whispers, but different ones. Growing up in the fifties with Communist parents (named and featured in the pages of all three Washington newspapers) made Carl an outcast. If Bob's youth was a dark episode of the sitcom *Happy Days*, Carl's was the ultimate Philip Roth novel.

The Bernstein family joined the Jewish migration to the northern suburbs of Washington, settling in Silver Spring, Maryland, just over the District of Columbia line. They moved on Carl's eleventh birthday, February 14, 1955.

The street on which Carl's family settled, Harvey Road, was largely populated by Jewish families, though it could certainly have been called eclectic. Next door to the Bernsteins was Nevada's Democratic senator, Alan Bible. Another nearby neighbor was Herbert Stein, a Nixon adviser and chairman of the President's Committee for Economic Development. David Scull, a prominent Maryland politician, was near the end of the Harvey cul-de-sac. The boys who would become Carl's closest school friends—Philip Berg, Herb Stein's son Ben, Gene Daumit and Jerry Akman—lived a few steps away.[4]

The Bernsteins' new place was the smallest house on Harvey Road, a redwood contemporary that backed onto Sligo Creek Park. The creek was downhill from the back of the house. From the street, the modern structure was partly concealed by a large grassy mound of earth. At first glance one might say it was the residence of an artist, or at least of someone with artistic pretensions.[5]

Carl's life on Harvey Road soon settled into a prematurely jaded—for a budding teenager—routine. His prepubescent education included learning to smoke, drink, play poker and shoot pool. Carl soon acquired his own cue—a two-piece screw-on job. His "hustling headquarters" became a dark second-floor walk-up pool hall on Thayer Avenue, two miles from his home. By the eighth grade, Carl began to get into trouble. The first time he was expelled from school was for throwing a tray of food, which he threw because he had lost $25 playing poker. The expulsion lasted three days. Later Carl would be given detention for smoking on the grounds of his high school. At the "trial" before the student body, he pleaded insanity, a defense that delighted his peers.

Unlike Bob Woodward, who had been named the outstanding student in the eighth grade, Carl Bernstein's lone claim to recognition in the secondary schools of Montgomery County, Maryland, was the grace he showed with his feet.

A former eighth- and ninth-grade friend, Gay Gerson, remembered that "Carl was great on the dance floor." Carl Bernstein, the boy, had graduated from the daily inanities of Pick Temple and Piccolo the pony to become one of a group of adolescent dancers on another local television time-filler. Now, three days a week, he was one of the first through the doors in downtown Washington at the studios of WTTG, Channel 5, where he was a regular on *Milt Grant's Record Hop*. The show was one of the many local imitations of the national TV afterschool show *American Bandstand*. The station's studios were on the top floor of the Raleigh Hotel, a tall building midway between the White House and the Capitol.[6] Playing the role of an afternoon television Ginger Rogers to Carl's Fred Astaire was Sharon Barbara "Bobbie" Parzow. Together, they won several jitterbug contests. Their joint effort usually got them a trophy, a bottle of cologne and a few gift certificates from the show's sponsors—heady bounty for teens of the fifties. The petite Bobbie was a perfect partner for Carl. She was an even five feet tall, and he towered over her, something he enjoyed with few members of the opposite sex.

Milt Grant's trademark was unabashed commercialism. During each show he would holler at this charges, "What's your favorite drink, kids?" and forty thirsty voices would scream, "Pepsi!" Then he would ask, "Where do we buy hit records?" with Carl and company yelling the correct answer: "Music Box Music Stores!"

During high school, Carl's scrapes with the law increased. He broke most of the windows in the home of what he termed "a local anti-Semite." That got him fined $1,500 by a county judge. Another time he lost his driver's license for speeding.

His academic career began to falter. Now there was summer school, to repeat failed classes. This distressed his mother, and in turn Carl, who wanted to please her. His popularity among girls nose-dived as well. He was shorter than most members of the opposite sex, in addition to his male peers. His freckles competed with acne, a handicap no teen needed. His knowledge of the twist and the stroll—the dances of the era—could no longer compensate for his physical appearance. The whispers about his parents' eccentricities didn't help.

He had found solace and a sense of belonging in his religion. The thirteen-year-old Bernstein began to lobby his parents for a bar mitzvah. Al and Sylvia Bernstein, who were atheists as well as Communists, tried to buy Carl off with a trip to San Francisco. He wouldn't go.

"But I want to be Jewish," Carl railed at his parents. "I want to be bar-mitzvahed." Against their wishes, he joined the Montgomery County Jewish Center. The only son of Al and Sylvia Bernstein took a cram course in Hebrew with a tutor. He looked forward to really belonging to his faith and to receiving all the presents—the rightful bounty of a Jewish boy reaching manhood.

The party after the synagogue service was held in the Bernsteins' modest house on Harvey Road. Hoover's FBI agents marched up and down the street recording the numbers of the license plates. "I remember the FBI coming to our house and speaking with my parents about the Bernsteins," Carl's friend Gene Daumit recalled. "It was talked about in the neighborhood."

A young Carl, viewed as being somewhat different because of Al and Sylvia Bernstein's Communist backgrounds, wanted to feel he belonged—to something or somebody. It was not to be. He asked his parents if they would join a country club. Sylvia and Al said they didn't believe in country clubs either.

There were no obvious artifacts of Judaism in the Bernstein house. The only nod to their heritage was Al Bernstein's rule that nothing German-made was allowed in the home. Carl rebelled by installing his yarmulke and the other Judaic trappings he had received at his bar mitzvah on the top shelf of the front hall closet. When visitors arrived, they observed that at least one member of the family carried on the faith as they took off their coats.

Carl also discovered AZA, Aleph Zadik Aleph, not a country club or a fraternity, but the B'nai B'rith male youth division, a large national Jewish boys' club whose distaff side was the BBG or B'nai B'rith Girls. After a year or two of AZA activity, Carl became its newsletter editor and ran for chapter president. He lost the election, but the practice from writing the newsletter helped him get a C in a 1958–59 high school journalism class.

In his boyhood memoir, *Loyalties*, Carl said that he often wrote of social change in the AZA newsletter, particularly civil rights. His platform, when he ran for regional AZA president in December of 1959, according to Carl, was based on Jews joining the civil rights movement. Carl said that he won the regional election, winning on the "fifth or sixth ballot" against his friend Bruce Fingerhut. Fingerhut, who in 1991 was a distributor of philosophical and university press books in South Bend, Indiana, remembers it somewhat differently.

"Although we both wrote editorials for our chapters on civil rights, there were no 'platforms.' It was more of a popularity contest. What helped Carl win was a bawdy skit he did while playing his guitar. This won him instant fame."

Carl is standing in front of his peers—a gaggle of gangling sixteen-year-old Portnoys. The adults and girls have left the room, and Carl sings a duet with Ben Stein to his AZA brethren.

> *I'm a lonesome cowboy—*
> *I've got gonorrhea.*
> [a falsetto voice] *Syph, too!*
> *I'm a lonesome cowboy—*
> *I got it from Maria.*
> *I'm a lonesome cowboy—*
> *It hurts when I pee-a.*
> [a falsetto voice] *Syph, too!*

"Carl's AZA chapter was also a powerhouse and it had twenty-five members present. I was the only one from my chapter," said Bruce Fingerhut.

Philip Berg, a neighbor who was present at the election meeting, also didn't recall any "platforms" by the candidates but couldn't recall the risqué song.

"I was the one who broke the tie," Berg said. "I changed my vote to Carl because I felt that the AZA responsibilities might hurt Bruce Fingerhut's grades."

Carl's ascendancy to the AZA regional presidency may have produced some other flights of fantasy. In chapter 18 of *Loyalties* he wrote movingly of his participation in a civil rights demonstration in Greensboro, North Carolina.

In this episode, he wrote of riding on a train with a group of a hundred AZA boys and BBG girls to a B'nai B'rith summer convention in the North Carolina mountains.[7] The train, according to Carl, stopped in Alexandria, Richmond, Danville, Chapel Hill "and on down the line." Carl wrote that the train broke down in Greensboro, North Carolina, at two in the morning. Although he does not give an exact date or year, it would have been either 1958, 1959, or possibly 1960.[8]

Carl described the sleepy teenagers making a mistake and entering the black waiting room and its still-open restaurant in the train station rather than the white side of the depot. Moments later, Carl wrote that "a cop burst through and said that we couldn't be served, that we had to move to the other side. He was out of breath from running, and his belly heaved over a garrison belt that sagged with canisters and batons and a holstered revolver. We weren't moving, I said—without considering the implications. The policeman seemed confused, and went to a telephone. A few minutes later, a large contingent of the Greensboro, North Carolina, police force arrived, threatening to arrest all of us for being in the black waiting room. Again we were told to leave. I said nothing in reply; by then I had had time to consider the situation. To the group, I announced that anybody who didn't want to get arrested should get back on the train. Everybody stayed. And waited."

Carl then wrote in *Loyalties* that an hour later either the police chief or his deputy came to the train depot with a woman who the police leader said was a Jewish bondswoman by the name of Goldstein. Carl said the woman told the B'nai B'rith youth that they were endangering the Jewish community of Greensboro and that they should get back on the train.

Carl wrote that when he got to the North Carolina mountains, he was hauled before the B'nai B'rith adult leaders. He said he told the adults that he had done a great thing, but the B'nai B'rith said otherwise. Carl called the lack of racial commitment by the Jewish organization "a scandal."

This adventure by Carl and the B'nai B'rith youth would be ennobling if it had happened. It didn't—certainly not the way Carl remembered it. (See "The Greensboro Appendix" on page 221.)

Greensboro marked the start of the civil rights movement in the South. On February 1, 1960, four male black students from North Carolina A&T College sat down at the lunch counter in Woolworth's downtown Greensboro store seeking service, which up to that time was available only to whites. The white waitress said, "I'm sorry, we don't serve colored here."

One of the young men, who had purchased school supplies at a cash register a minute before, said, "I beg your pardon, you just served me at a counter two feet away. Why is it that you serve me at one counter and deny me at another?" A black dishwasher working behind the lunch counter then told the four students that they weren't supposed to be there and that they were "a disgrace to your race."

This was the beginning. Within days, the movement spread to fifty-four cities in nine states. The revolution was on. When Carl's train came through, whether it was 1958, 1959, or 1960, the train station would indeed still have been segregated. And the black lunch counter or "restaurant" at the depot did stay open all night while its white counterpart (both used the same kitchen) closed before midnight.

But Carl's fellow AZA members have little or no memory of such an incident. Philip Berg, who read Carl's account in *Loyalties*, said he remembered hearing about a demonstration but didn't know anyone who participated.[9] Berg recalls taking a train to a B'nai B'rith convention in the North Carolina mountains. But he recalled a long layover in Greensboro much earlier in the evening and that he went to the movies during the stop with a group of AZA boys and BBG girls.

"It was the first time I had seen a segregated theater, and there was a rope between where the blacks and whites sat," Berg said. "The blacks sat in the back behind us."

Asked again about the Greensboro racial incident, Berg said, "Carl may have embellished that story."

Another Harvey Road resident and AZA member, Marty Stein, who was on the train, remembered only that "the train was crowded and there were about a hundred of us crowded into a car that seated fifty. I slept in the bathroom. I remember waking up in the middle of the night, getting off the train and seeing white and colored bathrooms for the first time. As a lark, Carl and I decided to go into the colored bathroom. A policeman stopped us and said we couldn't go in there."

"It would be incredible that I've never heard anything about it," Carl's friend Bruce Fingerhut said, "and I was at the camp. It is apocryphal at best."

Carl's AZA activities gave him a sense of belonging he'd never achieved at his Silver Spring, Maryland, high school, Montgomery Blair, on Wayne Avenue. Built in 1929, and (when Carl attended) with more than two thousand students, the "Blairite" tradition was one of the strongest in the Maryland suburbs of Washington. The Blair Blazers were at that time always near or at the top statewide in football and basketball. The diversity of the school was amazing. Blair was one of the few schools in the country to have a Latin Scrabble team—when Carl attended, it won the county championship, surely one of the most obscure high school competitions ever.

Carl would have liked to have been a jock. But he was too small for football, too short for basketball. He already smoked too many Kool menthol cigarettes even to consider track. Instead, Carl's credits included a year in the school's United Nations organization and two years in the Broadcaster's Club. As a young broadcaster he hyped upcoming dances and football games over the school's public address system. And like most teenage boys, he wanted to be seen as a ladies' man. He wore the right clothes and had the requisite high "aircraft carrier" flattop haircut of the day. But he was short, and his physical appeal was further damaged by the severe acne that later pitted his face, creating a lifelong moonscape.

"Carl was the class cutup," a female class member recalled. "You couldn't take him seriously."

Another Montgomery Blair coed put it more bluntly: "Carl was the class fuck-up."

"Nancy Immler, the head of the Keyettes, would never go out with me," Carl later remembered in a speech to the 1976 class.[10] Nor would Goldie Hawn, with whom I once rode to the Hot Shoppes after the Bethesda–Chevy Chase game in the backseat of Pete Oldheiser's chopped-and-lowered Buick."[11]

These rejections might have been transferred into an overcompensation in academics, but Carl remained a classic underachiever at Montgomery Blair. Combining a smile with guile, he stayed unfocused and got by with a minimum of effort. In his three years of high school, he was mostly a C, D and F student which was sometimes followed by more remedial classes in summer school. One subject in which he did show promise was English.

"He wrote journalistically," his composition teacher, Sylvia Wubnig, recalled in 1991. Was he a C student? she was asked. "Well, he definitely wasn't an A," she said. "I remember one paper. He wrote very easily. He was very bright, but indifferent. Outrageously indifferent. He was snippy. He was glib and contemptuous of the whole bit. About five or six years ago, I saw him rush by me at the Kennedy Center. He was there for a special ceremony honoring a movie star. I said his name and he turned and said, 'Mrs. Wubnig!' And then he hurried off.

"When I read his first book—it was so flimsy, but well written in a very glib way—it was just the sort of thing he turned in to me."

It was Carl's best American history paper, Alma Davidson, his teacher, thought. The essay, a total of fourteen pages, complete with footnotes, was neatly typed and well written. The subject was that famous South American political hero Salvador Lopez. That puzzled her. She had never heard of Salvador Lopez.

A few days later Carl got the paper back. He received an F. Everything in the paper had been made up. Indeed, there was no Salvador Lopez.

By his senior year, Carl's high school routine was settled. After the third period, he had a free hour to work on the high school paper, the *Silver Chips*. One might expect to learn that Carl would have been the editor or its star reporter. He was neither. The young Bernstein was the circulation manager, a nice way of saying he was the school paperboy, dropping off copies every third Friday to each homeroom and the principal's office. Carl used his free hour wisely by walking over to Jim Myers' pool hall and getting a stick off the wall to practice eight ball. Carl stopped returning from the pool hall. He had gym fifth period and chemistry sixth. Carl flunked both.

When he went to put his deposit down for his graduation cap and gown, the principal of the school told him to forget it—he wasn't graduating. "There was intense lobbying by me and my parents," Carl recalled in his 1976 speech. "The faculty reached a decision to get me out of Blair rather than put up with me another year. The night before graduation, Mr. Shaw, the principal, called my parents with news of the dispensation. The Bernstein family escaped disgrace, at least for a little while."

Al Bernstein, perhaps foreseeing that the world of academia would not be where his son would be spending the next four years, decided to get Carl a job. Ben Gilbert, an editor at the *Washington Post*, had been a next-door neighbor. Joe Young, the federal columnist for the *Washington Star*, was someone Al knew from his days as a union leader. The family felt that the *Post* had maligned Carl's mother when she testified before the Eastland committee, so Carl went to the *Star* to work as a copyboy. It was September of 1960. The salary was $44 a week. Carl, who had recently celebrated his sixteenth birthday, joined the ranks of employed workers.

"He had just started to let his hair grow long," Jerry O'Leary, a former *Star* editor, remembered. "He became our resident hippie, but I thought he looked more like Alfalfa in the 'Our Gang' comedies. He always had a cowlick in the back that wouldn't lie down. The bridge of freckles across his nose was just like Alfalfa's.

"Carl wore a white corduroy suit to work the first day on the job. We pulled the oldest trick in the book on him. His first task was to wash out all the carbon paper. He ruined the suit."

Executive Editor Newbold Noyes saw Carl washing the carbon paper in the men's room and ran into an editor's office demanding to know who the idiot was rinsing the carbon paper. When Noyes found out about the prank, he threatened to fire the editors if it ever happened again. The newsroom gang wasn't intimidated. They sent Carl up to the composing room the next day to search for "type lice." Carl didn't mind. For the first time in his life he had found a place where he felt he belonged.

3

[Bob, 1961–65]

Bob and Man at Yale

A COMMUTER TRAIN from New York deposited Bob Woodward in
New Haven, Connecticut, during the waning days of the summer
of 1961. He was now eons away from the narrow ideas of Wheaton, Illinois, entering an arena of academia generally populated by
prep school swells, pupils of privilege. The eighteen-year-old boy
from the Midwest was as green as foot-high spring corn, and it
showed.

Yale was still an all-male bastion of Eastern elitism in the early
sixties. It would not go coed until 1969. The total population of just
under ten thousand undergraduate and graduate students was,
perhaps even more so than Harvard, America's main source for
leadership in the corporate world and politics.

The school had been chartered in 1701, three-quarters of a
century before American independence. For its first decade and a
half, the college taught students at various locations in Connecticut. In 1716, after receipt of more than a thousand books from a
wealthy British benefactor, it was decided that the school needed a
permanent building. New Haven was the village chosen to host
the English colony's school for higher education. A trader from
Boston who had been successful importing goods from India then
donated more books and a large selection of East Indian textiles.
His name was Elihu Yale and his gifts were generous enough to
move the trustees to name the college after him at the 1718 commencement.

More than two hundred years later, in 1933, a series of residen-
tial colleges was established at Yale, patterned after the system

favored by British universities. Each college was to provide accommodations for undergraduates beginning in their second year at the school. They were headed by a "master" who was assisted by a group of faculty members.

The college Bob Woodward entered in the fall of 1962, Ezra Stiles, was a new building, part of a recent expansion program. It was still partly unfinished when the sophomore students moved in after their obligatory first year in the freshman quad. It should not be surprising that at a school like Yale, Ezra Stiles college was built with a grant from the American billionaire philanthropist Paul Mellon, or that the land was donated by the media magnate John Hay Whitney. Unlike the ancient Gothic architecture that dominates most of Yale, Ezra Stiles was a polygonal, modern structure meant to blend with its surroundings by being clad in an exterior of sand-brown stone and mortar. The building, with its solid facades and narrow window slits, was designed by Eero Saarinen, a Yale School of Architecture graduate. This youngest member of the famed Finnish family of architects had also been responsible for projects as varied as the once-avant-garde Dulles Airport in Virginia, outside Washington, D.C., as well as the Yale hockey rink.

Ezra Stiles's master at the time, Richard B. "Dixie" Sewall, was a Yale English professor and probably America's foremost authority on the literary works and life of Emily Dickinson. Sewall remembered the young Woodward as "quiet" and "doing nothing remarkable at Yale that I can remember." Sequestered on one of the upper floors at Ezra Stiles, living alone in a single room, the "quiet" Bob Woodward began to write a novel in his sophomore year.

The 1964 edition of the Yale *Banner*, the student yearbook, described Bob's literary efforts: "The work of Buchman and Richmond in the visual is complemented by the writing of Bob Woodward. In his secluded room on the fourth floor above the arch, he writes and revises his novel. When we visit him from time to time, he will usually turn his attention from the novel to the postcards on his wall which reveal the life and loves of a strange lady named Lulu Anderson."[1]

Bob Woodward once described the novel as "brooding and dark" although he would later call it "silly." Writing it may have served as a catharsis of sorts. The manuscript was a disguised autobiography about growing up in Illinois and contained the angst and pain that Bob had experienced in childhood—the trauma of his parents' divorce and the turmoil it had created. Bob alternated writing styles, doing one chapter in florid Faulknerian prose and the next in the bare, monosyllabic style of Ernest Hemingway. The four major characters in the book merged in the final chapter into a single individual. The main character's name was Dake, and if one eliminates the "a," the consonants form the letters of the Yale "jock" fraternity. The pages were sent off to Charles Scribner's & Sons in New York where they languished until being politely sent back.

Bob didn't take rejection well. He put aside his literary ambitions and concentrated on his studies. Though a dual history and English major, he also made enough time to throw himself into Yale's social life. A photo published in the *Yale Daily News* shows a young Bob Woodward in the thick of the annual rite of "bladderball," a school sporting tradition.

He also began to demonstrate a compulsion for practical jokes. One, which backfired, involved Bob's arranging a blind date for a classmate who was already on a date with a woman from another college. The three students, realizing Bob's attempted prank, then arranged for a campus security guard to go to Bob's room at Ezra Stiles, tell him that his classmate had been arrested for raping the woman and handcuff Bob as an accessory before telling him of the turnabout gag. Bob's longstanding girlfriend, Kathy Middlekauff, visiting from Smith College, was said to burst into tears as the handcuffs were produced by the uniformed guard.

Ezra Stiles was unique in producing writers. Author Taylor Branch once suggested in *Esquire* that journalist David Gergen, a former White House speechwriter, was a Watergate source to Bob and possibly the illusory Deep Throat. Writing in the magazine in 1976, Branch said Bob and Gergen attended Yale and had both lived at Ezra Stiles at the same time. Branch quoted a source saying this about Ezra Stiles: "There was one special thing about our college. It was almost all single rooms. Our students tended to be loners, not flashy. I noticed the other day that the *New York Times* recommended ten books to read this fall, and four of them were by Ezra Stiles men."

Bob continued to see Kathleen Middlekauff. She was less than two hours away at Smith, a Yale "dating" school. By the time he reached his senior year, they had been romantically involved for nearly eight years. Unlike his performance at Wheaton, at Yale he was just an average university student at old Elihu and would never make the dean's list. But Kathy did garner academic honors. One year after Bob, she would graduate magna cum laude in economics from Smith and belong to Phi Beta Kappa.

Yale, though, is more than a place to get an education. Grades and academic standing are, in the final analysis, less important than acceptance by one's peers. Rather than just a place to learn, Yale to many has been both a private club and a career.

Sports and clubs were more important to those making a "social profession" at Yale in the early 1960s than today. The university was still primarily attended by white males who had received their secondary educations at private preparatory schools. Vietnam and Woodstock were yet to change American campuses. Many Yale students still wore jacket and tie to class. The earnest, closely cropped young Yalies of that time were seemingly light-years away from the long-haired, scraggly bearded young faces staring out from the pages of the Yale yearbook just ten years later. By then, Yale's ranks would also include young women with straight, freshly pressed hair.

The undergraduates of Bob Woodward's era belonged to more accepting times. Fraternities were important entities at Yale then, and Bob joined Phi Gamma Delta. He also added to his Yale social standing by working on the staff of the *Banner*, the umbrella organization of all official Yale publications, with the exception of its daily newspaper. In his senior year he became chairman.

"Heading up the *Banner* isn't as prestigious as being the editor of the *Yale Daily News*, like Bill Buckley was," said Robin Winks, the author and Yale professor of history, adding, "It's more ceremonial." Nevertheless, Bob was referred to as a "*Banner* mogul" in the 1965 edition of the yearbook.

According to a Yale poll one year before, 30 percent of all students claimed to belong to a fraternity of some sort. In these fraternal groups, the pecking order placed Greek houses second to the seniors' secret societies, which have thrived at Yale since the early nineteenth century. The secret societies are loosely derived from covert male clubs that existed in Italy centuries ago. In a way, they could be seen as distant relatives of the American Mafia "families," which have also survived and involve similar mumbo-jumbo rituals. To be "tapped" and invited to join one of the nine secret societies at Yale was and still is a pinnacle attainment for seniors. Each club selected only ten to fifteen members from the graduating classes.

The most prominent of the secret clubs is Skull and Bones, which was made even more famous in recent years when the press learned that Yale graduate George Herbert Walker Bush was a member.[2] Skull and Bones, founded in 1832, has Bonesmen who were previously even better known than the former president. Averell Harriman, Henry Luce, William F. Buckley, Supreme Court justice Potter Stewart, William and McGeorge Bundy and William Howard Taft were all Bonesmen. It is no small coincidence that David Boren, chairman of the U.S. Senate Intelligence Committee, was also a member or that his daughter Carrie would become one of its first women members in 1992.

Bonesmen at Yale were stern and serious. Alcohol was not allowed inside the windowless Skull and Bones building. The senior members would meet, sequestered, twice weekly to discuss, in hushed tones, how they intended to make their marks on the world outside New Haven. As a symbol of how they were expected to lead others, all clocks inside were set ahead by several minutes. It could not always have been so purposeful. Nude wrestling and ritual masturbation among members is rumored to have taken place within the Bonesmen's tomb.

Next to Skull and Bones came Scroll and Key, a more liberal group, if any of Yale's secret clubs could be termed "liberal." Alcohol was permitted inside the Keymen's meeting place, and its members were diverse. The roster has included both Cole Porter and career diplomat Dean Acheson.[3]

The third of the "prestige" secret societies was Wolf's Head. The men there also were allowed libations. Wolf's Head had an inner courtyard where the Wolfmen played a game called roof ball. When balls went over the roof to the street outside, it was whispered that Wolf's Head had its own inner tennis court. All the rest—Elihu, Manuscript (the choice of David Gergen), Book and Snake, Berzelius, St. Elmo's and St. Anthony Hall—were considered "second tier" or "new."

Book and Snake, which tapped Bob Woodward, was founded in 1843. Considered at the top of the second tier, this "newer" club was actually older than Wolf's Head. Its stark marble mausoleumlike structure stands on the corner of Grove and High streets at the edge of the Yale campus. Four fluted columns and a tall door distinguish the otherwise inscrutable exterior, which faces a sea of ancient graves in a cemetery across the street. The proclamation on the cemetery's entry arch reads, "The dead shall be raised," and it is the first thing one sees when leaving the secret society of the Book and Snake.

Bob, by becoming one of fifteen seniors selected for Book and Snake in the spring of 1964, was establishing himself as being among the very best of Yale undergraduates. A Yalie could almost always count on an interview and an obligatory "free cup of coffee" when applying for a job, so powerful was and is the university's name. As media critic Jeff Greenfield (Yale 1964) put it in *M* magazine in 1992: "Elite institutions give you that push up the ladder regardless. . . . We are talking here about the venerable tradition of an 'old boys' network of which Yale . . . was and is very much a part."

But a member of a Yale secret society went beyond privilege, inheriting lifelong bonds with other members of the group who came before and after him. Book and Snake members include Washington insider Nicholas Brady, the former secretary of the treasury in the Bush administration, and President Bill Clinton's Defense Secretary Les Aspin, a member of Congress from 1971 to 1993, who was the House's most influential force on military affairs and weapons procurement.

Bonding at Book and Snake was achieved through intense sessions of marathon group discussions similar to ones held by Skull and Bones. Every subject from politics to sex was intimately debated. This mass form of psychotherapy was and still is prevalent among all nine secret clubs at Yale.

Yale—especially its secret societies—was a fertile recruiting ground for the U.S. intelligence community, particularly the Central Intelligence Agency. The list of Yale graduates who have become high officials of the agency and its predecessor, the Office of Strategic Services, predates World War II. Former director of central intelligence George Bush (Yale 1948) as well as the current leader, Robert James Woolsey (LL.B, Yale 1968) and the legendary CIA counterintelligence chief James Jesus Angleton (Yale 1941) are but three Yale men who have led America's spy forces. William McBundy was a top CIA officer who served concurrently as a trustee of the Yale Corporation (which manages the university's grounds and buildings) during the year in which Bob Woodward graduated.

Nathan Hale (Yale 1773) is considered America's first spy. Before he was hanged by the British in 1776, he bravely spoke the words that would make him immortal: "I only regret that I have but one life to lose for my country." A bronze statue of Hale stands in front of Connecticut Hall on the Old Campus of Yale. Another statue of Nathan Hale stands to the right of the main entrance to the CIA headquarters in Langley, Virginia. It was erected in 1973, the bicentennial of Nathan Hale's graduation from Yale, and is an exact copy of the Yale original sculpted by Bala Lyon Pratt in 1915. The agency paid the university $6,000 for the privilege.

In the early sixties, the CIA interviewed between twenty-five and fifty Yale seniors each spring. History majors and secret-society members were prime candidates. According to the book *Cloak and Gown* by Robin Winks, Yale's involvement with both the OSS and the CIA was personified by the Yale history professor and OSS/CIA master spy Sherman Kent.[4] The Yale history department, led by Kent, believed that it was important to reshape the world in a way beneficial to both America and Yale. This idea was prevalent among faculty throughout the school. The coach of Yale's rowing team, Allen "Skip" Walz, for example, was a paid CIA recruiter for fourteen years, receiving equal salaries from both the university and the intelligence agency.

That the university at New Haven was enamored with secrecy and intelligence matters was tellingly described by a member of Bob's class in the Yale *Banner* as he recounted their 1962 sophomore winter semester: "When Ian Fleming's *Dr. No* came to the New Haven screen during the year, it mattered little whether our hero was James Bond or Frank Merriwell, 007 or 1965; *we worshipped in earnest the star who embodied the essence of what it was to be a Yale man* [emphasis added]."

However, the movie-screen image of spies and spying had often given way to harsh reality. For instance, during the early part of the Korean War, the CIA ran an exercise called Operation Bluebell. It involved parachuting Chinese Nationalists and CIA agents into China, where their mission was to link up with anti-communist Chinese and send back intelligence. The exercise was a fiasco; all the CIA agents were either killed or captured. Most of them were Yale men from the class of 1950.

Certainly, with the CIA encouraged to recruit on the Yale campus, particularly among history majors and secret societies, it is more than reasonable to assume Bob may have been one of those approached by the agency, or by a military intelligence unit, especially after four years of naval ROTC training.[5] Although it would answer a lot of questions that have been raised about Bob Woodward, at this point one can only speculate as to whether he was offered the chance to become a "double-wallet guy," as CIA agents who have two identities are dubbed. Or did he agree to go dormant and inform on an "as needed" basis? It would certainly be understandable if he decided not to adhere to the straight and accepted the submerged patriotic glamour and extra funds that such a relationship would provide. It would also explain the comments of Pulitzer Prize–winning author J. Anthony Lukas, when he wrote in 1989 that Bob Woodward was "temperamentally secretive, loathe to volunteer information about himself," or the *Washingtonian*'s remarks in 1987: "He is secretive about everything." As *Esquire* magazine put it, summing up in its 1992 article on Bob, "What is he hiding?"

In one of his final deeds for Yale, Bob Woodward wrote a summary of life at Ezra Stiles college for the Yale *Banner*. While not necessarily secretive, the writing was perhaps a little puzzling:

"Stiles is quite inevitably an array of loose ends: fragments of broken glass much like the broken jars glued to a piece of plywood and displayed in the buttery our sophomore year. Then we may have stopped before the jars, turned our heads to one side, examined, maybe even felt a little humbled before them and wondered why we had not thought of it first. Now we are glad we did not— and if our heads turn to one side, it is only a foreshadowing of a violent no. Broken jars fixed to plywood only now conjure up images of a neobarbaric asymmetry; the surface supports the weakest of metaphors, and fails to blend with the jagged mistake of broken glass."

The author, who read the piece to several Yale professors in an attempt to decipher its somewhat cryptic meaning, was told by one, "Perhaps he was trying to twit the master. It's somewhat traditional among seniors." But when the former master of Ezra

Stiles, Richard Sewall, was read the passage, he disagreed and thought it might have something to do with the unfinished condition of Stiles when Bob moved in three years earlier. It may also have been an unconscious aping of Bob's college literary idol, William Faulkner. On page nine of Faulkner's novel *Intruder in the Dust* one finds: "The footpacked strip running plumbline straight between two borders of tin cans and empty bottles and shards of china and earthenware set into the ground, up to the paintless steps and the paintless gallery . . ."

In the same precious writing style, Bob also wrote revealingly in the Yale yearbook of being alone in a large university: "The vast majority of single rooms thrust most into an unaccustomed loneliness. This isolation brought many out into the open, where the essential exposure could take place; mind not only met mind, or person only person, but often person met mind, and the personable became more mindful, the mindful more personable. A few concluded that person and mind are not always compatible. For some loneliness and solitude led further inward, and some others died of overexposure."

Bob then quoted lines from Irish poet William Butler Yeats:

> *Civilization is hooped together, brought*
> *Under a rule, under the semblance of peace*
> *By manifold illusion; but man's life is thought*

Bob concluded by observing, "Thought is lonely."

4

[Carl, 1961–70]

Village Swordsman

"WHERE'S THE PARTY?" yelled Carl Bernstein as he joined the *Star* table at Duke Zeibert's restaurant in downtown Washington.[1] It was a rhetorical question because if there were a party, it was Carl who would have known where it was and who was there.

By the early 1960s, Carl had found a home at the Washington *Evening Star*. It gave him the sense of belonging he had never found with his family, in the public schools of Montgomery County or even AZA. There were the raucous lunches at Duke's, where the tabs always seemed to add up to $7.50, no matter what one ordered. And after the paper was put to bed, the *Star* newsroom would reconvene at Harrigan's, a dark, boozy bar on the waterfront in southwest Washington. Harrigan's had two drawing cards: the place offered some of the cheapest martinis in the city and was the closest place, and stayed open late, unabashedly advertising itself as an "old-fashioned saloon."

The owners of the *Star*, the Noyes and Kauffmann families, didn't know it yet, but their newspaper was doomed. It would be a slow, tortured death that would take two more decades. But it was ordained to happen no matter what scoops their reporters got, what the front page said, or how deep their coverage. The *Evening Star* could have been a combination of the *New York Times*, the *Los Angeles Times* and the *London Times* and it wouldn't have prolonged its life a single day.

The *Star* had been outflanked by the *Washington Post* for years. It had been the *Post* that had dared to buy the larger *Washington Times-Herald* in 1954 and then had surprised everyone by keeping

most of its circulation. The first Sunday edition of the combined
Post-Times Herald weighed in at two and a half pounds and 228
pages. The new daily never looked back.

On the other side of the *Star* was the tabloid *Washington Daily
News*, owned by Scripps Howard and priced at five cents. Its two
competitors sold for twice that amount. Readers called it the *Nickel
News*. The *News* too, was a morning paper.

And that's why the *Star* was doomed to bleed red ink until it
finally closed down after two new owners gave it money and ideas
that ranged from new page formats to "stealing" *Doonesbury* from
the morning competition. The *Star* was an *afternoon paper* and
people's habits had changed with the advent of television. Before
a blue cathode glow came to illuminate nearly every living room in
America, reading a paper when one came home from work was a
ritual. Now the face of Walter Cronkite was inside the house, a
fatherly figure who read the news of the day to a chorus of moving
pictures. Working hours had changed as well after World War II.
A more industrial America of the past had worked from six to
three—factory hours—leaving little time for morning papers. In
the emerging service economy, the hours were nine to five, and
workers actually had time to read a paper before going to work or
at the office, during the morning coffee break.

The *Post*, unprofitable for decades, went into the black in 1955.
By the late 1960s it would have two-thirds of the city's advertising
linage. The *Star* would never recover.

Still, the *Star* was a scrappy paper. Its owners were content to
squeeze out profits through understaffing and cutting back on
circulation promotion. This helped make the shorthanded third-
floor newsroom a delight for Carl. There were usually bursts of
frenzied action during which editors really did yell "Copy!" and
rip stories out of their typewriters as if staging the second act of
The Front Page.

Carl loved it. He thrived on the daily tension of getting a large
daily newspaper with five separate editions written, laid out and
delivered to hundreds of thousands of homes. He moved swiftly
from copyboy to dictationist to obituary writer to part-time reporter. Eventually he was paid an additional $7.50 for each story the
paper published under his byline.[2] And after his shift ended, he
didn't go home. It was on to Harrigan's, with a fake ID card in his
hand, where Carl cadged drinks. His hair, radically different from
his high school flattop, now hung below his collar line. Carl was

everywhere—a hyperactive, feral young newsman who couldn't sit still.

The washing-the-carbon-paper prank which took place on his first day at the *Star* had long been forgotten by Carl, and now it was he who played the tricks. Manning the obituary desk one day, he phoned the *Post* and created a made-up death notice of a "handicapped one-man band" who had "played for Woodrow Wilson." Knowing that the *Post* had callback policies for confirmation reasons, Carl passed himself off as the son of the deceased man, saying he was telephoning from Washington's Union Station while traveling with the body en route to a Florida burial. The *Post* ran the item in its first edition on page one before having second thoughts and pulling it. Carl became a hero for a day in the *Star*'s newsroom.

By 1964, Carl was a reporter of sorts. His first byline, which also made page one, was an appreciation of a woman street peddler who sold newspapers and talked to the office workers downtown. Carl had befriended her. When she turned up unclaimed at the city morgue, it was Carl who identified the body and who wrote an homage to her.

After that debut, Carl's byline began turning up about once a week. Most of the stories were routine. He would write about a housing shortage for troops returning to a Maryland Army base from Germany or about a "Space Cadet" program for "deprived children." But some were pure scoops, such as Carl's uncovering of an Episcopal Church on Capitol Hill that had canceled a concert because of the controversial content of some of its songs.

An example of Carl's ingenuity in creating a story was the page-one article he wrote on July 15, 1964. Carl had read that the leading Republican presidential candidate, Barry Goldwater, was a ham radio operator and kept a set rigged up in his hotel room at the GOP's headquarters in San Francisco. Rushing to the home of a nearby ham radio enthusiast, Carl called up Goldwater and talked to him, which Carl billed as the first newspaper interview of a presidential candidate over a ham radio.

Goldwater: "This is a Kilowatt Seven Uncle George Able Portable Six from the Mark Hopkins Hotel in San Francisco."

Carl: "Kilo Two Zulu Romeo Kilo here. Go ahead, Barry."

Goldwater: "I'm working A column S line with a Thirty L One. It's better than the rig in Washington. That rascal's always acting up. But up here I've got about thirty-five feet of wire stuck out the window for an antenna. How's the signal and where are you calling from?"

After Carl told Goldwater he was calling from a suburb of Washington, he asked about the ham radio outfit Goldwater had in his Corvette and then got the Republican senator to admit that he hung twenty feet of wire out of his campaign plane so he could indulge his hobby on the way to the convention. Carl then got Goldwater to tell him he had eight hundred convention votes and it "looked pretty hitched."

Goldwater ended the conversation with Carl by saying, "Hope to do it again. This is King Seven Uncle George Able Portable Six from the Mark Hopkins in San Francisco signing clear."

The young Bernstein now ached to be a full-time newspaper reporter. He enrolled at the University of Maryland, having gotten accepted on probation because of the excellence of his writing on the essay portion. The conditional acceptance was because of his mediocre high school grades. But it didn't last long. "I started working at the paper five days a week," Carl would remember in 1976, "and I stopped showing up for classes unless there was an exam and flunked out the next semester. It went on like that for a couple of years—readmitted on probation, middling grades, up and down—and then came the final straw. The university suspended me for having too many [illegal on-campus parking] tickets. I never went back."

But Carl was blocked at the *Washington Evening Star*. William Hill, the managing editor, perhaps as a convenient way of silently implementing a hiring freeze, announced a new policy instituted by a superior, Sid Epstein—all new reporters had to have college degrees. Stopped at the *Star*, Carl learned that a copy editor, Coit Hendley, had been offered the job of managing editor of the *Daily Journal* in Elizabeth, a gritty New Jersey town just across the Hudson River from New York City.[3] The daily had a circulation of 63,000. Carl begged to go along. Coit took him to New Jersey in the summer of 1965 as his personal assistant and told him he could write about anything he liked in his spare time.

A twenty-one-year old Carl moved into a walk-up, two-bedroom, apartment in Greenwich Village in the summer of 1965, directly above O'Henry's restaurant, a longtime New York landmark. He shared the apartment with three women, one of whom, an airline attendant, was a cousin of the film actress Ann-Margret. Two of the women shared a bedroom, another slept on the living room sofa bed and Carl was given the other bedroom.

"He literally brought home a different woman every night, mostly older than he was," one of his former roommates remembered. "They'd keep me awake a lot. He must have been quite a swordsman.

"If you had it, Carl would use it. If there was food in the refrigerator, Carl would take it. Once I had a borrowed green Triumph convertible. I parked it down on the street. Carl took the car keys and disappeared for three days. When he came back, he raved about driving over the Verrazano Narrows bridge with the top down. He never apologized."

Despite the temptations of Manhattan, Carl still found time to become both a prolific and a good newspaper reporter in New Jersey. He took Coit Hendley at his word, and within weeks after his arrival at the Elizabeth paper instituted a three-times-per-week column that he titled "Of This and That." The column chronicled the daily adventures of a young reporter, one Carl Bernstein.

Often Carl would spend the day with an Elizabeth worker, describing what he or she did—"John Kachurak has been painting signs in New Jersey for 35 of his 54 years," began one piece about a billboard painter. Young Bernstein sought out the unusual. This was Carl writing about the Maplewood, New Jersey, "Happening" Festival on September 10, 1965: "One of the more interesting pieces of sculpture at the Maplewood festival was a triple-torsoed Maidenform display mannequin with a Zenith indoor television antenna atop it. 'I call this *Modern Woman*,' said its creator, Ron Kramer."

On November 9, 1965, opportunity presented itself. The break proved to be a turning point in his newspaper career. He was at the northern reaches of Manhattan with a friend when the historic New York City blackout began. Carl roamed around town in cabs and on motorcycles absorbing the drama. Then he caught a bus to Elizabeth and pounded out his impressions on a typewriter. The stream-of-consciousness story read like a discount version of Jack Kerouac crossed with Tom Wolfe, but Coit Hendley allowed the five-thousand-word piece to run virtually untouched. It absorbed the entire front page of the November 10, 1965, *Elizabeth Daily Journal*.

"I was at a friend's apartment at 110th Street and Riverside Drive," Carl began, "and the lights fell asleep and I woke up.

"We looked out the window and—Dig We Must—this crazy unbelievable scene with half the lights in Manhattan out.

"Half the lights hell! We made our way up to the roof by candlelight and someone had stolen the Empire State Building. And the Chrysler Building and Harlem, and Jackie Kennedy's apartment house and Lincoln Center and Temple Emanuel . . ."

Carl went on that way for a thousand words with exclamation points, dots, dashes—every punctuation mark he knew. Later in the account, he described himself hitchhiking around Manhattan:

"Then came Tom Sabatino, a truck driver of 233 Hillside Avenue, who owns a big Checker stationwagon which seats nine. Mr. Sabatino, as his grateful nonpaying patrons made clear, is clearly one of the world's greatest sports.

"He loaded 15 of us into the oversized automobile and started heading uptown. Every time we would stop to let somebody out, others would crowd around the big Checker wagon. 'You going to Flushing?'

" 'How about the Bronx?'

" 'Mister, I'm only going to 42nd Street, but I've been walking since Wall Street.' Even at our final stop at 47th Street, the car was still loaded.

"And what a ride! By now the police had put up huge searchlights at some important intersections and people were walking in the middle of the street and hitchhiking. Grown men in Brooks Brothers suits walking backwards on Eighth Avenue with their thumbs out like they were sailors on the turnpike.

"The hotels. Who could ever forget the hotels on the night of the Great Blackout? I walked into the lobby of the Americana, that grand monument to the nation's conventioneers, and it was a human parking lot.

"One thousand people, the hotel's PR man said, were sprawled out in the lobby. It looked like two thousand and it was the damnedest thing I have ever seen in my life. The hotel had provided them all blankets and they were sleeping, talking, joking, drinking, crying, kissing in every imaginable nook and cranny of the Americana's multi-level lobby."

"How many people were in the Americana's lobby?" asked Leonard Downie, Jr. (who would become one of Carl's first editors at the *Washington Post*), in his 1976 book, *The New Muckrakers* (today he holds the top editorial position, Executive Editor). "How many of the hitchhiking executives were wearing Brooks Brothers suits? Were there really fifteen people packed into Tom Sabatino's Checker? With Carl, you could never be sure about the little details."

Carl rambled on with this colorful account for column after column. He concluded with a sixties-style coffee chant that would have made Allen Ginsberg proud.

"So I boarded the bus at Port Authority for New Jersey and settled back to try and catch some sleep.

"Then Boom! Brighter than a thousand suns! A billion-zillion-trillion candlepower. Dazzling, blazing, burning, positively blazing! Magnificent, splendiferous, overpowering, glittering, gleaming, flashing, brilliant!

"There it was! Weehawken, New Jersey! Weehawken, the City of Light!"

Ersatz Kerouac/Wolfe or not, the piece won Carl the New Jersey Press Association award for best news writing under deadline. He won another for an exposé of underage teen drinking in Manhattan and, after being rejected for a job on a New York daily, used his clips as a ticket home. In October of 1966, Carl got a reporter's job on the *Washington Post*, the newspaper he had avoided six years earlier because it had defamed his mother.

"He had to leave New Jersey," said a veteran of the *Journal* newsroom. "He was behind in his rent in New York and owed half the people on the paper five or ten dollars. He wasn't popular here. We called him 'the rotten kid.' "

Upon his return Carl moved into a seventh-floor apartment at 1808 Connecticut Avenue in northwest Washington. He quickly served notice at the *Post* that he wasn't about to write just a straight news story and file it. His first assignment, a press junket for reporters who were invited to go sixty-five feet underground to get a look at the beginning excavations for Washington's new subway system, was Carl at his alliterative best. Carl's story, which ran on page seven of the second section on October 26, 1966, described the hole in the ground as "dirty, damp, dark, and deep." The reporters on the tour were "spelunking scribes." Carl ended up saying that Washington's subway system "may turn out as sturdy as Gibraltar."

The next day, on October 27, 1966, Carl came up with a scoop that ran top right on the front page of the second section. He had been told that a $30-million appropriation for area post offices was being funneled into the postal bureaucracy to hire extra employees because mail was being delivered late. Carl uncovered company after company whose dated sale materials hadn't gone out in time and were still buried in the back of the post offices.

Young Bernstein soon discovered he had a certain advantage over other *Post* reporters covering the city. Though nearly everyone had college degrees from prominent universities such as Columbia or Northwestern and could write well, Carl was one of the few who had lived his entire life in Washington. He had the most precious commodity of all: an interlocking web of sources—men and women with whom he had gone to high school, worshiped with and who were now at least low- or mid-level government or corporate bureaucrats.

Still, Carl's forte was his colorful writing, much to the consternation of his older WASP editors, who liked both their bourbon and their city stories straight and unadorned. A piece on a new mini-train tour bus on the Washington Mall had this fifty-one-word single-sentence lead: "Winifred Smith started the motor, the vehicle went bump-bump-bump, horns honked because she drives on 14th Street at 12 miles per hour, and George Vasjuto recited his lines about the 898 stairs and the 555 feet, 5½ inches of Maryland and Massachusetts marbel [sic] that is the Washington Monument."

In a city newsroom where "no vivid writing" was an unspoken policy, Carl was an anomaly. Additionally, he was often late with stories, could never be found, turned in outrageously high expense accounts and became the office moocher. He didn't have a car and ran up huge taxi bills when he wasn't tooling around town in his imported racing bicycle. *Post* staffers remember marveling at his dexterity—interviewing a source on the phone while simultaneously bumming cigarettes by sign language, supplicating like a Bombay beggar. His editors felt he didn't fit in. He didn't. But he could write.

In fact, Carl had many other assets. Besides knowing the city and its suburbs like the back of his hand and having a burgeoning network of contacts, Carl would somehow always magically materialize in the newsroom at the time a major news story was breaking. When Lyndon Johnson, faced with bad polls and discouraging results from Vietnam, surprised the nation with his statement, appended to a speech on March 31, 1968, that he would not seek, nor accept his party's nomination for reelection, it was Carl who appeared at the center of the story. He had been at the Uptown Theatre on Connecticut Avenue attending a black-tie sneak preview of *2001: A Space Odyssey*. During the intermission of the long movie, he caught the breaking news on television and hurried to the *Post*'s fifth-floor newsroom. A still-new executive editor, Ben Bradlee, finding that Carl was one of the few reporters around wearing a tie, sent him to the White House. Carl was on the cusp of a big story, but there was no byline. Instead he played a supporting role to the *Post*'s national team. It was Hobart Rowen, Carroll Kirkpatrick, Richard Harwood, David Broder and Murrey Marder whose bylines were on the front page the next day. At the top levels of the *Washington Post*, Carl was still an invisible man.[4]

Carl started romancing a fellow *Post* reporter in the city, or "Metro," section of the paper shortly after he began working there. Carol Ann Honsa was Carl's type—slightly older, nearly six feet tall and Junoesque. She had begun at the *Post* only two months before he had. Carl married her on April 20, 1968, and they moved into an apartment at 1940 Biltmore Street in the colorful, partly Hispanic section of the city, Adams Morgan.

Carol didn't know what she was getting into. Carl's inability to manage his finances and his unorthodox nocturnal lifestyle wore her out. Their loud arguments soon were heard by neighbors, the noise permeating the apartment walls. The marriage blew up at a bawdy, rowdy New Year's Eve party given by a *Post* editor. The party, which was credited with ending at least three marriages, featured both excessive drinking and wifeswapping. Carol and Carl officially separated in August of 1971, and Carol filed for divorce in December of 1972. She asked for her maiden name back, $175 for her attorney and a jumble of furniture she had left behind when she moved out on Carl. The property included two used air-conditioners, a cube table, some curtains and an "antique pitcher and washstand." She got her name and the money but none of the furnishings when the judgment was finally given on October 4, 1973.

Later Carol left the *Post* and moved to India for a while where she filed free-lance stories on women's issues. Eventually, she married another *Post* reporter, Stuart Auerbach, and today lives in semi-anonymity in Washington. From time to time she still contributes articles for the *Post* but always avoids any discussion of her first husband.

5

[Bob, 1965–70]

The *Wright* Stuff

BOB HAD even more reason to be lonely in Norfolk, Virginia, a city surrounded on three sides by water and nothing like Wheaton, Illinois. He was sent there by the U.S. Navy three days after his graduation from Yale on June 13, 1965. Robert Woodward was commissioned as an ensign, just before the university's commencement exercises, by U.S. senator George A. Smathers of Florida.[1] The twenty-minute ceremony took place in the law school auditorium.

In Norfolk, Bob was assigned to the U.S.S. *Wright*. The ship, at first glance, might have seemed a relic from another era. It had been designed to be a heavy cruiser in the mid-1940s, but had quickly been converted to a small aircraft carrier, thus the name (after the two pioneers of flight). When Bob boarded the twenty-thousand-ton vessel in Norfolk, it had been reborn again, costing the taxpayers $25 million, rebuilt in 1962 at the Puget Sound Naval Shipyards in Bremerton, Washington. Its newest incarnation was that of a National Emergency Command Ship. One of three NECS vessels, to use the Navy acronym, the *Wright* was said to be a sanctuary for the president of the United States and his cabinet officers in case of nuclear war.[2] The *Wright* was described by the military publication *Jane's Fighting Ships* in an American edition as having "elaborate communications, data processing and display facilities for use by national authorities. The command spaces include presentation theatres similar to those at command posts ashore. The *Wright* has the most powerful transmitting antennas ever installed in a ship." According to the specifications for the

43

Wright, the tallest antenna mast was "eighty-three feet tall and designed to withstand hundred-mile-per-hour winds." A Navy spokesman for Cruiser-Destroyer Flotilla Four in 1963 said it more emphatically: "It has the most extensive communications facilities ever put aboard a ship."

In actuality, the *Wright*'s role as a haven for the president and his cabinet was secondary. According to Navy intelligence sources and a highly placed U.S. government official who helped implement the White House "hot line" telephone to Moscow, the "floating White House" description was, for the most part, a decoy. The ship was really an elite "at sea Pentagon" with a "smaller replication of the Pentagon war room on one level, built into a former airplane hangar below deck." It was described by the *Norfolk Virginia-Pilot* just after its maiden voyage in December of 1963 this way: "Packed into the 684-foot vessel are spaces for war operations, plotting, charts, conferences and projection of battle situations. Radios, Teletypes and facsimile transmitters provide worldwide communications." And according to other declassified records, there were also facilities for "producing and displaying maps, photographs, and other intelligence . . . an entire wall is used to display large status boards and maps, mounted on tracks so that they can easily be called into view."

Said the government source, "The *Wright* operated under SIOP, which stood for Single Integrated Operation Plan. SIOP was the plan the United States had to wage nuclear war on specified targets within the Soviet Union, China and Eastern Europe. The ship got the same sensitive intelligence information as the Pentagon war room got. It was part of the nerve network. The *Wright* was an alternate site that would have coordinated the launching of nuclear missiles—particularly from Polaris submarines in the early 1960s, and later the Poseidon class of submarines. It was also one of the locations the president and the top brass of the military might have gone in case of imminent nuclear war—if they could have made it in time. In the sixties it was the second preferred location for the president—the first for the Pentagon—after a hollowed-out mountain on the Pennsylvania-Maryland border [Raven Rock] and before a similar such bunker was established in the Virginia foothills of the Blue Ridge Mountains [Mount Weather].

"Under SIOP, the Strategic Air Command in Omaha would have given the command to nuclear-armed piloted aircraft. The

North American Aerospace Defense Command (NORAD) was in charge of launching land-based intercontinental ballistic missiles (ICBMs). But if either had been knocked out, that responsibility would have fallen to the *Wright*.

"If you can imagine the level of intelligence General Schwarz-kopf was getting during the Iraqi war—well, that's the kind of information the *Wright* would have gotten twenty-five years ago."

Declassified records bear this out. The command ship recorded an astounding 146,093 incoming messages in 1966. There were 277 phones aboard. The *Wright* was one of the first U.S. ships to get a satellite communications system, which gave it instant rapport with intelligence contacts worldwide. Before the installation, long-distance radio calls were initiated by a helicopter that towed an antenna wire several hundred feet into the air, then hovered there until all the secret communications were completed.

The satellite system was inaugurated on October 26, 1966, by Rear Adm. Robert Weeks. The first 36,000-mile earth-to-sky-and-back call—bouncing off the SYNCOM III military satellite—was made to the Pentagon.

The SIOP had three teams on the *Wright*, which would alternate watches. There were forty to fifty men in the unit made up of uniformed men from each of the military services, the U.S. Central Intelligence Agency and military intelligence. The crack unit operated autonomously from the rest of the ship. The SIOP groups were headed by a navy captain. Because the SIOP squad could begin nuclear Armageddon at any time, the ship was also laced with free-lance "fail-safe" informants, poised to report any aberrant behavior.

If nuclear war was about to begin and the order was given to strike, the team would have been commanded to begin launching nuclear missiles. If nuclear war was in progress, and there was no word from the Pentagon, the SIOP team on the *Wright* would have had the discretion to act on its own.

Could a massive nuclear strike have been launched from the ship? According to the source, "One person can't implement a nuclear strike. But if the SIOP team or a correct number of ranking officers were aboard, yes, they could. The *Wright* would have begun the process, and if the codes and prelaunch instructions were correct, then the missiles would have been armed with two men turning silver firing keys to let loose the nuclear weapons."

How elite then, was an assignment aboard the *Wright*? "Very elite. Virtually everyone aboard had a classified clearance. Certainly every officer. Most would have been top secret."

And would the Central Intelligence Agency have an informant or agent aboard? The source concluded, "Absolutely. The CIA would have had a liaison officer aboard at least. Probably covert informants in addition to the men on the SIOP team. Rivalry between the services was intense."

A former government official claimed that animosity between the CIA and the military was at a high level in the 1960s because the CIA had insisted Francis Gary Powers make his U-2 intelligence flights deeper into Russia and change his flight pattern, going from south to north or from Pakistan to Norway. The CIA wanted photos of the deeper route, dubbed Operation Overflight, because it needed shots of a Soviet ICBM missile construction site. Powers was shot down in May of 1960, captured and, after a show trial, held for two years before being bartered for a Soviet spy. The U-2 flights were curtailed, with the military blaming the CIA for its interference.

The SIOP, begun by Dwight Eisenhower, was formally drawn up in 1962 by Defense Secretary Robert McNamara and a group of assistants known as the "whiz kids." Further theories on SIOP came from the Rand Corporation, which had been "loaned" faculty members from Ivy League schools. One former Yale historian, Bernard Brodie, authored the modern theory of nuclear deterrence. But it was a Princeton academic, William W. Kaufmann, who created the "purposeful restraint" theory of nuclear war. Kaufmann believed that each side would begin with a few nuclear missiles—fired at Moscow or Washington—and then escalate if the other side responded. Thus if Washington (including the Pentagon) was leveled, an alternate command center such as the *Wright* would be needed to give the orders to fire the next deadly salvo of missiles.

The *Wright* also contained "lead caves." This was a holdover from a previous incarnation in which it viewed nuclear tests in the Pacific. The "caves" were lead-lined areas of the ship used to store or handle radioactive materials.

A quarter of a century later, Bob Woodward would write in his sixth book, *The Commanders*: "During his 18 months as Secretary [Defense Secretary Richard Cheney] had spent many hours delving into the top-secret Single Integrated Operation Plan (SIOP) for nuclear war with the Soviet Union and Warsaw Pact nations, the most important war plan by far . . ."

How was Bob Woodward chosen for this assignment? When interviewed by writers Len Colodny and Robert Gettlin in March of 1989 for their book, *Silent Coup,* he was asked that question. According to the taped transcript, Bob laughed and replied, "No idea. I was a radio ham when I was a kid. And it was a communications ship. Maybe that was the connection." He also downplayed the duty, telling Colodny and Gettlin that the *Wright* wasn't "one of the prestigious assignments."

That was a facetious, false answer, but an understandable one if Bob had pledged never to reveal the true nature of the ship. Certainly he was in a ham radio club in his sophomore year of high school, but not during his junior or senior years. His days of tapping out Morse code had ended seven years before. It's doubtful that the U.S. Navy would have chosen an NROTC officer on the basis of a boyhood ham radio hobby. But Bob did possess the small-town, conservative, Yale-educated background that the government looks for in assigning men to secret missions.

Several other naval officers called Bob's assignment aboard the *Wright* a "plum" and a "top job." Bob's skipper, Captain Frank Romanick, told this writer (after confirming the presence of the SIOP team) that an assignment on the ship was considered "choice . . . select." But retired rear admiral Frank Corley had a more pragmatic explanation: "On that kind of ship, they would also be looking for couth people, no 'wild' men. A Yale man would be considered couth."

Bob's listed title on the *Wright* was circuit control officer. He said he supervised a group of fifteen to twenty enlisted men and has admitted his position required getting a high security clearance. Aboard were eleven hundred enlisted men and fifty-three officers. According to declassified records, two hundred of them worked in "communications."

There are three common levels of security clearances in the U.S. military—in ascending order of importance they are confidential, secret, and top secret. Bob's clearance was top secret "crypto" clearance, which allowed him access to nearly any classified document as well as codes. He also ran the ship's newspaper, which gave him an excuse to speak to anyone aboard. There were other clearances above Bob's, but they were for single intelligence missions and extremely rare. Bob Woodward has insisted in other interviews that a top secret crypto clearance is not necessarily an indication of intelligence work. This is certainly correct, although that kind of clearance and Bob's position as a naval officer would have given him entrée for viewing the ultrasensitive messages that flowed to and from the *Wright*. Bob Woodward, holding a top secret crypto clearance, would have been one of the few aboard able to decode an order commanding the SIOP team to wage nuclear war.

A study of the *Wright*'s 1965 and early 1966 deck logs showed that the majority of Bob's duty aboard the ship during that time was while the vessel rested in drydock at berth 55 of the Norfolk Naval Shipyard in Portsmouth, Virginia. When the ship did go to sea, it mostly roamed Chesapeake Bay or hugged the Eastern seaboard. Its main exercises away from shore were to test and retest helicopter landings on the converted aircraft carrier, a crucial event that would have occurred in a national emergency. The Pentagon brass would have attempted to evacuate from the District of Columbia to the *Wright* via helicopter, a forty-minute flight.

The ship operated under Atlantic Command DEFCON, which in military parlance stood for defense conditions. There were five levels of DEFCON. Level five was considered "routine or normal." Level four was "standby with strengthened security measures." Level three was "alert status." Level two was "declaration of war or an increase in force readiness." And level one was "war—maximum force readiness." In Norfolk, the ship operated under level five.

After more than a year of sea duty with the *Wright*, Bob wed his high school sweetheart, with whom he had now been romantically involved for nearly a decade beginning with the ninth grade and through her four years at Smith College. The marriage to Kathleen Middlekauff was a formal ceremony on June 27, 1966, at a Presbyterian church in Summit, New Jersey, near her parents' home. Bob's best man was Jonathan Leader, an Ezra Stiles college resident who had graduated a year before Bob, in 1964.

Jon Leader had gone to prep school, was a lifelong resident of New York City and was not a member of any Yale secret society, so he would seem to have little in common with Bob Woodward. He was though, like Bob, a history major. He told this writer in

1992 that he was "surprised at being selected." And although he lived in Manhattan, less than 250 miles from Washington, Bob's "best man" said he had not had any contact with Bob for "at least ten years."

Bob's ushers at the wedding seemed to be more logical choices. David Nochimson, a 1965 Yale classmate, was both a history major and a Book and Snake man, and thus an obvious choice to "stand up" for Bob. (Nochimson, who today is a Los Angeles entertainment lawyer, politely but firmly refused to be interviewed for this book.) Scott Armstrong, Bob's longtime boyhood friend from Wheaton, then attending Yale, also ushered. Kathleen's former cheerleading partner from Wheaton, Carolyn Billingsley, was maid of honor. Bob's sister, Anne, was a bridesmaid.

After a short honeymoon in Manhattan, Bob and Kathy moved into an expensive new waterfront high-rise apartment building in Norfolk at 330 West Brambleton Street, near the Norfolk Naval Yard. But Kathy hated the small apartment and its downtown location. After a few months they changed address, moving to the Crown Point Townhouse Apartments. There they rented a new two-bedroom unit for $110 a month. A 1966 ad for the Crown Point development touted the "dishwasher, disposal, range and hood." Crown Point promised "colonial charm with the best of comforts."

The second year of duty aboard the *Wright* found Bob at sea, unlike 1965. The NECS ship did cruises that ranged from Cape Cod to a trip to Uruguay ordered by the Joint Chiefs of Staff. According to the logs, the ship was often followed by "Soviet trawlers" and "Soviet merchant ships." The deck logs also recorded Bob's two "special" in person courier missions while the NECS ship was berthed in Boston and Norfolk.

Nearly five months before the South American cruise, and more than four years after the ship was rebuilt for the SIOP dreams of President Eisenhower and Robert McNamara, a "presidential quarters" was hastily designed by a Norfolk interior decorator on the cheap for $7,000. In a publicity story, complete with picture, the designer told the *Virginia-Pilot* that he didn't realize the suite was for the president until he was partly finished. The presidential "suite" contained no seal or presidential trappings and was used by flag-rank officers. Shortly after the Norfolk decorator finished his work, the *Wright*'s log would note that President Lyndon Johnson helicoptered out from an Alliance for Progress conference in Uruguay during mid-April of 1967 and "passed alongside starboard beam, range 100 yards. President waved to crew assembled at quarters." But Bob's memory, as expressed in a recorded 1989 interview, was that "the President came aboard."[3] That was untrue and obfuscating. While off the shores of Uruguay, the *Wright* operated under "standby" or DEFCON four status, handling all communications—confidential and otherwise—for the president and his staff.

There is some evidence that the U.S. government was fearful of violence toward Lyndon Johnson at the Uruguay conference. In renegade CIA officer Philip Agee's controversial published diary, he wrote that he was one of sixty agents sequestered in the South American country during the president's visit.

A twenty-year veteran of naval intelligence told the author that the *Wright* also had intelligence collection equipment aboard. Although not a pure "spy ship," in the absolute sense of the word, such as the *Pueblo* or the *Liberty*, the NECS vessel was capable of directing its mammoth communications equipment toward trailing Soviet ships to overhear their conversations or codes. A slow-moving object at sea, in international waters, would seem the last place to put the top brass of the Pentagon, or even the President, given the choice of a command aircraft flying in its own airspace or a protected bunker inside a mountain, the other two available options. However, the ship was indeed intended to be a supersecret Pentagon in the Atlantic Ocean. The U.S. military, at the time, believed that a floating command ship could hide in the vastness of the sea.[4]

During the long cruises, Bob took correspondence courses from the University of Wisconsin and began another novel. Neither newlywed fell in love with the culture of the eastern-Virginia-peninsula city of Norfolk. When Scott Armstrong came to visit, Bob's idea of a good time was to give him a private tour of the *Wright*'s open-to-the-public facilities.

After nearly two and a half years of duty based in Norfolk aboard the *Wright*, Bob was assigned to go to Vietnam. According to David Halberstam in *The Powers That Be*, Bob got orders to go to Can Tho province, in the Mekong Delta, an assignment that raised the chances that he could be killed or wounded.[5] This is where a friend, David Charles Miller, Jr., was working as a CIA operative in 1967 and 1968 (more about Mr. Miller in chapter 6). Bob, now promoted to lieutenant junior grade, did not want the duty and no longer believed in the war or the direction it was taking. According to David Halberstam, the first evidence of Bob's avoidance of Vietnam duty was that he wrote a letter to everyone in the Pentagon who might have a bearing on his fate and told them he was ready to go career Navy and wanted to serve aboard a destroyer. Leonard Downie tells a similar tale in *The New Muckrakers*. But in Bob's 1989 recorded interview with Gettlin and Colodny, Bob told a different story: "I made a trip to Washington to talk to my detailer . . . I'd rather go to a ship." Bob said the detail officer made the arrangements for him.

According to a veteran naval captain, Bill Brinkmann, "that sounds kind of reasonable. If someone had served two and a half years at sea, he might have had a little leverage to get out of Vietnam." But another former naval officer said, "Nobody got out of going to Vietnam in 1968."

Bob's new duty, aboard the U.S.S. *Fox*, based in San Diego and Long Beach, California, was about as close as one could get to the South Asia mainland without actually being there. The six-month tour, which began on October 17, 1968, included three weeks of joint cruising with the U.S.S. *Galveston*—stopping to get a final briefing at Pearl Harbor—from San Diego to a site in the South China Sea about 125 miles off the coast of North Vietnam. The staging area, midway between the Chinese island of Hainan and the enemy, near the center of the Gulf of Tonkin, was known as Yankee Station.

That destination was where a convoy of ships would gather to support U.S. Navy bombers and fighter jets that made strikes from aircraft carriers into both the North and South Vietnamese war zones. At times, Bob's ship would cruise within twenty miles of the coast. The ship was considered a PIRAZ vessel in Navy parlance—the acronym stood for Positive Identification and Radar Advisory Zone. The *Fox*, classified as a guided-missile frigate, carried missiles and experimental communications equipment. Its mission was to determine whether enemy aircraft, possibly MiG-17s or MiG-21s, were following U.S. jets back to their sea-based aircraft carriers. There was also an intelligence team aboard that listened to Vietnamese communications using the ship's antennas. Most of the team spoke Russian or various Asian languages learned at the armed forces language school in Monterey, California. The intelligence mission was to attempt to deci-

pher North Vietnamese and Viet Cong radio communications. The
enemy was considered relatively unsophisticated in transmitting
codes.

Bob's half-year cruise aboard the *Fox*, to the Yankee Station
area, included four months spent in the Asian Pacific theater,
including R&R—rest and recreation—stops in Yokosuka, Japan,
and Hong Kong. Minor maintenance was done at the U.S.'s Subic
Bay base in the Philippines. Bob spent Christmas day of 1968
aboard the *Fox* in the Gulf of Tonkin.

Bob's title now was communications officer. As a full lieutenant, promoted in late July of 1968, he ran the radio team. Bob was
one of twenty-seven officers out of the nearly four hundred men
aboard. The commanding officers of the *Fox* during Bob's tour
were Captains Robert Welander and M. D. Ward.

Life aboard the ship could be grueling, according to David
Juarin, the communications officer of the *Fox* from 1969 to 1971,
after Bob Woodward's tour. The communications officer shared a
six-by-twelve-foot stateroom and did eighteen-hour shifts with six
hours off for several days in a row. There were movies and card
games during the off hours, but those activities quickly wore thin.
After doing what Juarin remembered as "thirty to sixty days at a
whack," the ship would head to an Asian port for liberty.

The communications officer had one major perk. In a crowded
ship, privacy at sea was nearly impossible. Bob had access to the
crypto vault, a small room to which he was given the key and
codes. Inside was a desk and the codes of the ship. Each month,
and sometimes more often than that, Bob's responsibility entailed
destroying the old codes and installing a series of new ones at the
direction of naval intelligence. It was an excellent place to study,
and Bob read and reread classic literature. After returning to San
Diego on April 2, 1969, Bob was awarded the Navy Commenda-
tion Medal for his communications work aboard the frigate.

Certainly the new longer absences were a strain on Bob Woodward's first marriage. But the young couple made plans for the
future. Bob's four years in the Navy were to end in the middle of
1969. Bob and Kathy planned to move north in California where
each could do further study at the University of California at
Berkeley. Bob intended to write when not taking courses. Kathy
would work and support him.

According to Kathy Woodward, Bob came home one day,
shortly before his four years were up, and said, "I've been ex-

tended for another year. I have a choice of being stationed in San Francisco or Washington."

At first, Kathy thought that didn't pose much of a problem. She assumed they were staying in California and began preparing for the movers. Berkeley and San Francisco were minutes apart. So she was amazed when Bob told her, "I'm going to Washington. It's better for me."

Bob said he would be working at the White House, according to Kathy Woodward. This account has been confirmed by Al Woodward, Bob's father.

Shocked that Bob would scrap their plans, Kathy refused to head east, and that effectively ended their marriage. Kathy Woodward, without the funds necessary to make the move to Berkeley by herself, then arranged to get a job as a teaching assistant at the University of California at San Diego in exchange for a salary and courses.

Bob has said in interviews that he served an additional year because the chief of naval operations extended *all* regular officers, beginning in 1967. Bob was mistaken. Extensions were done on a selective rather than blanket basis. Doctors and other crucial occupations were the officers most likely to be extended. While technically Bob served "at the pleasure of the president," it is surprising that he was forced to serve an extra year, particularly in light of his long and honorable duty at sea over a four-year span.

That he chose Washington over San Francisco would seem even more puzzling, particularly because it clearly jeopardized and in the end terminated his twelve-year relationship with Kathy. She visited him once in Washington, but their marriage was over. They were divorced in 1970.[6]

On his own again—as he had usually been during his years in high school, at Yale, and at sea—Bob had plenty of time to ingratiate himself with the nation's military leadership inside the Pentagon, across the Potomac River from the nation's capital. It was like a reunion week at Yale. The chief of naval operations was the powerful Adm. Thomas Moorer, who could have met Bob when he visited the *Wright* on December 2, 1966, and who would later become chairman of the Joint Chiefs of Staff. The former commander of the *Wright*, Francis Fitzpatrick, now a rear admiral, was Moorer's deputy. And it was perhaps more than sheer coincidence that the other top aide to Moorer was now Rear Adm. Robert Welander, the former commander of the *Fox*. One could easily theorize that either Moorer, Welander, Fitzpatrick or all three requested Bob for "special" duty at the Pentagon because of his experience aboard the *Wright*. It may also have been a sort of penance, a year of duty at the nerve center of the U.S. military, ordered by the same government agency that was responsible for getting him out of going to the Southeast Asian mainland.

Bob has described his job at the Pentagon as that of a communications watch officer. He explained that he was in charge of "all the communications coming to the CNO, or actually to the whole Navy Department, including the secretary of the navy."

So he was again in a unique situation. Moorer was a friend of two of the most powerful Nixon administration appointees, Henry Kissinger and John Mitchell. Besides the sensitive data that flowed in and out of the Pentagon relating to the Vietnam War, Kissinger used the Navy's communications center to communicate with Peking. It was also the top-secret SR-1 channel of naval intelligence, inside the communications center, that was used to make arrangements for Kissinger's secret trip to China, which led to renewed relations between it and the United States.[7] Kissinger also used the Navy Department's clandestine communication channels to initiate negotiations with North Vietnam. Meetings with the Soviet Union were also arranged through the CNO communications room. Richard Lugar, the Republican senator from Indiana who would later serve on the Senate's intelligence committee, was one of Bob's predecessors. Lt. Robert Woodward, then, was in the same place he had been on the *Wright*. He had the opportunity to be privy to the secrets of a nation.

Did he also go to work in the White House, as he told both his wife and father?

"I had courier duty there occasionally. . . . Carrying some documents or a folder," said Woodward in his taped interview with Gettlin and Colodny in 1989. Bob so downgraded his White House duties, calling them "scut work," that in reading his remarks it's as if he were trying to equate his duties at the White House to that of a pizza delivery man.

But although Bob Woodward has emphatically denied it, there is now a significant body of evidence that points to him as a very special type of naval officer. One top military official with whom Bob reportedly did face-to-face, sensitive briefings was Gen. Alexander Haig, who then worked for the National Security Council in the basement of the White House. The chief of naval operations,

Adm. Thomas Moorer, and the former secretary of defense Melvin Laird, are both on tape in 1989 interviews as saying that Bob Woodward briefed Alexander Haig at the White House. Later, Moorer attempted to back away from his recorded statement, making contradictory statements and sounding befuddled. Laird said he was "aware that Haig was being briefed by Woodward." Laird's assistant, Jerry Friedheim, said, "Woodward was there." Roger Morris, who worked for the National Security Council at the time, reported he saw Bob outside Alexander Haig's office several times. And Jim Hougan, in his 1984 book, *Secret Agenda*, and also in interviews with this author, said Bob admitted that he had been a briefer, although he wouldn't say whom he briefed. Nevertheless, Bob Woodward, after being asked by Colodny and Gettlin whether or not he briefed at the White House, responded with a strong no. Considering the evidence, Bob Woodward's denial more strongly suggests intelligence than it does his uninvolvement in White House briefings.

When Kathy Woodward was asked why Bob would choose to end their four-year marriage by accepting the Washington assignment, she said, "Well, that's Bob, isn't it?" Kathy Woodward said that Bob was "very ambitious . . . ruthless . . . controlled." She told another interviewer that Bob was "severe in his relationships" and that "his vulnerability is hidden by his desire to be in control."

The U.S. military does not take lightly its choice of men who work in communications at the Pentagon, deliver documents to the White House or brief the nation's leadership. As Roger Morris added, "People who go to the Pentagon and act as briefers usually wind up as someone's protégé, whether or not they stay in the service." Bob Woodward's selection for these assignments was a result of his entire life to that date: small-town Republican boyhood, a "loner," the Barry Goldwater–like speech at his high school commencement, continued conservative expressions at Yale—*the* school of choice for intelligence-community recruiters. It was at Yale where a professor would label him "a crypto-fascist" and where he had chided Kathy for empathizing with the radical SDS—Students for a Democratic Society. And it was at Yale where Bob joined a one-hundred-and-twenty-two-year-old secret society.

Although Bob Woodward only reluctantly speaks to the press, preferring controlled television interviews where time is measured by thirty-second sound bites, he has continued to deny any friendship with Alexander Haig, saying he didn't meet him until 1973. He has vociferously fought all attempts to link him with White House briefings while working at the Pentagon. Bob portrays his background in such a way that his initial success as a writer and a reporter, particularly during Watergate, seems to have come from simple hard work, from knocking on doors in the dark of night and from talking with low-level government secretaries. Nothing could be further from the truth. While Bob certainly worked hard, he also had a network of contacts that began at Yale and continued at the Pentagon, a powerful combination that would serve him well over the next two decades. Bob denied knowing Alexander Haig because Gen. Haig would be one of his more important government sources when Bob became a newspaper reporter, and because Alexander Haig is one of two or three men who fit the description of Deep Throat. When Robert Woodward left the Pentagon, he was completely plugged in, or, to use one of his book titles, Bob was *wired*.

6

[Carl and Bob, 1969–72]

The Sentinel Files

Whenever you run a clandestine operation, you run two things at the same time: you prepare the team for the hit, and you keep it so small there's nobody to spread it all around. And across the hall is a big staff working on what we call special plans. They're preparing the cover story. The cover story is what they want people to believe and to talk about, and to argue about.

—From a 1992 speech by Col. Fletcher Prouty, former chief of special operations, Joint Chiefs of Staff

AFTER FOUR YEARS at the *Washington Post*, Carl had firmly established his reputation. It wasn't good. Arguably, he was one of the more talented writers at the paper. His long pieces on the neighborhoods of Washington were keenly observed, almost poetic. He did investigative pieces uncovering exploitation of the poor in the inner city by greedy landlords. He wrote reviews of rock groups ranging from the Rolling Stones to Blood, Sweat and Tears. Many of these pieces were unassigned, the type of reporting others were calling the "new journalism." It was the kind of writing that Nicholas von Hoffman and Tom Wolfe did. It was what Carl wanted to do but what the *Washington Post* didn't want him to do.

Rolling Stone—now there was a magazine where he thought he could have sparkled. Writing and reviewing the new music, that was Carl's aspiration by 1970. And he could have succeeded there had they found a place for him when he wrote to them, asking for Hunter Thompson's political beat. Jann Wenner turned him down. Didn't they know the drop-out, the rotten kid, could write? Consider his knowing review of this rock group in August of 1969:

> Iron Butterfly's sound always seem to border on anarchy, a characteristic which is both the group's greatest asset and liability.
> The music is full of fine elements—good lead vocal, the use of arpeggios and other classical techniques on lead guitar, spine-chilling dissonance that somehow holds together, Bach-like organ chorales, and in part, a mysticism that few groups incorporate in their sound.

Two weeks later Carl had a long piece on the Washington neighborhood of Cleveland Park. It took up nearly the entire front page of the Metro section and ran over to page two:

> Cleveland Park is a neighborhood based on comfort—not Georgetown comfort or Embassy Row comfort or Watergate comfort, but the easy comfort of the small towns where most of the New Dealers were raised. It is the relaxed comfort of ample porches, hammocks, tree houses for children, spacious homes of five and eight bedrooms, broad walkways and shaded streets where cars are parked on the wrong side of the road.

Writing such as this was what kept Carl in the newsroom. If executive editor Ben Bradlee had had his way then and ignored the fuss that would have been made by the reporters' guild—of which Carl was an active member—Carl would have been out the door. Carl offended Bradlee. The executive editor, now into his fifth year of remaking the *Post* in his own image, was always immaculate, clad in striped pure-cotton shirts with stark white collars. He wore red suspenders—Carl said they looked as if they belonged in a firehouse—and pleated wool trousers. Bradlee didn't think a reporter should come to the office in old army fatigues and long greasy black hair. What demonstration was this kid going to anyway? The *Post* spent millions of dollars building a modern newsroom, and Carl's work area was soon surrounded by little black holes, the pitted desecration of cigarettes dropping from his desk, landing on the floor and burning through the new carpeting. It was Carl who put two desks together to make a Ping-Pong table, installing a table tennis net. And it was Bradlee who noticed during one of his insouciant yet calculated tours of the newsroom.

The Bradlee tour: Ben would pause to talk to the favored writers, one foot on the floor, the other resting atop the edge of a reporter's desk, verbally stroking them with praise while dominating them through body language. He was nearly fifty then and in his prime. He tried to notice something about each one of the 379 members of the news department. Certainly young Bernstein was hard to miss. His desk was marked by a lone imported bicycle wheel at the side of it and parodies of Nixon family life—Tricia's wedding photos propped up on its top surface. Still, Bradlee respected Carl's writing. He could have fired him when he was reported sleeping on an old couch in the press shack at city hall during the mayor's press conference. He nearly let him go after Carl left a rented car in a garage in Richmond, Virginia, and forgot about it for several months—the bill the *Post* received was equal to half the year's state travel budget.

Carl just didn't fit in. He wasn't close to being a free-agent superstar journalist such as Ward Just, Haynes Johnson, Stanley Karnow, or David Broder. Bradlee had seduced those men from other papers with a combination of promises and cash. Carl wasn't a bright young Ivy League Turk, the likes of Bob Kaiser. At the *Post*, Carl Bernstein was a fringe player. But he could write.

Now across the river from Washington at the Pentagon, Bob Woodward read the *Post*. He studied it. Writing for a Washington newspaper was a far cry from writing the novels he had once aspired to do. In 1970 his father would be elected a circuit court judge. Al Woodward led the ticket with 90,434 votes; the nearest Democrat got 52,576. The most Republican town in the nation did well for Bob's dad even though Democrat Adlai Stevenson III was sweeping the state and winning a U.S. Senate seat. The victory decided Bob's future. He would follow in the footsteps of his father and be an attorney. He applied to Harvard Law School and was accepted. At the age of twenty-seven it was time to do something with his life.

But Bob also read another respected daily newspaper, the *Wall Street Journal*. He grew to idolize and then became friendly with its top Washington investigative reporter, Jerry Landauer. In downtown Washington a prominent lawyer also read the *Journal*. The attorney's name was Richard Copaken and he worked for one of the city's leading law firms, Covington and Burling. He, too, knew Jerry Landauer and wanted his help—he had a story to tell. Copaken's story was about an island, Culebra, off the coast of, and part of, the Commonwealth of Puerto Rico. U.S. Navy air units had used portions of Culebra for bombing and strafing runs since 1936. The Navy wanted to expand the area's bombing territory, and the natives wanted it stopped. Five people had been killed and children injured when Navy jets descended from the sky without warning.

Copaken had a glittering resumé. He had been editor of both the Harvard *Crimson* and the *Harvard Law Review*. He had also been a White House Fellow under Lyndon Johnson. As a White House Fellow he had met the aforementioned David C. Miller. Miller was in the Fellows program after serving in Vietnam as a member of the CIA. He had been recruited by the Agency straight off the campus of the University of Michigan. As a White House Fellow, Miller worked in the office of Atty. Gen. John Mitchell and then John Dean. He was a friend of both Bob Woodward's and Richard Copaken's. But what did Bob Woodward know about Culebra? "He knew a lot," Richard Copaken told the author. "He knew all about the secret spy program, Task Force 157, for example."

Task Force 157 was a U.S. Navy intelligence program that used current and former CIA "free-lancers" to further U.S. interests around the world. It monitored access to major world ports and was active off the coast of Vietnam. Task Force 157 was responsible for helping Henry Kissinger pull off his secret 1971 visit to China. It monitored nuclear weapons being transported on Soviet ships. It recruited foreign espionage agents.

The secret spy corps was given a verbal go-ahead in 1962 by President John F. Kennedy as a way to extract information from Cubans who worked for the Navy at its Guantánamo Bay base. It was formally sanctioned by Lyndon Johnson in 1968. The budget was small, less than $10 million a year. T.F. 157 (initials were used by members) finessed the lack of money by hiring "part-timers," Americans overseas and patriotic college types who were already entering a line of work where they could be useful to the unit.

In 1968, T.F. 157 was part of several intelligence groups that helped to get a wealthy conservative candidate, Luis A. Ferre, elected governor of Puerto Rico. Ferre owned the island's largest cement factory, several plantations, and had some key media holdings. Ferre had never won an elected office; he had previously been rejected three times by the voters. The CIA wanted him governor because it felt that, as a conservative, he would be a forceful antidote to Fidel Castro in the Caribbean. The Navy wanted Ferre in and had agreed to support him in exchange for being given continued bombing rights to Culebra. The two teamed up even though Puerto Rico was considered domestic and technically outside the CIA's operating charter. Part of the Navy's support included padding food-supply bills to its Roosevelt Roads Base and then funneling the extra money to a third candidate, splintering the vote and thus helping Ferre. The Navy even let the Ferre campaign use its printing presses for fliers and brochures. The CIA and T.F. 157 chipped in with a dirty-tricks program that included a goon squad and a rumor mill that spread negative stories about Ferre's opponents before the election.[1]

After Ferre was elected in a surprise upset, the bombings on the island increased. In 1969, a total of thirty-five thousand target runs were made on a nine-hours-per-day basis, with three hours for Sunday strafings. In addition there were 228 days of missile firings, 42 days of mine-dropping exercises, and 123 days of naval gunnery practice.

At this point, Ferre acted duplicitously, promising to help the Culebrans and intercede for them, but in actuality doing little. After Ferre's promises proved to be empty, Copaken stepped up his services on behalf of the island.

Copaken was representing the Culebrans on a *pro bono* or charity basis. He had been told that Bob Woodward had a lot of information about Culebra, and he had tried to get help directly from Bob's friend David Miller. Now he asked a friend to introduce him to Bob Woodward. Bob's hero, Jerry Landauer, was invited to sit in as both reporter and "bait" to ensure Bob's presence. Copaken, Landauer, and Bob Woodward met several times. The first time was at the Hotel Washington, across from the U.S. Treasury. They also met for dinner at the Golden Ox, a downtown steak house. Still another time they arranged to meet at Bob's apartment, which Copaken recalled as "a tiny studio high-rise apartment, somewhere off Dupont Circle." At Bob's place, according to Copaken, he was shown information Bob had on Culebra that had been compiled in a leather-bound diary. "It was clear," Copaken said, "that Bob Woodward was keeping a daily log of what he saw and heard at the Pentagon."

Covington and Burling later asked Bob Woodward if he would take a lie detector test to verify what he had told and shown them; Bob became indignant and refused.

Jerry Landauer wrote two articles about Culebra and Puerto Rico for the *Wall Street Journal*. The first ran on June 10, 1970. The second, which ran just before the Puerto Rican elections of 1972, used information supplied by Bob and was helpful in getting Ferre defeated in his reelection bid. Copaken then got the Navy to cease the bombing runs. A few years later Jerry Landauer exposed the bribes and income tax evasion of Spiro Agnew and was credited with forcing the vice president to resign. David Miller went on to other cloak-and-dagger exploits. At one point he reportedly told a requestor of information that it would be dropped off in "a plain envelope in the dark of night." In the late 1970s he sometimes playfully signed memos to friends as "Deep Throat." Later he would serve in the National Security Council, monitoring world terrorism. By 1990 he was President George Bush's staff assistant for national security. And of course Bob Woodward eventually got to be an investigative reporter just like his idol, Jerry Landauer, topping him by getting a U.S. president to resign.[2]

The question, then, begs itself once more. Was Bob Woodward ever a free-lance or retained Central Intelligence Agency liaison officer, informant or operative between his graduation from Yale and his separation from the U.S. Navy? Was he a free-lance agent for Task Force 157? This author got various forms of affirmative opinions from intelligence experts. It would explain his assignment to the *Wright* and his misleading statements to interviewers. It would make more understandable his being able to get out of going to Vietnam in 1968, his extension for an additional year at the Pentagon, his being chosen to brief at the White House and his denials as well. It would also help explain his subsequent high-level friendships with leaders of the U.S. military and the CIA. But the final answer lies within Bob Woodward. Bob, whose professed favorite author is Charles McCarry, a former CIA covert operator, has said many times that he is a mere "gatherer of facts." Fair enough. The facts that have preceded us to this point as well as those that follow certainly create a body of circumstantial evidence. It is up to Bob to address them.

After he began working at the Pentagon, Bob Woodward leased a sixth-floor apartment in downtown Washington. The small studio,

495 square feet, at 1718 P Street, N.W., was some six blocks from the *Washington Post*. It was a relatively new building, constructed in 1968. There were 182 apartments—mostly studios and one-bedrooms—built for young professionals on their way up. On the roof there was a small pool, with showers and a sun deck. One could even see the top of the *Post* building from the roof garden above the eleventh floor. Bob's apartment, number 617, stared down into a small canyonlike courtyard created by several equally tall office and apartment buildings. The structure had been designed in an L-shape with the front and back sides of the building facing the street and an alley.

A month after leaving the Navy Bob applied for a reporter's job at the *Washington Post*. It was now August of 1970. Harvard law was put on hold. He was interviewed by Harry Rosenfeld, who was then the assistant managing editor of the metropolitan desk—the local news department. Rosenfeld remembered being startled when Bob Woodward told him how much he wanted a job as a reporter and that he was willing to work without salary until he proved himself.

Such an offer from a Yale history and English major, who had just served honorably in the U.S. Navy, seemed too good to be true. Rosenfeld brought him aboard for a two-week trial and threw him at a lesser editor where Bob was left to flounder. Bob's two-week tryout lasted three, but it was for naught. He wrote seventeen stories; none were printed. The former Yale poet and novelist was deemed too clumsy to write straight city copy at Washington's largest newspaper. Still, his news sense was good. One story, about a new policy by gas stations of accepting only exact amounts of money after dark, appeared in another paper soon after Bob's three-week career at the *Post* was over.

Rosenfeld told Bob that a job for a reporter was available at the *Montgomery County Sentinel* in nearby Rockville, Maryland. The *Sentinel*, the leading suburban weekly outside of Washington, had a paid circulation of just under thirty-five thousand.

Bob was interviewed by Roger Farquhar, the paper's editor. Farquhar, who now lives in retirement in Maine, remembered, "There were forty applications for the job and I interviewed twelve. I hired Bob partly because he was from Yale. But I remember him standing in the doorway of my office with his hand on the knob as he was about to leave. He told me, 'I want to work here so bad I can taste it.' "

The new reporter, said Farquhar, showed his prospective editor some recent Navy discharge papers and a letter of recommendation from Rosenfeld. But it wasn't necessary to get the job. "We were sort of a farm club for the *Post*—Tom Shales started here."[3]

Although Bob displayed "a great work ethic" and would "work for hours and hours" and "take on a story like a bulldog," according to Farquhar, all for $110 a week, he didn't move to Montgomery County and join the community. Each day he would drive to the newspaper's Rockville offices, a twenty mile trip each way, in a 1970 Volkswagen Karmann Ghia sports sedan (replacing an older VW Beetle). The new reporter continued to live in his apartment six blocks from the *Washington Post*.

"He replaced Knight Kiplinger, who was going back to work for the family magazine [then called *Changing Times*, now *Kiplinger's Magazine*]," a former *Sentinel* staffer, David Bartlett, recalled. "There were two openings and I got the second one. I became the news editor and drama critic."

Bartlett, who developed a close working relationship and friendship with Bob at the weekly paper, remembered that Bob seemed to have a "knack" for getting information. "You can get good stories with contacts and persistence, but some people have a gift for getting information out of people. Bob had all three—contacts, persistence and the 'gift.' "

Bob Woodward's first story for the *Sentinel*, on September 24, 1970, with the prescient headline "Rockville Council 'Bugged,' " was still clumsy. Bob Woodward was no Carl Bernstein.

> ROCKVILLE—The subject was roaches Monday night [Bob was punning a recent Broadway play, *The Subject Was Roses*] as a plastic bag of roaches allegedly fresh from a refrigerator in the Rockville Gardens apartment was paraded before the mayor and council.
>
> A large clack [sic] was organized by Marjorie B. Gilbert, head of the Rockville Gardens tenants union, to give testimony at the city council citizen's forum concerning the conditions in and around the apartments.

Bob soon let it be known that he had contacts in the government.

"He used to come in the newsroom and tell us some wild stories," Farquhar told this writer in much the same version he has told others. "He'd tell us there was going to be a revolution in some banana republic in a week, and sure enough, there would be."

Bob Woodward was soon perceived as different by the staff of the *Sentinel*. "He was considered wealthy," David Bartlett remembered. "At least he was a lot better off than the other reporters. He was never short of money. He was able to go to New York City at least two weekends a month. We never knew where he was getting it from. He had a nicer apartment downtown . . . it was the kind you couldn't afford on a *Sentinel* reporter's salary."

After a few weeks Bob's output at the *Sentinel* became one-half local stories and the other half either state or national pieces that he researched and wrote entirely himself. Bob Woodward also became the *Sentinel*'s motion picture critic. Most of the films were viewed on his New York City weekends. *Sentinel* staffers recalled a romantic interest in Manhattan that drew Bob Woodward there.

Bob's movie essays showed a predisposition to "art house" and serious American films. They were also personally revealing, even autobiographical, and eerily prophetic. In reviewing *Carnal Knowledge*, the 1971 motion picture directed by Mike Nichols and starring Ann-Margret, Jack Nicholson and Candice Bergen, Bob described the Ivy League character played by Bergen as "an enigmatic Smithie from down the road." He also wrote that the film was "unsatisfying for the same reasons upper middle class life never lives up to its expectations. . . . The important moments seem to have been left out, and maybe never existed."

In an even more arty work, the Italian film industry's version of *Death in Venice*, Bob led his review with this: "Just suppose Richard Nixon had lost the 1968 election, retired pouting and alone to die in some place like the exotic Hotel Del Coronado in San Diego, Calif., and Italian director Luchino Visconti made a documentary movie of the event, and jazzed it up, calling it, say, 'Death in San Diego.' Well, then Visconti might, indeed, be forgiven with Nixon as a subject." Near the end of his piece, Bob Woodward wrote that Dirk Bogarde, the film's star, "seems no more profound and just as pathetic as a Richard Nixon giving a 'Checker's speech.' "

That Bob, who had voted for Richard Nixon just two years before, and who was a by-the-book Republican from a conservative household, would have written such scathing remarks indicated that a change of heart and mind had taken place while he was working at the Pentagon. He told his friend David Bartlett more than once that he was "annoyed" that he had been made to serve an extra year in the Navy. He had also become disenchanted with the war in Vietnam, as evidenced by some of his 1971 stories for the paper.

As he became more assured at the weekly, he began to disdain the library board meetings and the "council plants a tree ceremonies" assignments, focusing instead on probing investigative pieces that had both national and state implications. One such story was about the black militant leader H. Rap Brown. Bob's story revealed that Brown had been charged with arson during the 1967 Cambridge, Maryland, riots, guaranteeing that he would be on the FBI's most wanted list if he skipped out on his bail before the trial. Bob got the prosecuting attorney in the case to admit that the arson charge had been fabricated in order to put him on the list.

"The *New York Times* woke me up at six in the morning when the story broke to ask if they could pick it up," Farquhar recalled. Bob wrote several follow-up stories and was eventually subpoenaed to Howard County, Maryland, along with Farquhar, to give a deposition on his series.[4] He also seized the opportunity to apply for a reporter's job at the *New York Times*. He was interviewed but wasn't hired. But he didn't give up. He continued to solicit both the *Post* and the *Times* by sending them his most recent clips.

He also composed colorful, albeit hyperbolic, feature stories on local and state figures. He once described a local attorney and power broker, Bob Linowes, as "the Perry Mason, Voltaire and Ivy League Kublai Khan of land development in Montgomery County."

In the final three months of his one-year stay at the *Sentinel* Bob Woodward's stories took on a national bent. They also had a news-breaking tone. There were pieces on wiretaps and the new national political organization Common Cause. Given the context in which they appeared—a community paper filled with recipes, high school sports and county political posturing—the stories were astonishing for their content.

An interview with retired U.S. senator Wayne Morse conducted by Bob Woodward began with Morse saying that a 1963 study of American Vietnam policy had made President John Kennedy "fear the Pentagon, State Department and CIA would suck him into a Bay of Pigs in Vietnam." Bob also quoted Morse describing President Richard Nixon as "a slicker . . . an evil man" and "an ego-maniac.".

A few weeks later, Bob followed up the long story on Morse by getting an exclusive interview with John Kenneth Galbraith. Galbraith admitted to Bob that he had written the report about which Morse had talked. In the interview—Bob reached Galbraith in Vermont—the former ambassador to India in the Kennedy administration bemoaned not saving a copy of the report and then said in a conspiratorial aside to Bob that the report was filed "from Bangkok through CIA channels. It was top secret, eyes only . . . I would love to see it if you get a copy."

With so many mentions of the CIA by famous people one might then expect to learn that Bob produced a favorable feature story on the Central Intelligence Agency itself for the suburban newspaper.

He did.

On the back page of the first section of the *Sentinel* on April 22, 1971, Bob wrote an unassigned article titled, "The Non-Selling of the Central Intelligence Agency." It was the only story on the page. In the complimentary piece on the Virginia-headquartered agency for the Maryland-based weekly, which he wrapped around a speech by CIA director Richard Helms, Bob described everything from recruitment on college campuses to the image of the Agency.

At one point in the story, Bob wrote that a CIA spokesman would not "disclose how many employees the CIA has or even discuss the CIA budget." In the next paragraph, Bob wrote that "an informed government official estimated that the CIA has over 10,000 employees in the U.S., several thousand abroad on the payroll and spends well over $500 million in a year."

Bob also said that "an informed government source" had told him that CIA director Helms, a Democrat, would be kept on as CIA chief and "Nixon has been pleased with his work, though initial intentions were to keep the Johnson appointee on for one year after Nixon took office."

The first high school reunion is usually the worst of the three or four one attends in a lifetime. Each attendee is still in his twenties, still hungry, still eager to make it. The more successful class members strut, posture and preen, pulling their new cars to the front of the building and lingering during their arrivals and departures. The ones who haven't made it are combative, argumentative, still grasping and stretching for the brass ring of life.

At Wheaton High's ten-year reunion in 1971, there were whispers about Robert Upshur Woodward. Where was he? Where was Kathy? The women speculated. Bob had come home from sea to an empty apartment and a Dear John note, one said. The marriage was kaput, over, asserted another. Bob was working for a weekly paper in Maryland, said still another. "Oh my," was heard from one of the women.

The boy voted most likely to succeed had become the class failure of Wheaton Community High School.

Bob's stories continued to find their way to the desks of the *Post* editors. Bob would call Harry Rosenfeld every few weeks, often at home. Rosenfeld soon learned that Bob was, if not a superb politician, a persistent one.

That young Woodward also continued to politick with his former mentors at the Pentagon came through on the pages of the *Sentinel*. In July of 1971, Bob wrote a feature story detailing where officials lived in the Washington area, gleaned from the pages of the new edition of the *Congressional Directory*. He noted that most elected officials chose to live in Virginia. He also wrote, "Residence at the Watergate, the post downtown cooperative apartment complex, is the listing for many of the top Nixon officials including, of course, Attorney General (and Mrs.) John N. Mitchell. Also Secretary of Commerce Maurice H. Stans and Secretary of Transportation John A. Volpe live at the Watergate."[5]

The long article was illustrated with three photos chosen by Bob. They were of Adm. Thomas Moorer, Secretary of Defense Melvin Laird (Bob described Laird knowingly as living in a "humble residence in Bethesda") and Health, Education and Welfare Secretary Elliot L. Richardson. The inclusion of the Admiral Moorer photo was especially peculiar as he was not even named in the story.

Bob Woodward's search for what would later be called by his *Post* editors "Holy shit!" stories eventually got him in trouble. Bob had read a story in the *Washingtonian* magazine in which the publication rated the area's judges. Bob and another reporter, Bill Bancroft, got the idea to run a story rating the area's high school principals. The story ranked each principal from "outstanding" to "poor" and characterized two of the principals as "unsuited." The ratings, which were arbitrary, forced the paper to publish several pages of letters to the editor. It wasn't enough. The paper and Bob were sued by one of the "unsuited" principals, Fred Dunn. The educator eventually won $356,000 in the courts, but the local verdict was overturned by an appeals ruling from a jurist at the state level.

Bob still wanted in at the *Post*. During the deliberations over the Pentagon Papers—documents that revealed the United States' secret role in Vietnam—he was given the Supreme Court's decision by a source two days in advance. Bob went to the newspaper and fed it to an editor. He was not believed. A young kid simply couldn't get that type of information was the reasoning.

Still, Bob continued to lobby with Rosenfeld. On a Saturday during the late summer of 1971, Bob learned that the editor was vacationing at home. Bob went to his house and caught Rosenfeld up at the top of a ladder painting the gutters of his house. The young *Sentinel* reporter climbed the ladder until his face was even with Rosenfeld's paint can. From that level, Bob Woodward made yet another pitch for a reporter's job on the *Post*. This time he won.

Hired by Rosenfeld, he began working as a reporter for the Metro section on September 15, 1971. The salary was just under $13,000 per year. His first bylined story ran two days later, on Friday, September 17. The single-column item, which ran on page three of the City Life section, was a routine piece about the possible disbarment of a lawyer in Silver Spring, Maryland. No one in the newsroom at the *Washington Post* was moved to say, "Holy shit."

7

[Bob and Carl, 1971–72]

In Tandem

"I told Bob Woodward recently I didn't believe there really was a Deep Throat. . . . He was understandably offended. So I asked him if he had revealed Deep Throat's identity to at least one person who didn't *have* to know. He said he had. That one person would have told one other person, who, in turn, would have told two more. The informant's identity would have become public in days."

Playboy: "Then why would he invent such a character?"

Heller: "I believe they had *many* sources inside the government, and the best way to protect them was to create one person who didn't exist."

—Joseph Heller in a
Playboy Interview, June 1975

BY THE TIME Bob Woodward began his job as a reporter for the *Washington Post*, Carl Bernstein had been shipped out. Now considered somewhat of an affront to the still new, more conservative regime (at least in style of dress and manners) of Ben Bradlee, the young Bernstein toiled on the Virginia legislative beat. He spent his days following the populist campaign for lieutenant governor of the Commonwealth's first truly liberal Democrat, a fiery speaker known as "Hollering" Henry Howell.

Howell, whose slogan was "Keep the big boys honest," won his race for the second-highest office in the state but would lose a quixotic race for governor a few years later. Carl admired Howell. He was the kind of politician whom his parents would have revered. Carl liked Howell so much he wrote six separate stories about him during the fall of 1971.

A week after Bob Woodward turned in his small initial story on the Silver Spring lawyer, he scored his first page-one byline. It was a tragic yet routine piece about five family members killed in a fire. Fires and robberies involving death were a necessary inclusion in the *Post*'s city pages, and the hoary slogan "If it bleeds, it leads" was still a big part of the paper's daily content. Bob quickly discovered another way to make page-one news. He began to uncover one scandal after another about the unsanitary conditions in area restaurants and at farmers' markets. Rat droppings and roach infestations discovered near food became his beat. In his first three months at the *Post*, he scored fifty-six bylines, more of them making the front page than those of any other city reporter.

His editors also learned that Bob had "connections" in the government. At first the source was referred to as his "friend" or "Mister X," later becoming known as "Bob's friend." When Alabama governor George Wallace was shot in a Laurel, Maryland, shopping center while campaigning for president on May 15, 1972, the *Post* couldn't get any government authority to release the name of the would-be assassin. "Bob, would you call your friend?" he was asked by the city editor, Barry Sussman. Bob dialed his "friend" but couldn't locate him. The name of Arthur Bremer was eventually supplied to another editor by Kenneth Clawson, who worked in the Nixon White House but had once been a *Post* staffer. The friend did supply Bob with other information on Bremer later, giving details that enabled him to write a series of articles about Wallace's assailant.

Bob became Bradlee's new "fair-haired" favorite on the city section. The executive editor said Bob was "all over the paper" with his potpourri of fire, real-estate-fraud, restaurant-sanitation and George Wallace attempted-assassination stories. The new guy's a comer, Bradlee told the other editors, and he took "the kid" to lunch at Chez Camille, a French bistro on DeSales Street, Bradlee's favorite restaurant at the time. The two discovered much in common. Both had been in ROTC programs, both had served as officers in the Navy and both had gone to Ivy League universities (Bradlee to Harvard).

Bradlee's confidence in Bob Woodward was verified when the new reporter was awakened a month later at nine A.M. on Saturday, June 17, by Sussman. We want you to come in and help on a breaking story, he was told. The Democratic headquarters at the Watergate hotel/apartment complex had been burglarized. Five men had been arrested. Bob walked from his apartment to the paper's newsroom. It took him ten minutes. Carl Bernstein was already there, on the phone.

In the past two decades there have been nearly two hundred books written on the subject that came to be known as Watergate. It is not this author's aim to give a complete retelling of the Watergate story. What has always fascinated most observers was how two—albeit talented and tenacious—young newspaper reporters were, seemingly alone, able to unravel the entire labyrinthine scheme of political sabotage, defamatory acts, income tax fraud and the resulting obstructions of justice by the administration of Richard Nixon.

There is no specific starting point to the Watergate saga. The popular date is that of the break-in itself, but with hindsight it could be said to be the initial discovery of a pattern of illegal political abuses. More accurately, one could go back to 1969 or choose the New Hampshire Democratic primary race of 1972 and detail some of the covert actions taken by saboteurs for the Republican Committee to Re-elect the President, or CREEP. The grand design for the guerrillas of CREEP was to provide Richard Nixon with the weakest possible opponent for his 1972 reelection campaign. Thus, by taking actions that discredited Sen. Edmund Muskie, perceived to be the strongest candidate for the Democratic Party, CREEP paved the way for a landslide victory. Most damaging was a letter to the editor that appeared in New Hampshire's largest newspaper. It created an impression that Muskie condoned the racial slurring of French Canadians who lived in the state. The letter was written by Ken Clawson, the president's deputy press secretary and a former *Post* reporter. CREEP had also prepared a huge dossier on Edward Kennedy, in case he entered the race.

G. Gordon Liddy, who had worked for the president's assistant for domestic affairs, John Ehrlichman, either led a series of burglaries or masterminded burglaries whose purpose was either to bug or copy documents from the offices of Nixon's enemies. At one point, in late May of 1972, Liddy appeared at the rear of George McGovern's headquarters in Washington and, with an air pistol, shot out the floodlights there in order to lay the groundwork for a future break-in. Liddy supervised the Watergate burglary of June 17.

The initial story on the Watergate break-in appeared on Sunday, June 18, 1972. It ran on the top left of the front page under the byline of Alfred Lewis. Lewis, a veteran reporter for the *Post*, had used his contacts with the city's police department and spent the entire day inside the Democratic headquarters at the Watergate, observing the investigation firsthand. Eight other reporters, including Bob and Carl, were given contributing bylines at the end of the story for the work they had done Saturday. Carl also contributed a smaller, related story on the five men who had been arrested.

On Monday, June 19, Bob and Carl's first joint byline appeared in the top left-hand column of the paper. The story named James McCord, one of the five arrested, as the "salaried security coordinator for President Nixon's reelection committee." The caption under a head shot of McCord described him as a "retired CIA employee." Bob wrote the story on Sunday afternoon, and Carl rewrote it, adding refinements.

There was no doubt that the *Post*'s coverage of Watergate, personified by Bob and Carl for the next two years, was far ahead of its competitors. The Alfred Lewis–bylined story was picked up verbatim the same day by the *Los Angeles Times* and other papers. The chief competitor in Washington, the *Star*, never assigned a permanent team to Watergate, contrary to other reports. It purchased the *Washington Daily News* on July 12 in one last attempt to regain the dominance it had once enjoyed; much of the summer of 1972 was spent digesting that acquisition. The *Star* was distracted. Editors and reporters were being reassigned, and the Watergate opportunity was for the most part missed.

The *Star* got small scoops here and there—such as revealing that Watergate conspirator and former CIA agent H. Howard Hunt was the project director of a recent Julie Nixon charity film financed by the government. But more typical was an error-filled front-page story making fanciful claims that the Watergate break-in was financed by a group of right-wing Cubans who believed that the Democrats were pro-Castro. But at least the *Star* reported the Watergate drama. In the early stages, many of the nation's newspapers failed to follow the developments the *Post* uncovered. Even many of the dailies that were part of the *Washington Post*'s news service syndicate dropped the evolving story from their pages. Certainly the television networks failed to follow up. It wasn't visual. Only the *New York Times* and the *Los Angeles Times* joined in the chase.

It was the *Los Angeles Times* that got the exclusive interview with Alfred Baldwin, a key Watergate participant. The story, written partly in the first person with the help of reporter Jack Nelson ("I could see men with guns and flashlights behind desks and out on the balcony"), was a great read that a jealous *Post*, which had first rights in Washington to reprint *Times* material, refused to use. When the *Star-News* called California and said they would like to run it, the paper was given the okay with the caveat of clearing it first with Ben Bradlee. An enraged Bradlee, who didn't want to admit he'd been scooped but was smart enough not to let it fall into the hands of his crosstown rival, agreed to run it the next day.

Most of the *New York Times'* best stories came with the byline of Seymour Hersh. He alone would rival Woodstein as a Watergate chronicler. A rivalry soon developed between them. In *All the President's Men* Carl and Bob referred to Hersh as "pudgy" and described him as wearing "a frayed pinstripe shirt" and "rumpled beach khakis." Later Hersh would tell *Post* editor Leonard Downie, "Bernstein should talk about how somebody dresses." Carl retaliated by visiting Hersh's office at the *New York Times* when he was absent and leaving a written message which startled the reporter. It concluded: "By the way, I went through your files."[1]

And why was the story assigned to Bob and Carl rather than the established stars—such as David Broder, Murrey Marder or Lawrence Stern—who regularly graced the *Post*'s front pages? Because at first few saw it as a story that would expand and last. And besides, the national "names" were already committed to following a presidential candidate or were scheduled to cover one or both of the two upcoming national political conventions. Even Bradlee was musing over which of the recently unhitched *Washington Daily News* reporters to approach. Should he hire one of the tabloid's best, Nina Hyde, to take over the fashion beat? Finally, it was nearly July, and employee family vacations were being planned. Carl and Bob didn't have families; they weren't even married.

Carl and Bob's byline next appeared on July 8, 1972, and then regularly in August, helping them immeasurably in lining up sources. Disgruntled Republican campaign workers, following the unfolding story in the *Post*, soon knew whom to call. And when they came looking for their sources, Bob and Carl were legitimized from the moment they spoke their names. When knocking on CREEP doors, little introduction was necessary.

But even the *Post* at first ran dry on Watergate. Less than a week after the break-in, follow-up stories were relegated to the Metro section, and Bob was spending part of his time back in the city section writing assigned stories on the District of Columbia's heroin problem. Carl got reassigned to the Virginia beat. In July of 1972, Carl and Bob still were far from working in tandem, contrary to popular myth. Bob wrote a Watergate story with veteran city reporter Paul Valentine on July 11. It was Robert Levey who broke the story on G. Gordon Liddy's firing by John Mitchell on July 23.[2]

Bob took advantage of the lull to go home to Wheaton in mid-July. Dutifully, he had mailed copies of most of his bylined stories home. His father had filed them in a large manila envelope. Al Woodward was still only vaguely aware of Watergate and his son's role in reporting on it. In Wheaton, Watergate may as well have been a foreign word. Al Woodward was a little surprised when Bob filled him in and, being a loyal Republican, somewhat concerned. At the family's summer cottage on Lake Michigan, Al Woodward urged his son to vote for Richard Nixon in November. A month later, jurist Woodward would tell a local newspaper, "Investigative reporting can reach a point where people are on trial in the newspapers rather than in the courtroom. What concerns me is the press could deprive people of a fair trial."

Carl and Bob's first breakthrough came in late July. It began when Carl noticed a series of articles in the *New York Times* by Walter Rugaber that detailed phone calls to CREEP from one of the burglars. At that time, Carl was telephoning his then steady girlfriend, writer Marie Brenner, in New York City each evening at eleven P.M. Brenner's task was to read him the headlines in the first edition of next day's *Times*, which had just hit the streets. Carl, who was acutely aware of being beaten by the competition, had told her just after the break-in, "I can't come up this weekend because I'm working on a story that can bring down the president."

A second story in the *Times* said that $89,000 in checks had been placed in a bank account of one of the arrested men by a Mexican lawyer. A Miami district attorney had subpoenaed the man's phone and bank records.

Carl, acting with dubious legality, used a contact at the phone company and acquired a list of the burglar's calls. Then he located the state's attorney in Miami through a series of smile-and-dial calls. The attorney, Richard Gerstein, invited Carl to come to Miami to see some of the checks in his possession.

Gerstein, a flamboyant lawyer, kept Carl cooling his heels for most of the day. Eventually Gerstein saw him, but Carl got nowhere. Gerstein said his investigator, Martin Dardis, had the checks. After nearly an hour, Carl went back to Gerstein and reiterated his request to see them. This time Gerstein walked him over to Dardis's office and told him to show Carl the documents.

Most Watergate buffs know that this was the point where Carl discovered the $25,000 check from Kenneth Dahlberg—a donation the Minnesota banker had given to CREEP but that had instead gone directly to one of the burglars. Bob followed it up from there with a phone call to Dahlberg. Bob and Carl had made their first completely independent revelation.

Many people remember the motion picture of *All the President's Men*, in which Carl was portrayed as leaving Gerstein's office in frustration and tricking his secretary into going away from her desk. In the film, Carl then raced back past her reception area into Dardis's office. That didn't happen in the real story but was just one of many expedient plot devices used to make the movie more exciting. It was also one of the few scenes Carl wrote instead of William Goldman, the scriptwriter.

Gerstein later felt he had been shortchanged. His name wasn't mentioned in the motion picture, and he threatened to sue Warner Brothers when he wasn't allowed to see a rough cut of the film in advance. "I fail to understand why Bernstein and Woodward . . . find it so difficult to share any credit with us for the information we produced, which then broke the Watergate case open," Gerstein said.

When he was asked why his name wasn't mentioned in the movie, Gerstein replied, "I don't know. Perhaps they feel giving credit to someone else might detract from their superstarring role."[3]

The Dahlberg $25,000-check story was written by Bob with the assistance of the city editor, Barry Sussman. Sussman was becoming the chief appendage to "Woodstein"—the term by which the team was known in the newsroom. It could be argued that the team was often a troika in 1972–73, with Sussman as the head.

"Woodsteinman" would have been more accurate. Triumvir Sussman rewrote Woodstein's stories, editing them to fit the "news holes." He became Bob and Carl's walking clip file and was turned to anytime they or the *Post* needed to check a fact.[4] But the Dahlberg check story may have been overlooked by many of the newspaper's readers. It ran on the same day Thomas Eagleton resigned as the Democratic vice-presidential candidate after his past psychiatric treatment had been revealed in the press. Much of the Dahlberg story's impact was lost.

Bob befriended the Democratic candidate's camp a few weeks later. Campaign manager Frank Mankiewicz let Bob sit in on McGovern strategy meetings in Washington during the summer of 1972. Although it helped his Watergate investigation very little, Bob was able to so charm the McGovern organization that after the election Mankiewicz would travel with Bob to Wheaton, meet his parents and stay overnight.

Just after the check breakthrough, Carl and Bob began their nightly door-knocking campaign at the homes of CREEP workers and conducting frequent interviews with a major source, former CREEP treasurer Hugh Sloan. Carl would later say, "It was like selling magazine subscriptions. One out of every thirty people will feel sorry for you and buy one."

The list of CREEP members was given to Bob and Carl by a *Post* staffer. With Woodstein now assigned to the Watergate story exclusively, they became the repository for countless leads—some good, some fruitless—which helped them widen the Watergate crack. One lead, from one of Ralph Nader's attorneys, created a link with the Pentagon Papers when the lawyer leaked to Carl that one of the Watergate burglars had attacked Daniel Ellsberg physically during a demonstration in May, shortly before the break-in.

In mid-September 1972, seven men were indicted for the Watergate break-in. To the original five who had been arrested inside the Democratic headquarters, G. Gordon Liddy and Howard Hunt were added. After reporting the story for the *Post*, Bob wrote in the duo's 1974 book, *All the President's Men*, he "broke the rule" and telephoned his source in the government known as Deep Throat.[5] The source told him that the go-ahead to give funding for the break-in had come from officials who were above CREEP employees.

Bob's "rule," of course, was the now-legendary signaling ritual made famous to everyone who read the book or watched the movie of *All the President's Men*. If Bob wanted to talk with his source, he would pull a flowerpot, into which a red flag was stuck, back to the rear of his sixth-floor apartment balcony. If the source wished to meet with Bob, he would mark page twenty of his *New York Times* with a hand-drawn clock before it was delivered. Bob would then meet the source by taking two cabs to be sure that he wasn't followed and then rendezvous in an underground garage late at night.

This does strain credulity! We are asked to believe the skulking around, taking two cabs, meeting in man-made subterranean caverns, and after all this are told Bob would cavalierly break the rules on a whim by telephoning to read him a story he had just written. This author has been on every floor of 1718 P Street, N.W.—Bob's former apartment building—and has been inside Bob's sixth-floor apartment and has stood in the courtyard several times. He found the following discrepancies between Bob's account in *All the President's Men* and what was physically possible.

Bob's apartment, number 617, faced into an inner sunken courtyard, a small area that, stepped off, is approximately one hundred feet in length and thirty feet in width. Bob's unit was the second one in from the alley, yet its balcony couldn't be viewed from there—one needs to get deep into the courtyard in order to just see part of it. The balcony floor is a single slice of concrete with an opaque divider set in the middle to separate another apartment's share of the same cement slab. Bob's half was the innermost one.

In order to have a chance of spotting a flowerpot, one would have to walk far into the courtyard and crane one's head sharply up to see the sixth floor. The flowerpot would then have had to be pulled against the rear and all the way to one side, up against the metal railing. Otherwise it couldn't have been seen on the balcony from any angle inside the courtyard. So if one made it into the courtyard and if the flowerpot were at the outside angle of the balcony, it could be seen, but one wouldn't have gotten away with such an action more than a few times. There were eighty apartments that looked down into the tiny courtyard, and anyone staring up to an apartment and daily lurking around in the enclosure would have been observed and likely reported after more than one visit. If Deep Throat had checked daily, as Bob said on page 72 of *All the President's Men* he would have been noticed within weeks.[6] The author knows from firsthand experience. The few times he came to the building and looked up to the sixth floor, a resident came out, leaned over the railing, and engaged him in friendly, sometimes suspicious, conversation. This was during the daylight hours. The author didn't have the nerve to try it at night.

To get to the courtyard one had to pass through two locked doors and within view of the reception desk. The building was heavily secured. But there was another way to view Bob's apartment in 1972, and that was by entering from the alley, walking fifty-six steps and then looking up. This was an even steeper angle, yet was more accessible. It was much harder to see anything on Bob's balcony floor from that angle, and again a daily intruder would have been on display to eighty apartments. For "a source in the executive branch," as Bob described him (page 71), to attempt either gambit on a regular basis would have been an unacceptable risk, given the many alternatives. The flowerpot adventure was the stuff of spy novels as the reader shall soon see.

In a June 17, 1992, twentieth-anniversary story in the *Washington Post* on Watergate, Bob said he couldn't remember his apartment number. Then he misled Karlyn Barker, the *Post* reporter, by saying, "606 or 608 or 612, something like that."[7] In *APM*, Bob vaguely described it as a "sixth-floor apartment" (page 72) even though he had long moved out by the time the book was released. On the other hand, he described a single visit to Martha Mitchell (page 93) precisely as "room 710, Marriott Suite." By giving equal-numbered digits to Karlyn Barker, Bob placed each unit on the outside of the building and in a location able to be easily seen without ever entering the premises. But the even-numbered red herring was simply that, a false clue. The author acquired documents handwritten by Bob Woodward updating his resumé in 1972. He had clearly written "Apt. 617" on those papers. That Bob—a master recordkeeper—would somehow forget the number of an apartment in which he lived for several years and where such historic events took place is surprising.

Bob said he never knew how the *New York Times* got marked. Fewer than ten residents usually subscribed to the paper. Thus, the *Times* was not delivered to his door, but left at the reception desk, unmarked and stacked with several others in the lobby. In 1972, the front door was locked at night for security reasons. This author also doesn't know how Bob's paper could have been "marked with a clock." Other parts of *APM* fail to add up. Bob said he once had to walk for "fifteen blocks" (page 195) to meet with his source because he couldn't find a cab. But Bob knew that three of Washington's largest and most prominent hotels—the Mayflower, the Capital Hilton and the Madison—were all within six blocks of his apartment. All normally have taxis lined up in front twenty-four hours a day. Each had an all-night doorman available to summon or whistle a cab.

So why were there so many questionable cloak-and-dagger scenes in *All the President's Men*? Money. It was that simple. Carl had the idea to write a book and the two dutifully began their work on it.

"At first we were going to do it about the Watergate burglars," Bob said in a 1974 *Los Angeles Times* interview. "We had a chapter about Howard Hunt. Carl wrote one about the 1970 elections." The book that Bob and Carl originally intended to write also included chapters on G. Gordon Liddy and John Mitchell. It was about the men and women closest to Richard Nixon. According to Bob, the original title was simply *Reporting Watergate*.

What changed it all was a phone call from Robert Redford. He wanted to make a movie about Watergate. He had just finished making a political film titled *The Candidate*, and he had gotten into an argument with some Washington reporters about Watergate and whether or not Richard Nixon had been involved. Redford, who had met Nixon when he was thirteen—Redford was awarded a tennis trophy by him—had a low opinion of the president. Always political, Redford began following Bob and Carl's byline in the *Post* and became fascinated with the odd pairing. The coupling of the classic Ivy League WASP and the dead-end, dropout Jewish kid was, to Redford, as if Martin and Lewis had gone into journalism rather than comedy. He checked them out and was further impressed with the chemistry—Bob's iceberg-lettuce crispness and Carl's seething volatility. There was a movie to be made here, Redford told friends.

But he suggested to Bob Woodward the movie should be about two reporters and how they cracked the Watergate mystery. If that's how Redford wanted it, then that's how the book would be written. Redford was willing to pay $450,000, plus profit participation, for the privilege. For that, Bob and Carl could take poetic license.

8

[Bob and Carl, 1972–74]

Read the Book

From the October 1973 *Yale Alumni Magazine*—news from the class of 1965:

> In case you hadn't noticed, there's been a good deal of legal activity in the Nation's Capital recently, and some of it involves members of the Class. I've already mentioned the fact that the whole sordid tale was originally exposed by Bob Woodward (along with another *Post* reporter) but I haven't revealed that Tom Marinis turns out to be a member of the President's new legal staff under Fred Buzhardt. . . . Regardless of the outcome (and at this writing, in August, there's just no telling about that), it's going to be quite an episode to have behind you when it's over, from the legal p.o.v. No argument there.[1]

By early 1973, Bob and Carl had a web of sources everywhere. Bob's were on a high government level, but Carl's army of boyhood connections was nearly as valuable. The dome of the Capitol was, figuratively, now inverted like a sieve, and leaking badly.

Woodstein had received a big break in late September of 1972 when Carl got an unsolicited telephone tag. The call came from a Tennessee lawyer and helped Carl and Bob establish the pattern of dirty tricks that led to Donald Segretti, a southern-California attorney. Leads like this were multiplying as the repetition of the joint byline penetrated the consciousness of more than a million metropolitan newspaper readers. The Segretti revelations began when one of the *Post*'s California stringers, Robert Meyers, made contact with the recent USC graduate. Meyers located and confronted Segretti directly, getting only photographs, which didn't come out because the camera had been loaded incorrectly. A few weeks later Meyers led Carl to the lawyer's Marina Del Ray apartment, and Segretti told Carl he had been employed by the president's appointments secretary, Dwight Chapin.

The stories ran in mid-October of 1972 and were the first to link the dirty-tricks campaign to the White House. The story also said that Ken Clawson, the former *Post* reporter who had worked for the White House, was the author of the New Hampshire "Canuck" letter that was instrumental in destroying the Muskie campaign.[2] Bob wrote in *All the President's Men* that he telephoned Deep Throat at home to arrange a meeting prior to the stories. However, the book maintains it was still necessary to take two taxis to meet his source, even though he had just arrived at National Airport from New York and had called him on a pay phone after getting off the shuttle. A few days later, Bob claimed, he dragged the flowerpot in front of the balcony to signal yet another meeting with Deep Throat.

All the President's Men is often contradictory. The book would have us believe that contact with Deep Throat was so sensitive, so dangerous, that elaborate markings via the *New York Times* and signals with flowerpots were necessary to arrange a meeting. Two different cabs were necessary to arrive at a destination. Yet after all this elaborate and thrilling drama, Bob wrote that he called his source more than once at both his office and his home. So much for consistency.

In the film of *All the President's Men*, Ben Bradlee tells Bob Woodward that he needs another source before he feels comfortable with a story Bob and Carl had just written. The two were linking Robert Haldeman, the president's top assistant, with those who controlled the political espionage fund. Carl then went into an office and telephoned a source in the Justice Department where he got a confirmation. Woodward got on the phone and also made a call. The phone is answered, "Dr. Kissinger's office." Woodward asks for "the deputy general's office," but his source isn't there.

Of course, the deputy general's office is where one might have found Alexander Haig in the fall of 1972. Could this have been an accidental slip by the writers? Or a mischievous false clue that would later lead to further speculation about Deep Throat's identity? Or could it have simply been convenient to write the truth and believe that no one would get the connection? Since Bob and Carl had both worked on the script and had had consultation rights, one can be assured that the location wasn't just a lucky coincidence created by a scriptwriter.

Certainly the physical characteristics of Alexander Haig were written into both the book and the movie. Both Deep Throat and Haig were heavy smokers, at least until Haig had triple-bypass heart surgery in 1980. Scotch was Haig's drink of choice—the general sometimes kept a bottle in his desk at the White House—and Deep Throat is portrayed as a scotch drinker. Hal Holbrook, the actor who played Deep Throat in the film, even resembled Haig. And, of course, the *APM* descriptions—"in the Executive Branch," "at the White House," "veiled references to the CIA and national security," "incurable gossip"—all fit the general. After all, who but a military man answers "affirmative" instead of "yes," as Deep Throat did with Bob on page 270 of *All the President's Men*.

APM even dropped a gratuitous aside absolving Haig of any wrongdoing on the last three pages ("Haig himself, the reporters learned, had come to doubt the wisdom of the President's course"). The transparent clues to Haig as a source do not set him apart. Some of the references could fit David Miller, Washington "public relations" man Robert Bennett or Adm. Bobby Ray Inman. All had intelligence links, and all have been accused of supplying information to Bob Woodward and helping his newspaper career.[3]

It's clear to this author that Bob used a hybrid of three or four main sources to construct the fictional Deep Throat character for *All the President's Men*.[4] But Bob has said he revealed just one name to Carl and possibly to Bradlee.

Possibly? Yes. It is the author's view that Bradlee himself was never told Deep Throat's identity by his reporter even though the former executive editor has said he does know. Bob told *Time* in 1976 that he never revealed the identity of Deep Throat to any of the editors at the *Post*. Carl said in a 1986 *Playboy* interview, "I think Bradlee knows, but I'm not sure. My recollection is that Ben was never told who it was, but I think he's got some pretty educated guesses." And former *Post* reporter Chuck Conconi told this writer that Bob once told him that Bradlee was a gossip and he would never tell him any secrets. Bradlee himself said in an interview with David Frost in 1991 that he knew, but when asked

if he would reveal the identity after Deep Throat died, he replied
that he probably wouldn't.

Carl broached the idea of a book about Watergate during August
of 1972. As their bylines increased and the story expanded, Carl
approached an agent of sorts, a far-left counterculture type who
represented Daniel Ellsberg. The agent, David Obst, had once run
Dispatch News Service, the syndicate that broke Seymour Hersh's
piece on the My Lai massacres (the story that made Hersh's name
as a reporter). The Watergate story was hot and getting hotter,
was Carl's pitch to Obst, and the three of them—Carl, Bob and
Barry Sussman, who wanted in on the project—would chronicle
it. But Carl cut Sussman out of the book deal shortly afterward.
That, and other events, would earn him Sussman's lasting enmity.
Obst, Carl and Bob wrote a twelve-page proposal in mid-October
1972. It was a difficult pitch to write. Few publishers would have
known the names of Woodward and Bernstein. Book editors (as
most everyone else in America) were still only vaguely aware of
the Watergate saga. And, more to the point, it was a story whose
ending was still unknown.
    Obst sent the confusing, still unresolved proposal to four pub-
lishers. But he was a friend of Simon and Schuster chief Richard
Snyder—the two vacationed and "played" together. According to
former S&S chairman Peter Schwed in his memoir, *Turning the
Pages*, the relationship was extremely close. Schwed said Obst
thought of Snyder as an "older brother and mentor."[5] Thus, even
though Simon and Schuster's final bid of $55,000 was topped by
New York publisher David McKay, Obst convinced Bob and Carl
to go with S&S because it had more clout. So excited was Bob on
getting the contract that he updated his job description for the
Post's personnel department, spelling the name of his publisher
"Simon and Shuster." (Said second wife Francie Barnard, "Bob's
a terrible speller.")
    Snyder was lukewarm to the project at first. The advance was
exceedingly generous for such a book, but Snyder paid it because
he believed his friend Obst had a pipeline to Washington journalists. S&S wanted to print more books on political matters because
the firm believed doing so would enhance its prestige. Besides,
Obst told Snyder adamantly that if he didn't publish the book,
they would never do business again.
    Obst tried to get Snyder behind the project by arranging a lunch

on October 25, 1972, at the Hay-Adams Hotel, across Lafayette Park from the White House. The meeting was a fiasco. Snyder, behind in his sleep, was in a nasty mood. And Bob and Carl, after supposedly staying up all night revising their proposal, had just been discredited, reporting on the front page of the *Post* that morning a revelation which indicted presidential assistant Bob Haldeman as the fifth person who controlled CREEP's political espionage fund. Though technically correct, they wrote that one of their best sources, Hugh Sloan, had told the Watergate grand jury about Haldeman. Sloan's attorney was denying it, and their newspaper was being denounced. The mistake was being attacked by White House press secretary Ron Ziegler at a press conference as the two traveled to the lunch.

In *All the President's Men* Bob and Carl wrote about the lunch with Snyder as being "strained" and that they "barely touched their food." Then, on page 187, there was a poignant picture of their walk back to the *Post* in the rain after the lunch—holding copies of the newspaper over their heads to keep dry. When they arrived at the newspaper, "soaked and shivering," Bob phoned a source. Those scenes, as written, were saturated with symbolism: David being cut down to size by Goliath. Which is why it becomes harder and harder to believe *All the President's Men*.

It didn't rain that day.

On October 25, 1972, the day of that famous lunch with Richard Snyder and the day the Haldeman story ran, the front page of the *Post*, in a box above Carl and Bob's Haldeman story, said that there was a "near zero percent chance of rain." Indeed, the next day's edition confirmed that no precipitation had fallen in the Washington area on October 25. A check with the National Oceanic and Atmospheric Administration in Rockville, Maryland, which keeps an hour-by-hour record of precipitation, revealed that there was only one day in the month of October 1972 on which it rained between noon and three—the nineteenth. Woodstein's description of walking back disgraced in the rain was pure fabrication. The lines fostered great imagery, but were made up.

If that were the only such instance in the book, the team might be forgiven, with the fabrication chalked up as a mistake. But on page 278 of *APM* the weather became conveniently metaphoric once more. Bob described March 27, 1973, as being a "warm, sunny day" and "working up a moderate sweat" in walking to an appointment at the White House "five blocks away." In fact, the highest recorded temperature for that day was 63, the average was 55, with a very pleasant 49 percent humidity average between nine A.M. and five P.M. It was also partly cloudy, with "65 percent sunshine." Could one work up a sweat in such weather? According to a weather expert at National Oceanic, "The only way you would sweat in a five-block walk is to run with a heavy load on your back."[6]

The anything-for-imagery style continues. On page 320 of *APM* is the famous meeting between Carl, Bob and Ben Bradlee on Bradlee's front lawn. The date and time are precise—May 17, 1973, between three-thirty and four A.M. The "chill was biting," they report, and they "spent a half hour on the lawn bouncing around to keep warm." The NOAA temperature reading was fifty-two at that hour with nearly still two-mile-per-hour winds, far from a biting chill unless someone had circulatory problems.

On page 79 Carl remembered that it took exactly "an hour and a quarter" to drive to McLean, Virginia, "late that afternoon" because of rain. He said it normally took one-half hour. Carl also wrote that he got "soaked" searching for the house of CREEP treasurer Hugh Sloan on foot. That date is September 18, 1972. Actually, it did rain that day. NOAA's reading at National Airport reported trace amounts of a tiny two-hundredths of an inch between four and five P.M. and four-hundredths of an inch between five and six. A weather expert called this amount similar to the amount of moisture in heavy fog. While a traffic snarl may have caused the driving time to be nearly tripled, precipitation definitely was not a factor—and certainly not nearly enough to get "soaked" looking for an address. Carl wrote in *APM* that he made a date to come back "in a couple of hours" because his source "would not be home until seven-thirty or so." Yet he would have us believe that "a few hours later," when he went back to the house, it was still raining ("he said and let Bernstein step out of the rain and into the hallway"). According to NOAA, there was no rain at all that day after six P.M.

Carl invented an even more dramatic "fact" in *APM*. On page 260—the day is February 26, 1973—he avoided being served a subpoena from CREEP in a civil suit by dashing up seven flights of stairs and calling Ben Bradlee. In *APM*, Bradlee told him to go see a movie and then phone the *Post* at five P.M. Carl wrote he went to see the hard-core pornographic film, *Deep Throat*.

That too was made up—it simply didn't happen. The film *Deep*

Throat had played Washington in the summer and fall of 1972, which is why managing editor Howard Simons coined the nickname for one of Bob's secret sources. But in February of 1973 there were no hard-core pornographic films playing anywhere in Washington. Some soft-porn pictures were showing, but not *Deep Throat*.

There were no porn films in the area because four months earlier, law enforcement authorities had raided a number of District of Columbia adult theaters, impounding several hard-core films. A trial awaited. All affected theaters had switched to action or soft-porn movies, and *Deep Throat* wasn't one of them.[7] There were no ads in the *Post* or the newly named *Star-News* that day or week for anything resembling the film. When these fabrications and embellishments are added to the impossibilities and incongruities of the Deep Throat flowerpot and *New York Times* exercises, and walking-fifteen-blocks-to-find-a-cab stories, one begins to react to such lines as *"Everyone's life is in danger"* (their emphasis) with mirth.[8]

Why would Bob and Carl invent or embellish such seemingly incidental details of their book? Why would they make up meetings with a character named Deep Throat? The answer is that Bob was consumed with naked ambition, anxious to prove that he could succeed at his newly chosen profession. There was money and fame at stake. Writing a book that assailed the senses, created empathy by pitting two plucky reporters against the system and the elements, was a carefully planned endeavor. The walking fifteen blocks to find a cab at night or being "terrified" because Bob had to spend an hour in a parking garage or ducking into an alley to avoid being followed was manufactured hokum that added drama and suspense to the book. It also created empathy for the protagonists. In Carl, who had been telling tall tales since he was a teenager, Bob had the perfect partner. That they got away with such recklessness would give them license to attempt it again. The unnamed source was the cover. And who checks the weather?

Carl is late for an impeachment hearing. "Carl, where are you?" Bob asks.
"Oh, the shuttle got jammed up in the wind coming back from New York," Carl tells his partner.
Bob dials Eastern Airlines. "All flights are on time? Thank you."
Carl had lied to his partner. Again.

After Bob and Carl won a Pulitzer Prize for the *Post* and when Watergate started to unravel in the spring of 1973, Dick Snyder began to suspect that his $55,000 investment might pay off.[9] According to Peter Schwed, Snyder said, "This is it! We're going all the way with it!" A powerful editor, Alice Mayhew, was freed up to work with the two reporters "day and night." Mayhew, who helped Bob and Carl write the book, kept urging them to "build up the Deep Throat character and make him interesting."

Thus, with Mayhew goading the two on one side and Robert Redford standing in the wings on the other, with nearly half a million dollars and a piece of the profits waiting for two reporters whose combined income was less than $30,000 per year, what Bob and Carl produced was a sort of Hardy Boys at the White House. Part of it—the impossible and lunatic Deep Throat cloak-and-dagger derring-do, and much of the literary effect—was dreamed up. Those parts were a hoax, a relatively harmless hoax designed to sell books and make a movie. The core of the book, the step-by-step rehash of the fall of Richard Nixon and the men around him, was written from their clips and reporters' notes. Those details were largely accurate. Bob and Carl certainly did have several important sources in the executive branch of government. Thus, while the contents were sound, at least some of the packaging of *All the President's Men* was phony.

However, part of the methodology Bob and Carl used to get many of their Watergate stories was unethical or bordered on criminality. Carl's acquisition of confidential phone records from a source inside the telephone company was highly questionable; they also misrepresented themselves to sources by not mentioning their employer, the *Washington Post*. At one point in their book Bob even intentionally lied to Deep Throat. Of course, that was probably just more embroidery.

They also asked members of a grand jury to reveal what had gone on during confidential sessions. They betrayed a secret source in the FBI by revealing his identity to his supervisor. Carl traded information with a law enforcement agent, promising to give out facts on another person that were to be used against him.

Bob and Carl were hungry. Both hated Nixon, so they believed their cause was just. Breaking "a few rules"—some of which they later regretted and said so—was expedient at the time. Thus Woodstein, too, was claimed by much of the same rationalized law-breaking fervor that claimed the men involved in Watergate.

Yet those men were sent to prison for their roles. Bob and Carl became heroes for it and prospered.

In her scholarly 1978 book, *Lying: Moral Choice in Public and Private Life*, Sissela Bok, a Harvard professor of ethics in medicine, prophetically wrote:

> In pursuing their investigation, the two journalists [Carl and Bob] came to tell more than one lie; a whole fabric of deception arose. Persons being interviewed were falsely told that others had already given certain bits of information or had said something about them. One of the reporters tried to impersonate Donald Segretti on the telephone. The other lied to Deep Throat in order to extract corroboration of a fact which this witness would have feared to reveal in other ways. And the newspaper was used to print information for which there was not always adequate evidence.
>
> It is not clear that, beyond the secrecy which had to surround the investigation, deception was actually needed. Yet it is certain that the reporters deserve great credit for exposing the misdeeds of the Watergate scandal. It can be argued that, in order for this exposure to be possible, deception was needed: but what is more troubling in the book than the lies themselves is the absence of a moral dilemma. No one seems to have stopped to think that there was a problem in using deceptive means. No one weighed the reasons for and against doing so. There was no reported effort to search for honest alternatives, or to distinguish among different forms and degrees of deception, or to consider whether some circumstances warranted it more than others.
>
> The absence of such reflection may well result in countless young reporters unthinkingly adopting some of these methods. And those who used them successfully at a time of national crisis may do so again with lesser provocation. The impression gained by the reading public is that such standards are taken for granted among journalists. The results, therefore, are severe, both in terms of risks to the personal professional standards of those directly involved, the public view of the profession, and to many within it or about to enter it.

Most of *All the President's Men* was written between July and December of 1973. Carl would rewrite Bob's drafts, and sometimes Bob his. In August, Carl told Bob, "We've got to get out of town."

They did, taking a five-week leave of absence to work on the book, spending much of the time at Bob's mother's posh house in Naples, Florida. Their paid researcher, Bob Fink, stayed behind in Washington.

But when it came to putting words on paper, Carl procrastinated. He would make excuses, leaving for three-hour trips to the grocery store for cigarettes, until finally Bob hid his mother's car keys. Then Carl would sit in the sun on the patio, wearing nothing but a pair of shorts, a typewriter in front of him on a glass-topped dining table. He sat for hours until inspired, whereupon he would pound out ten or fifteen pages of prose "so perfect" according to Bob, that no word changes were necessary. Bob wrote from inside the living room, keeping one eye on Carl. The first draft was more than a thousand typed pages. Alice Mayhew cut 40 percent of that while Bob and Carl battled to keep in their pet sequences. The final rewrite, with Mayhew hovering nearby, was done in two hotel suites at New York's St. Regis Hotel. "Most of the writing was Carl's," Bob said later about *All the President's Men.*

When asked about the novelistic approach Carl stated "writing in the third person, you can look at yourself with some detachment. You can be more honest."

Both were already discussing a second book. It would be about Patty Hearst and her recent kidnapping, the two said at the time. "There's no question that's the great story—it has everything . . . family, the police role—it's even got some sex," Carl told the *San Francisco Chronicle.*

"It's all there," Bob mused, "the role of the media, the race movements, the radical movements."

"Modern, nomadic California," said Carl, as if in a dream.

And what was in their immediate future? How were they planning to handle the fame and fortune? Carl told New York's *Daily News*, "We're either going to be Ross or Tom [Ross Lockridge, Jr., and Tom Heggen, authors of, respectively, the bestselling Civil War novel *Raintree County* and the smash stage hit *Mr. Roberts.* Both had committed suicide after completing their works] or we're going to be like Mark Spitz and do shaving-cream commercials."

In total, Bob and Carl got, besides the movie fees and the $55,000 advance from Simon and Schuster, another $25,000 for a *Playboy* magazine two-part serialization in May and June of 1974 and $30,000 from the Book-of-the-Month-Club. After the book became a bestseller, topping the *New York Times* list for fifteen weeks, they got a $1-million advance from Avon, the largest amount ever paid for a nonfiction paperback up to that time.[10]

But those were just the initial financial rewards. The first printing of 75,000 copies sold out in weeks, and a second printing of 150,000 copies was ordered. By the end of 1974, 193,000 copies had been sold, assuring them of royalties for years.

The book was also a critical success. The *Wall Street Journal* wrote, "It's one thing to know the butler did it, it's quite another thing to know how he did it, and who helped him pull it off." And the *Journal* added, "It's packed with the sort of suspense usually reserved for the mystery counter."

As the book was about to be printed, the *Post*'s principal lawyer, Edward Bennett Williams, attempted to get the book stopped. He had read the galleys and thought he was being portrayed as a drunk and a sleazy lawyer. There was a debate in the book between Williams, "clutching his drink in both hands" and then presidential speechwriter Pat Buchanan. Bob and Carl had included sentences that had Williams ranting, "Judge Sirica is some kind of pissed," and the attorney also saying, "We had to do a lot of convincing to keep your asses out of jail." Williams instructed his partner, Joe Califano, to call Richard Snyder and literally yell, "Stop the press!" Califano threatened to "send Bob, Carl and Bradlee to jail" if the book was printed. Snyder, who hadn't started the press, told him it was too late. He made vague promises about making changes in a later edition. The chance that Williams would sue could generate magnificent publicity, and the vision of the three Watergate heroes in jail was almost too good to be true. He ordered the presses to roll as soon as he hung up the phone.

When the book came out, Edward Bennett Williams stopped speaking to Bob and Carl for two years. But he forgave them. Later Williams, who served on a CIA advisory board, would tell a friend, attorney Bill Murphy, about Bob, "He has no right to know the amount he knows." But more than ten years later, in 1986, he would attempt to convince Bob Woodward to write his biography. Bob backed away from the project, claiming he was too busy.

All the President's Men had a publication date of June 17, 1974, the second anniversary of the Watergate break-in. The inside dust jacket photos of Bob and Carl looked raw, like home snapshots. Later, after several paperback versions of the book had been

released, the photos of the two were removed. The 1976 paperback cover featured photos of Robert Redford and Dustin Hoffman—below the title and authors' names was the phrase, "Now
a film from Warner Brothers." The same paperback book also
boasted "28th printing" in letters as large as the two authors'
names.

9

[Bob and Carl, 1975–76]

See the Movie

FROM *News Reporting and Writing*, fifth edition, the textbook for basic journalism classes at many colleges in 1992:

> No introduction to journalism would be complete without the book that describes how two young reporters, Bob Woodward and Carl Bernstein, toppled a president. . . . The most notable example of an unknown source is Deep Throat, the source for a considerable amount of information about Richard Nixon during his presidency. The reporters who handled the Watergate revelations, Carl Bernstein and Bob Woodward, never disclosed the identity of this key source—if indeed it was one person. Some reporters believe that Deep Throat actually was a convenient way to handle a number of sources who demanded anonymity as the price for information.

By 1975, Ben Bradlee was paying homage to his two stars: "Carl and Bob have a different problem than the rest of us. They're part of American folklore now. Everybody knows their names."

For a year after the publication of *All the President's Men* the two reporters who personified Watergate had been deified by the press and public alike. They could do no wrong. They had bestowed upon the *Washington Post* honors that drew the paper up to the level of—some would say ahead of—the *New York Times*. They had won numerous journalism awards, capped by a Pulitzer Prize. Now a movie was being made by Warner Brothers about their adventure. The screenwriter, William Goldman, declared it had "the greatest buzz in Hollywood since *The Godfather*." Producers and publicity people had descended upon the paper's newsroom, and suddenly there were Robert Redford and Dustin Hoffman, nosing around, making small talk with reporters in order to get the feel of a journalist's life. Redford was now following his subject around, attempting to duplicate Bob's walk, which he later described as "direct."

Bob, Carl and even some of the *Post* editors had gone Hollywood for the moment. Particularly Carl. He invited Hoffman to his parents' house for Passover dinner, and Hoffman reciprocated by asking Carl to his place in Greenwich Village to watch the Academy Awards. Managing editor Howard Simons showed Redford around Washington and took him on an arrowhead hunt in Virginia. For that he was rewarded by being invited to spend a week at the actor's ranch in Utah.

Apprehensive, unsure as to whether they had gotten themselves into a *Butch Bernstein and Sundance Bob* movie that would backfire and ridicule them, the top executives of the *Post* spent a year biting their nails in anticipation of the $8.5-million-budget film. Foremost among the early worriers was Carl Bernstein himself. Robert Redford had cast himself as Bob Woodward. The two were already being confused in the public's eyes. Was it Bob Redward or Bob Woodford? And it was Redford's movie. He owned it, for God's sake. The first syllable of "Woodstein" was sure to come out a winner. Before Dustin Hoffman was signed on to play Carl, there were rumors that Bernstein might be played by the unglamorous Michael J. Pollard, the scruffy, cretinous-looking actor who had been Warren Beatty's sidekick, C. W. Moss, in *Bonnie and Clyde*. With each name bandied about, Carl's mood rose or fell. Al Pacino? Carl could live with that. Ringo Starr? You've got to be kidding.

A slew of veteran actors were in the running to play Ben Bradlee, all of them first-rate. Kirk Douglas, Richard Widmark, George C. Scott, Henry Fonda and Gregory Peck were all being mentioned. Bradlee, tongue in cheek, suggested Fred Astaire. Jason Robards, Jr., was the pick, a good one as it turned out, for he picked up an Academy Award for his performance.

Who would get the role of Katharine Graham, now the Queen Victoria of journalism? The names Patricia Neal, Dorothy McGuire, Eve Arden and Alexis Smith were thrown out, leaving Lauren Bacall as the producer's choice. And would the John

Mitchell remark—"Katie Graham's gonna get her tit caught in a big fat wringer"—be in the movie?[1] In the end, that was the only element of the *Post* owner's persona that made the film. The doyenne of Washington's leading newspaper hesitated to be portrayed by any mere actress. Her character remained absent from the silver screen. One report claimed she got cold feet and legally tried to stop the filming after production had begun.

Certainly Bob Woodward never attempted to press Katharine Graham into being depicted on-screen. After Watergate, a love-fear relationship evolved between himself and the *Post* leader. In 1975 he told writer Laurence Leamer that he found her "very sensual. You get the feeling that if she loses faith in you, she'll cut your balls off or your ovaries or whatever."

Howard Simons, who was played by Martin Balsam in the film, was portrayed as meek and mild, unlike his real personality. He was also given movie lines that said he wanted Carl and Bob off the story when the opposite was true. Bob would apologize for the characterization at a memorial service in 1989, after Simons died of cancer. Veteran character actor Jack Warden, fresh from stealing scenes in the sex comedy *Shampoo* got a meaty supporting role as Harry Rosenfeld.

Barry Sussman, Bob and Carl's editor during the Watergate years, had a different problem. He *wanted* to be a part of the movie. He felt he *deserved* his place in history. Next to the two reporters, Sussman was the most important figure of the drama. Now he was being cut out of the film, his character merged with another. At first Sussman was merely annoyed. "If they want to accurately represent what things were like at the *Washington Post* and leave me out at the same time, there's something wrong," he said.

Two decades later, in 1992, on the eve of the twentieth anniversary of the Watergate break-in, the *Post* would acknowledge the Sussman slight as part of a week-long orgy of Watergate remembered. The newspaper would call it a "grievous example" of the facts deleted from the movie.

Sussman's annoyance would turn to anger when he became convinced that the filmmakers had stolen the opening scene of the movie from his 1974 book about Watergate, *The Great Coverup*. The opening paragraphs of Sussman's book described Richard Nixon landing in a helicopter to brief Congress on the nation's Strategic Arms Limitation Talks (SALT) in early June of 1972. Indeed, the opening shots of the finished film were identical to Sussman's book.

"They stole that right out of my book," Sussman said.

But couldn't it have been a coincidence?

"It was no coincidence."

But surely Bob and Carl weren't involved?

"They saw the finished script. They contributed. They had approval rights."

The original opening scenes were quick-cut staccato night shots of the Washington Monument, the Lincoln Memorial and the Capitol, culminating in a final shot of the Watergate building. That part of the script was written by William Goldman, who received the on-screen film credit and an Academy Award. Goldman had written a long string of successful novels, beginning in 1957 with *The Temple of Gold*. His screenplays for *The Great Waldo Pepper* and *Butch Cassidy and the Sundance Kid* had helped make Robert Redford a superstar. But the script he originally wrote for *All the President's Men* was roundly criticized. Alvin Sargent, a script doctor who had written the Ryan and Tatum O'Neil vehicle, *Paper Moon*, was brought in for an uncredited rewrite, although Goldman retained the screen credit by virtue of his contract.

Carl Bernstein wrote his own version of the film together with his new girlfriend, the writer Nora Ephron. They presented it to Redford in the presence of Goldman, who became incensed, not just because the pair had tried to usurp his work, but because he felt that Redford had sprung Nora and Carl on him without notice. Nora, who was part of a well-known theatrical family, had inserted love scenes between her and Carl into the script. Goldman was anxious to leave the project and begin working on the film version of his novel *Marathon Man*, and he did so as soon as possible. The only part of the script that Carl and Nora wrote that was finally used in the film was the sequence where Carl tricked Ruby, the Miami secretary of Martin Dardis and Richard Gerstein. Of course, that episode never happened—in the book or in reality. Carl and Nora, taking poetic license, made it up.

Many of the scenes that were left out of the shooting script provided romantic interests for the two principals. An early version had Carl in bed with two women. Bob was given a fiancée named Nancy, a pseudonym for his second wife, Francie Barnard. The final product was totally nonsexual in content, which caused the film's publicists great concern as it came closer to its release date. A movie with Redford and Hoffman and no love interest was like a Burt Reynolds movie without a car chase, they said. A scene filmed at the Washington "in" restaurant of the decade, *Sans Souci*, which had Bradlee/Robards saying to Woodward/Redford, "Our cocks are on the chopping blocks," was also excised.

Movies being movies, a liberal interpretation of Bob and Carl's saga was the rule of the day. Bob's Karmann Ghia was changed to a Volvo in the film because it was said to "fit his personality" better. The scene in which the two reporters met with Ben Bradlee on his front lawn in order to avoid "electronic surveillance" took place in the movie's own time frame, six months before it actually occurred. Bob's apartment became unit 519 for the movie. It was the one closest to the alley and one floor down. Future historians would be able to point to it and say that indeed Deep Throat could view a flowerpot on the balcony from the alley. Indeed they could, but of course they were misled; it was 617, not 519.

Director Alan Pakula shoved all issues of accuracy aside. "We're not doing *CBS Reports*," he said just before the film's premiere.

Bob added, "The movie does some compression. Everything they've done may not be literally correct. It's correct in the generic sense for a movie adaption—it's not a documentary."

Names were changed. Marilyn Berger, the *Post* reporter who tipped Bob and Carl to the Canuck letter, requested her name be switched. She had left the paper to work for NBC television and no longer wanted to be thought of as a *Post* reporter. Her name in the film was Sally Aiken.

The movie contained several hints that pointed to Al Haig as being one of the Deep Throat sources. There was the call to the "deputy general's office" next to Henry Kissinger's, the physical resemblance of Haig and Hal Holbrook, and a phone call made by Bob early in the movie. In that scene Bob says to Deep Throat on the phone, "We talked about Wallace," referring to the George Wallace assassination-attempt stories he had written and for which "Bob's friend" had supplied information.

There was even a biographical note that may have referred to Bob's troubled childhood. As Hoffman/Bernstein and Redford/Woodward walk toward a house in a suburban neighborhood, Hoffman mutters, "All these neat little houses and all these nice little streets. It's hard to believe that something's wrong with some of those little houses." Redford quickly answers, "No, it isn't."

Many necessary liberties were taken. The three meetings with Donald Segretti were compressed into one; a series of meetings with CREEP treasurer Hugh Sloan was shortened to two. The end of the film showed wire copy spewing out news story after news story, but some of the dates on the stories were wrong.

One truly authentic note was inserted, however. The security guard who made the initial discovery of the break-in, Frank Wills, was given a small cameo role, playing himself.

Some of Richard Nixon's still loyal supporters complained about the accuracy of the film. Kenneth Dahlberg told the *New York Times* that "the book was . . . relatively fair, the movie is grossly inaccurate. I was portrayed as a nervous, scared, and apprehensive man, somebody with something to hide. . . . I was very straightforward and up-front. It's too bad that honesty in presentation was forsaken for the self-aggrandizement and self-adulation of Woodstein and the imperial *Post*." Chuck Colson also had his own review: "It would have been refreshing, too, had the movie shown us Woodstein's mistakes . . . such as unauthorized access to grand jury records (a crime), allowing themselves to be used by the CIA in printing leaked smears (the Ervin Committee report documents this) and coercive tactics (practiced upon me and others)."

But *All the President's Men*, however factually inaccurate, was a superb, even masterful, motion picture. What made it so wasn't just the acting—many of the supporting roles were small gems—or the script. The greatness of the film came from a collaboration between Gordon Willis, the man behind the camera, and Alan J. Pakula, the director.

In spite of some fabrications or embellishments which Bob and Carl had added to the book, the core of *All the President's Men* was a series of phone calls, followed by a series of interviews, followed by meetings and ending with a newspaper story. It wasn't exactly riveting material for a film. The other problem was that the viewer knew the ending—Nixon had long resigned by the time the film was released—and the public had long been "Watergated" to death by the media.

Willis's contribution was to create a sense of danger where there had been none. The film meetings with Deep Throat and other sources took place shadowed in dim light. The camera angles were high, Hitchcock-like long shots. The only scenes brightly lit were the ones inside the *Post*'s newsroom, giving it a beacon-

of-truth appearance. Moreover, at the newspaper, the two protagonists are shown in close-up and the camera angle was lower,
making the subjects seem larger than life. David Shire's music
amplified the suspense. Pakula, in a speech after the movie was
made, said, "The hard light of truth is in the newsroom; no
shadows there."[2]

Pakula was careful always to portray Bob and Carl as the under-
dogs, the little guys against an unseen but sinister political machine. As they traveled through the city, the camera shot them
from a distance, making them seem small, swallowed up in the
vastness of the Washington establishment. In another scene, Red-
ford/Woodward was shown alone, walking through an empty
parking lot. The camera was pointed at him from a high angle far
away, and the character was reduced to miniature. The episode in
the Library of Congress main reading room, stunning in its kalei-
doscopic effect, focused on Bob and Carl sorting through records
while the camera rose above them slowly, gradually reducing
them to dots.[3]

While the filmmakers took many liberties with the book, the
salty language was left mostly intact. The several profane "holy
shit" and "rat fucking" phrases originally earned the movie an R
rating, which would have prevented many schoolchildren from
seeing the movie. This resulted in a massive last-minute lobbying
effort to the Motion Picture Association of America's ratings
board.

Richard Heffner, who headed the ratings board, wrote Robert
Redford a letter six weeks before the film's scheduled release
explaining the R rating apologetically, and calling the film "a most
important motion picture that surpasses in historical significance
even the innovative reportorial book on which it is based. I hope
that many Americans will see the picture with parents deciding to
take those younger children they believe will benefit from seeing
its dramatic revelation of American politics at its worst and American journalism at its best."

But Heffner upheld the R rating, saying the board "had no
option but to give *All the President's Men* an 'R' in the light of a
clearly stated Policy Review Committee."

The R rating was appealed and, without the producers' having
to change a single word of dialogue, was reduced to a PG. Whether the fact that a friendship existed between Ben Bradlee and
Motion Picture Association chief Jack Valenti, whose organization

controlled the ratings board, had anything to do with the reversal would be speculative. Certainly Bradlee and Valenti were cronies, attending Washington Redskins football games together. The MPAA chairman was also a Democrat, who had been a former close aide of Lyndon Johnson. Valenti, who chaired the appeals board, said after the decision that the rare reversal had no "precedent value." He noted the film contained "no violence, no sex, and if it weren't for the language factor, it would be a 'G' picture." The entertainment trade magazine *Variety* headlined the reversal PIX PROFANITY FOR WHOLE FAMILY. *Variety* asked, "Is the MPAA rating system designed to protect young children or 'ordinary parents'? And who can be designated as an 'ordinary parent'?"

The rating change by the MPAA more than enhanced the film's box-office appeal. It also assured the film playability in high school history classes throughout the country for decades.

Warner Brothers certainly tried to make the look of the film accurate. Former *Post* night managing editor John "Jack" Lemmon remembered a Warner's production assistant asking to borrow a musical triangle—used to summon editors to news budget meetings—because the wool yarn that was used to hold it was perceived to be unique. When Lemmon refused, the movie's producer promised him an identical one. The filmmakers were as good as their word. One was found so close to the original that Lemmon was left scratching his head as to why the switch was made in the first place. The triangle scene never made the screen.

Warner also spent $475,000 re-creating the *Post* newsroom, combining soundstages number eleven and four at its Burbank, California, studios (the combination was necessary because the *Post* newsroom was sixteen feet longer than Warner's largest soundstage). If they couldn't film inside the *Washington Post* ("Too disruptive," Bradlee decided) then the *Post* would be shipped to Hollywood. Much was made of the eventual 237 boxes of authentic newsroom trash that were shipped west. The newspaper charged Warner Brothers a dollar per box, but that was for the cost of the shipping carton; the trash was supplied gratis. A hundred and fifty duplicate desks were purchased from the same firm that supplied the newspaper, arriving on the soundstage painted in *Post* "regulation" shades of red, green and blue. Old phone books were recreated by Warner's prop department and combined with more than a ton of books and other directories. When Ben Bradlee visited the set, he was taken aback by its authenticity. Harry Rosenfeld was the only other executive of the newspaper to make the trip to California. One of the more notorious figures from the other side of the Watergate drama to visit Burbank was the president's former lawyer John Dean, and Dean's wife, Maureen. Ironically, the Deans got a VIP tour by Robert Redford, receiving more attention and stares than Bradlee or Rosenfeld, who were partly responsible for Dean's unemployment.

Prior to the national opening on April 7, 1976, a series of benefit showings were arranged. The biggest, attended by Bob, Carl and many from the *Post*'s newsroom staff, was at the Kennedy Center in Washington. The $25-a-ticket showing raised $25,000 for the Fund for Investigative Journalism. Robert Redford, Dustin Hoffman, Jason Robards, Martin Balsam and many of the other actors attended, provoking a near riot from more than a thousand tourists who focused on the flaxen locks and bronzed skin of Redford. On the other side of the entrance to the theater were some two hundred strikers singing "We Shall Overcome." The *Post* at that time was on the verge of breaking the pressmen's union. Management would eventually win.

Bob told the press covering the event that the film was "spectacular! I mean, when we sold the thing to the movies, we said we wanted this to be about reporting, and that's what it is." Later he said, "The movie's not just pretty damned true, it is true."

Five days later in Wheaton he would say much the same thing. A benefit screening held there, for the Central Du Page County Hospital, would net $20,000. Bob's father and stepmother attended the reception and movie. The *Wheaton Journal*, in its review, led by asking, "Who said the life of a reporter wasn't glamorous?"

All the President's Men opened the same day as two other popular films, *The Bad News Bears* and Alfred Hitchcock's last effort as a director, *Family Plot*. Of course, it was *APM*'s opening in a platform release of just 604, mostly urban theaters that got the majority of the attention, both at the box office and in the media. Warner Brothers' marketing plan called for a limited release in large-city theaters, which would draw on the sophisticated demographics the studio felt was its prime audience. But even Warner wasn't prepared for the ticket sales during the first weekend. In New York City, the film set house attendance records at both the Astor Plaza and the Tower East theaters. In Washington, playing at two theaters, the MacArthur and the Cinema, the film grossed just under $100,000. The total for the 604 theaters for the first three days was $4,565,820.

Thus the public's perception of Bob Woodward and Carl Bernstein was formed, not from their newspaper reporting or their books, but from the film of *All the President's Men*. Even though the combined sales of both the hardback and paperback copies of *APM* eventually reached more than 4 million copies, that didn't come close to the dent the picture made in the mass consciousness. In 1976, the average national movie-ticket price was $2.13.[4] The movie's domestic gross was more than $68 million through the end of the year, making it the second most successful motion picture of 1976, behind Sylvester Stallone's *Rocky*, and putting it, for the moment, on the list of the "top thirty grossing pictures of all time," according to *Variety*. Besides the nearly 34 million tickets sold, tens of millions would see the film later on television, another generation would see it on video cassettes, still others would view it in high schools and colleges as part of history or journalism classes. Bob Woodward would be forever bound with the actor who played him (they have remained good friends), as would Carl Bernstein with Dustin Hoffman.

The film's reviews were equal to the grosses. In New York, there were unanimous raves, with the lone exception being Penelope Gilliatt of the *New Yorker*. The usually grumpy John Simon of *New York* magazine urged everyone to "see it twice"; Gene Shalit on NBC's *Today* show suggested that the film should "win a Pulitzer Prize for moviemaking"; Vincent Canby in the *New York Times* called it "the thinking man's *Jaws*"; and Rex Reed gushed, "I could actually smell the carbon paper and feel the pulse quicken with the dreaded approach of a deadline."

Frank Rich, who had grown up working in his father's shoe store four blocks from the White House, wrote in the *New York Post*: "*All the President's Men* means to be about the power of the press, and it is triumphantly so. When, at the movie's end, those keys batten out a barrage of Watergate headlines that document the ultimate triumph of a free press over White House horrors, you may feel a rush of patriotism that makes your head spin."

One of the few mixed reviews came from the *Post*'s own critic, Gary Arnold. In a long, thoughtful essay Arnold pronounced the film "incomplete." Arnold called it "an absorbing movie that somehow fails to evolve into a rousing dramatically satisfying movie as well. *All the President's Men* lacks an expansive vision and an elemental spark of showmanship and inspiration." He also bemoaned the cutting of Sussman from the film and said that the audience would come away with an "ambivalent set of impressions" about Carl and Bob. "They get a little devious now and then, but invariably it's all in the line of duty."

The film's place in Hollywood history was secured when after making virtually everyone's best-of-the-year list, *APM* was nominated on February 10, 1977, for eight Academy Awards. Although it lost to *Rocky* (which had the same little-guy-against-the-system formula) for best picture, it won, in addition to the Bradlee depiction by Robards and the botched screenplay of William Goldman, two awards for sound and set decoration—the boxes of authentic trash, in effect, won it an Oscar. Film editing also got a nominating nod as did Jane Alexander, who played the bookkeeper source. *Rocky*'s John Avildsen stole best director from Alan Pakula.

To promote itself to readers and potential subscribers, the *Washington Post* quickly began running ads with photographs of Dustin Hoffman and Robert Redford. The headline of the ad read, "If you liked the movie, you'll love the original."

10

[Bob and Carl, 1974–76]

The "Final" Encore

As the royalty checks from Simon and Schuster began to arrive, Bob and Carl's lifestyles changed. Bob exchanged his 1970 Volkswagen Karmann Ghia for a 1973 BMW, while Carl replaced his sturdy Raleigh racing bike with an exotic Mercier touring model. Carl also purchased two apartments in the Hispanic Adams Morgan section of the city, knocked the walls out and made a living space of 3,500 square feet—he named it "the Xanadu of the barrio." One of the apartments, number 605, had personal significance. It was where his grandfather had delivered dry cleaning to a Washington judge when Carl was three. And the new living quarters sat just two blocks from where he had been brought after his birth.

Carl became obsessed with interior design. He added a stained-glass ceiling in a newly constructed "Florida" room, built a study and created a huge living room. The new co-op apartment had one of the best views in the city of the majestic Washington Cathedral. He began spending hours pouring over wallpaper samples in the *Post*'s conference room and consulting with the newspaper's home-decorating editors.

The Watergate movie and book money fattened their bank balances. It seemed to inspire changes in their appearance. Bob grew his hair longer; Carl had his trimmed (by Washington's "hairdresser to the stars," Charles Stinson) to above the shoulders. They began to merge physically, both of them wearing matching imitation Gucci loafers.

With fame and fortune came other pleasures. Women were

now even more readily available. Carl, whom one female *Post* reporter described as "persistent" before Watergate, no longer had to make that effort. Bob proudly told one interviewer that he had three girlfriends. He described two as reporters and the third as a teacher. He credited the newfound ability to have that many women friends to Carl.

One of Bob's first dates after finding fame was CBS Washington reporter Lesley Stahl, who had recently left WHDH television in Boston. Carl's liaisons were more hedonistic. With his fame and riches, he began attending "swingers"—group sex parties— where, after Watergate, he was treated as a celebrity. The sex parties Carl attended in Arlington and Fairfax, Virginia, attracted a lot of CIA members, one in particular being John Arthur Paisley, a CIA electronics expert who would die mysteriously in 1978.[1] When Bob Woodward found out about Carl's carnal escapades, he assigned another *Post* reporter, fellow Yalie Tim Robinson, to investigate. He told him to determine if Carl had any "special" relationship with the CIA sexual adventurers. Robinson's findings were inconclusive.

Frances Roderick Barnard, who became Bob's second wife, had the face of an angel. It was said that men fell in love with her fifteen minutes after being introduced. Francie had Texas blue-book breeding to go with her beauty. Her grandfather, Dorrance Roderick, owned the *El Paso Times*. Francie left Texas as a teenager and began to build a resumé. After Radcliffe, there was a sojourn at Little, Brown, the Boston book publisher, a short marriage, a year in Europe, back to Texas in 1972 to work for Congresswoman Frances "Sissy" Farenthold's historic bid to become the state's first woman governor, and finally a reporter's job at the counterculture Boston *Phoenix*.

Sarah McClendon, who operated a news bureau in Washington and served as a colorful White House correspondent for a chain of Texas newspapers, was asked to take Francie on as an intern. According to McClendon, "she was an intern for a week. At the end of that time, I made her a reporter."

Francie was next made Washington correspondent for the *Fort Worth Star-Telegram*.[2] It was in that capacity she met Bob Woodward. Except Carl saw her first.

Francie attended a press conference given by John Connally at Washington's Madison Hotel during the summer of 1972. The former Texas governor was in the capital to announce a new coalition called Democrats for Nixon. When it was over, Francie was introduced to Bob and Carl in the hotel's coffee shop. Carl asked her out, and the two went bicycling together on their first date. After the two had seen each other a second time, Bob asked Carl for Francie's phone number. At first Carl refused to give it to his partner, but Bob eventually prevailed, and Francie and Bob began to see each other regularly. The relationship might have stayed that way for years if Bob Woodward hadn't received a scare in mid-1974. After a doctor's examination he was misdiagnosed with leukemia. Two days passed before he got a correction, and by then he was severely depressed. He went away for a week with Francie to a country house he had bought on Gibson Island in southern Maryland, leaving Carl in the city to cope with the demands of fame. Carl promptly had an auto accident, cracked some ribs and quickly gained fifteen pounds due to the inactivity from the injuries.

When Nixon resigned on the warm evening of August 8, 1974, Bob and Carl were, by design, silent. Bob munched a sandwich, watching the speech on television in the *Post* newsroom. Ben Bradlee walked among the fifth-floor staffers, telling everyone he saw, "Don't gloat, don't gloat" (he had used the same phrase when Ehrlichman and Haldeman resigned), and chasing away a *Women's Wear Daily* reporter who tried to crash the scene. But the qualifications of the new president concerned Bob. He reacted to Gerald Ford's ascendancy by privately telling a friend, America had "traded a dishonest SOB for an incompetent."

Still, it was the brief hint of his own mortality that may have pushed Bob Woodward into deciding to marry Francie Barnard. In a hurried ceremony of under five minutes, the two were wed by a District of Columbia judge on November 29, 1974. Bob's high school chum, Scott Armstrong, who had ushered at Bob's first wedding, was promoted to best man this time. He arrived by cab with a box of Minute rice under his arm. Carl, who had only heard of the location for the nuptials an hour before, swiped two flowers from a hotel arrangement to use as boutonnieres.

Bob was asked by the judge, Harold Greene, if he wanted to think it over before the ceremony. Bob said, "We've thought it over. We decided a couple of days ago. We've been thinking about it for a couple of months." Bob was described as wearing "a well-wrinkled blue suit," Francie, a "brown tweed knit suit." Carl paid

Bob Woodward, 1961. At Wheaton Community High School he was chosen "most likely to succeed."

Carl Bernstein, 1961. His parents had to plead with his high school in order for him to graduate.

Bob (seated) with classmate Richard Jennings as "moguls" of their Yale classbook, the *Banner*, in 1965.

In Yale's madcap rite of bladderball, Bob (front right) leads the *Banner* staff into battle.

A drawing depicts emergency helicopter landings on the "floating Pentagon" U.S.S. *Wright*. Bob served aboard the *Wright* as a communications officer from mid-1965 to late 1967. (National Archives)

"Woodstein" working the phones in the *Washington Post* newsroom during
the Watergate period, 1973. (UPI/Bettmann Newsphotos)

General Alexander Haig, Bob
Woodward's purported men-
tor, 1973. Woodward became
his neighbor shortly after
Nixon's resignation in 1974.
(National Archives)

Martha Mitchell, wife of former U.S. Attorney General John Mitchell, interviews Bob and Carl on CBS television in 1974. Bob admitted on the program that he voted for President Nixon in 1968. (UPI/Bettmann Newsphotos)

Hollywood on the Potomac: (left to right) Dustin Hoffman, Carl, Bob, and Robert Redford at Washington's Kennedy Center benefit showing of *All the President's Men*, 1976. (AP/Wide World Photos)

Literary lions: (left to right) Nora Ephron, Lillian Hellman, Carl and Bob arrive for the New York premiere of *All the President's Men*. (UPI/Bettmann Newsphotos)

Carl and Nora surprise Rose Styron, wife of author William Styron, with the news that they are expecting their first child, at a New York publishing party in 1978. (AP/Wide World Photos)

Ben Bradlee, executive editor of the *Washington Post*, 1965-1991. (Cynthia Johnson/Gamma Liaison)

Bob with Scott Armstrong. The pair co-authored *The Brethren*. (Bruce Hoertel/Gamma Liaison)

Carl, during his four-year stint at ABC television in the early 1980s. (Diana Walker/Gamma Liaison)

Carl with Bianca Jagger leaving the Palladium, a New York nightclub, in 1986. (AP/Wide World Photos)

Carl with new steady, Faye Wattleton, the former president of Planned
Parenthood, in 1992 at a Committee to Protect Journalism dinner. At right is
Fred Friendly, former head of CBS News. (Steve Allen/Gamma Liaison)

Bob with his third wife, Elsa Walsh, in 1991. Bob says she has "brought balance
to my life." (Diana Walker/Gamma Liaison)

for the wedding dinner at the French restaurant Sans Souci. Located a block from the White House, it had been a favorite of top-level Nixon appointees.

Bob said that they were both too busy for a honeymoon. "Maybe in December," he said. "We're both going to stay here. We have work to do."

The only relative of either the bride or groom attending the ceremony was Francie's mother, who happened to be in town. Carl's by-now steady girlfriend, Nora Ephron, was on hand as well.

Bob and Francie moved into a house that Bob had selected in September. The house, at 4506 Edmunds Street in Washington's exclusive Wesley Heights neighborhood, backed onto Ben Bradlee's family home. On the same side of Bob's street, exactly three doors down, lived Bob's purported mentor, Alexander Haig. At the time, Haig's rented house at 4428 Edmunds had an electronic communications center installed in the basement.[3]

Carl met the writer Marie Brenner at a New York journalism convention in April of 1972.[4] Marie was just twenty-two, six years younger than Carl, and a graduate student. When Carl asked her what she did, Marie told a white lie and said she was a stringer for the *Mexico City News*. Carl asked her out and they had drinks at the Algonquin Hotel. But once Watergate became white-hot, Carl was unable to make it to New York to visit her. The romance cooled. Still, she had been a great help during Bob and Carl's Watergate period. Besides reading Carl the next day's first edition of the *Times* when it hit the streets in the evening, it was Marie who had located Martha Mitchell at the Essex Hotel for Bob. This paved the way for his 1972 exclusive interview with her after the press had reported her "in hiding." Carl even enlisted Brenner and her cousin, an editor in Mexico City, in a fruitless search to help find the source of CREEP's money-laundering scheme.

Later, Brenner gave a party at which Carl was introduced to Nora Ephron. Soon after that, Carl and Nora became inseparable and would become each other's second try at marriage.

In 1978, Nora Ephron put together a collection of her articles in a book titled *Scribble, Scribble*, dedicating it to Carl Bernstein. It was, perhaps, a metaphor for her life. She was the daughter of two successful writers of plays and films; her sister, too, was a writer. She had been named after the heroine of the Henrik Ibsen play *A*

Doll's House. Every experience she ever had she later turned into magazine articles and, eventually, books. She penned articles on the size of her breasts, feminine hygiene sprays, the Pillsbury Bake-Off and *Deep Throat* (the pornographic movie). She wrote about her friends, her lovers, even her first husband, all with the same revealing, tart wit. "Everything is copy" was her family's motto, and no one was safe—not even her best friends—from the often-caustic pen of Nora Ephron. When she met Carl Bernstein, she was writing a column for *Esquire*—it was a prestigious national soapbox. Soon Carl and Nora would be the toast of the New York literary set. Carl's name was on the bestseller list; Nora's would follow. They believed they could write a better script for *All the President's Men* than Bill Goldman, such was their conceit. Together, when they walked into an expensive restaurant, whether in New York or Washington, heads invariably turned as they were led to the most visible table in the house.

Unlike Bob and Francie, who shrank from publicity, Carl and Nora courted it. Bob Woodward didn't like Nora. In fact he "loathed" her. It was as if he were McCartney to Carl's Lennon, with Nora as the wicked Yoko Ono tempting him away into a New York world of parties and inflated egos.

But both Bob and Francie showed up for Carl and Nora's wedding on the afternoon of April 14, 1976, in Manhattan, a ceremony that was conducted by a New York City surrogate judge. Carl's friend and *Post* columnist Richard Cohen, and Cohen's wife, Barbara, then a newspaper editor at the rival *Star*, were the only others present. The nuptials took place one week after the opening of the film of *All the President's Men* and five days after the release of Bob and Carl's follow-up book, *The Final Days*. After the wedding Carl rushed off to an interview with *Newsday* and a taping with Tom Snyder for NBC television.

The idea for a second book, about the fall of the Nixon presidency, was Carl's, just as it had been his idea to write a book about reporting Watergate. In retrospect, that may have been his biggest contribution. Carl and Bob first titled the manuscript *Save the President* before changing it to *The Last Days* and then to *The Final Days*. The original plan was to tell the story of Richard Nixon's downfall through the eyes of six U.S. senators. When they didn't get enough senatorial cooperation, they scrapped the plans.

Bob and Carl worked with much more help on the sequel. They hired Bob's hometown friend Scott Armstrong and a young Colorado newspaper reporter who had become a free-lance writer, Al Kamen, to do research. Those two researchers eventually became more than that, collaborating on both the writing and reporting. By the time the manuscript was completed, Kamen and Armstrong would have done more interviews and written more of the book than Carl.

Scott Armstrong was from the south, or self-described "wrong" side, of the tracks in Wheaton. He had been two years behind Bob in school and they had met when he dated Bob's stepsister, Susan. At seventeen, Scott married a twenty-nine-year-old woman and fathered two children. Bob convinced Scott to follow him into Yale when he learned of his exceptionally high SAT scores. Unlike Bob, Scott worked his way through school and at one time had to take a year off from his academic studies in New Haven to take a full-time job. He eventually graduated in 1968. A year later, he was divorced.

After Scott arrived in Washington, Bob helped him get a job with attorney Sam Dash on the Senate Watergate Committee. In that position, he was said to have been a major source for Bob and Carl for their later Watergate stories. Not that Scott "leaked" information exclusively to Bob and Carl. In November of 1973 he was suspended for thirty days from his Senate job for giving unauthorized information to *Rolling Stone* magazine. Later, with Bob's help, he would get a job as a reporter for the *Post*.

The dust jacket of *The Final Days* said that "Woodward and Bernstein interviewed nearly 400 persons" for the book, but Scott Armstrong and others would later say that Carl Bernstein did less than his share of work on it. Carl did fifteen joint interviews with Bob, a few others alone, but generally spent more time living well in a newly discovered Washington–New York social life with Nora Ephron. "I'm sure Carl did twenty interviews, maybe twenty-five," Scott told *Post* reporter Walt Harrington years later. "But if you said he did thirty-nine, I'd call you a liar."

As the time dragged closer to the deadline for the completion of *The Final Days*, Bob became furious with Carl's sloth. At first Bob chalked it up to satyric drive—Carl still dated several different women even though he was betrothed to Nora Ephron. Once during that period Carl called a *Post* reporter at three in the morning and begged her to come over. The woman eventually succumbed to his supplications. The next day she told a few of her fellow staffers in the newsroom that "it was worth it."

When Carl had tried to inject love scenes of himself and other women into the movie script of *All the President's Men*, he had been told, "Carl, Errol Flynn is dead." The filmmakers were in error. In Carl, the deceased actor who had been known for his serial sexual encounters may have been reincarnated.

Carl would also attempt to impress women with his athletic prowess. One remembered waking up in the morning to have Carl tell her he was going jogging. She watched from his apartment window as the star Watergate warrior, a white towel tucked neatly around his neck into a sweatshirt, ran around the parking lot "exactly twice." Then she saw him slowly smoke a cigarette before walking back into the building.

As the book was being finished, Bob got into a series of profane shouting matches with Carl. Bob asked Simon and Schuster to replace Carl as coauthor and create a triple authorship—he, Scott Armstrong and Al Kamen. S&S, however, knew full well that Woodward and Bernstein were now to reportorial books as Lerner and Lowe were to musicals, or as Masters and Johnson were to sex, and wisely refused. The names, now embedded in the American consciousness, would stay. Carl's final contribution, in total, was said to be a small part of the book, less than 25 percent.

A total of five people contributed to the writing and research for *The Final Days*. In addition to Bob, Carl, Scott Armstrong and Al Kamen, Simon and Schuster editor Alice Mayhew was thanked for "the hundreds of hours" she spent with "the manuscript." Mayhew made numerous trips to Washington to help with the book. Additionally, Bob and his group, writing partly from a sixth-floor office in the *Washington Post* building and also from Bob's house, had full access to the newspaper's library and research staff.

If Woodstein and company were expecting the huzzahs that erupted when *All the President's Men* was released, they were quickly disappointed. *The Final Days*, full of gossip, questionable episodes, and unsubstantiated innuendos, met with a firestorm of criticisms.

Most cited was John Osborne's essay in *The New Republic* magazine, which called the book "the worst job of nationally noted reporting that I have observed during forty-nine years in the business." Christopher Lehmann-Haupt wrote in the *New York*

Times, "But can we believe *The Final Days*? . . . The experience of reading the book is credible. . . . Of course, to trust *The Final Days* one must read it with a predisposition to believe; yet not to do so is to put oneself in the curious position of doubting the very reporters who broke the Watergate story in the first place."

Peter Prescott of *Newsweek* said, "Woodward and Bernstein can only say: trust us. I do, for their past courage and enterprise; still, their book makes me nervous."

Prescott was referring to the 394 unnamed sources that were the basis for the information of *The Final Days*. The book was considered important, yet no sources, bibliography or substantiation was offered. It was the authors' contention that only by offering sources anonymity could they get candid and unfiltered information. The critics contended that a cloak of anonymity gave sources the right to slander and embellish. But everything was checked with at least two sources, Bob and Carl would answer. Finally, in an attempt to quell the carping, the two told *Post* ombudsman Charles Seib that they would give their notes and files to a library, to be opened in twenty-five years. No library or other repository was ever revealed.

Said political writer Richard Reeves, "I tend to think what they wrote is true. But they made a disastrous error in writing it the way they did. The issue is whether their story is credible. They are asking people to trust them. Why should people trust them? Readers should know who their sources are. What they have done is institutionalize Deep Throat."

One of the more positive reviews appeared in the *Washington Post* (predictably) by distinguished economist John Kenneth Galbraith. One might wonder whether the *Post* book editors would have chosen Galbraith had they known of his chummy interview with Bob at the *Sentinel* fewer than five years before.

Much of the maelstrom was in response to the perceived lack of taste in the book's pages. The revelation suggesting that Pat Nixon hadn't had sex with her husband in fourteen years caused shudders. Carl defended the material, saying that "it's very much about the loneliness, in some ways, of Richard Nixon. . . . I don't see how you can write accurately about what Mr. Nixon's travail was without an understanding of the distance in his relationships."

Bob said, "We know from our own private lives that things like that affect the way we do our job. And it's a fact that everything that affects the president affects his job and affects everybody in this country."[5]

Bob and Carl's disclosures of the Nixons' marital relations (or lack of them) and their supposed overconsumption of alcoholic beverages were some of the points that led columnist James J. Kilpatrick to write that the book was "brutal, needless, tasteless and profitable" and the *New York Times*'s William Safire to label the book "journafiction." Safire asked, "What motivates such outpourings of vitriol? 'We had to make a lot of it up, but there's two million bucks in it,' said one of the writers. (Actually I doubt whether either one of them said that, but somebody once told me that he overheard somebody else say that Woodstein said something remotely like that at a party which—by the new *Post-Newsweek* standards—means it can be turned into direct quotations and be accepted as true.)"

The unveiling of the Nixon's private lives claimed one serious casualty. Pat Nixon suffered a stroke two months after the release of *The Final Days*, reportedly just after reading the book. After that, Richard Nixon consulted lawyers and wanted to sue. He was told proving libel would be both difficult and costly. His attorney also cautioned that a lawsuit would also increase book sales further.

Still, Ben Stein, Carl's boyhood friend who worked as a speechwriter for Nixon during the months before his resignation, thought the book was "compassionate." Stein said Carl "had a lot of empathy for the Nixon family." At the same time, however, Stein claimed that there were several errors in the book, particularly descriptions of his actions and thoughts.

While Bob and Carl would not disclose their sources for the 195,000-word book, many were transparent. Over a period of time, many of the figures have either come forward or otherwise revealed whether or not they were interviewed. The following figures supplied information for the book: J. Fred Buzhardt, the president's legal counsel; Pat Buchanan, then a Nixon speechwriter; Barry Goldwater, the Arizona senator; Ollie Atkins, the president's photographer; Bryce Harlow, a presidential counselor; Ray Price, also a speechwriter; Lt. Comdr. Andrew Combe, skipper of the presidential yacht *Sequoia*; Leonard Garment, the White House legal counsel; Stephen Bull, an aide to the president; William E. Simon, then undersecretary of the treasury; Bruce Herschenson, then a public relations aide for the White House; Henry Kissinger, who had two different titles during the second administration—assistant to the president for national security and secretary of state; Kissinger's assistant Lawrence Eagleburger; speechwriter Ben Stein; David Eisenhower, the president's son-in-law; and David Gergen, also a White House speechwriter.[6]

Barry Goldwater was the source for a much disputed anecdote about a dinner in the White House on December 2, 1973. In the account, the authors described Bryce Harlow as telling Goldwater, after dinner, that Nixon was drunk, as an explanation for his incoherent behavior. But Harlow, Price and Buchanan all claimed that they did not tell their interviewers that Nixon was drunk. In fact, according to Pat Buchanan, "the president wasn't drunk. Nor was he exhausted . . . the president was relaxed and having a good time. And that's what I told Bernstein when he interviewed me."

That the authors of *The Final Days* chose to go with the Goldwater account, rather than that of Bryce Harlow, Pat Buchanan and Ray Price, showed a predilection for selected sensationalism. As Ray Price said, "Harlow, Buchanan and I all told them their version was untrue, but they used it anyway."

Bob told *U.S. News and World Report* in its April 12, 1976, edition, "We gave everyone the opportunity to comment. No rumor or gossip was used. Nobody has disputed any fact."

Journalist Tom Wicker, in his 1991 book, *One of Us*, pointed out that Price and other Nixon loyalists "may only have seen what they wanted to see," but it should also be noted that Bob and Carl held a point of view as well. It was Carl who had repeatedly attempted to add a "Nixon is guilty" paragraph to the early Watergate stories. And Bob had demonstrated a contempt for Nixon when he was with the *Sentinel*, *before* he got to the *Post*.

Edward Cox, the husband of Tricia Nixon, disputed the book's account that said he had told Sen. Robert Griffin that Nixon had talked to the pictures in the halls of the White House, a remarkable episode that would become a John Belushi skit on *Saturday Night Live*. Cox said he had refused to be interviewed but told Woodstein he would verify material, particularly sensational matter. He told a reporter for the *New York Times* that he was never called again.

Media watchdog groups began to pick the book apart. One such organization, the U.S. Citizen's Congress, claimed to find 146 factual errors in the first edition, including such minor mistakes as referring to Gerald R. Ford as Gerald L. Ford, and Frank Carlucci as a former HEW secretary (he was not—he was one of several assistants). Of course, all books contain errors. Francie Barnard said she caught several in the galley stages, such as a Senate office building being located on the wrong street. The pilot of the *Sequoia*, Andrew Combe, found his name spelled Coombs, even though he had been a Yale classmate of Bob Woodward's. He wrote Bob a letter, asking that it be changed in later editions. So many errors—particularly when a phalanx of five people was supposedly involved—raised eyebrows.

Shortly after *The Final Days* was released, Carl and Bob appeared on NBC's *Meet the Press*. The book was attacked by Edwin Newman, Jack Nelson of the *Los Angeles Times* and conservative columnist John Lofton. When Carl punctuated one of Bob's answers by adding, "Nobody has successfully challenged any of the facts in it," Lofton pounced.

"Well, let me take a whack at it," he began, and proceeded to question the accuracy of an account of a White House cabinet meeting. Bob and Carl had written that, at the meeting, cabinet members Elliot Richardson and William Ruckelshaus had agreed to post FBI agents outside the offices of the recently fired H. R. Haldeman and John Ehrlichman.

But, said Lofton, he had just spoken to Ruckelshaus, and Ruckelshaus had said he wasn't present at the meeting.

Backpedaling, Bob said he had "talked to all sorts of people involved" in the event and had "quadruple checked it." Carl said, "I don't think it is wrong . . . I think the account stands."

But the account was wrong. And because the mistake was pointed out in so public a forum, the paragraph describing the meeting was amended in later editions of *The Final Days*.

The people on record as refusing to be interviewed for the book included all members of the Nixon family, with the exception of David Eisenhower; Nixon's personal secretary, Rosemary Woods; Diane Sawyer, now a television journalist but then the assistant to press secretary Ron Ziegler; Ziegler; Dr. Walter Tkash and Dr. William Lukash, the two White House physicians; Lt. Col. Jack Brennan, a military aide to Nixon; and Alexander Haig.

Although the general came out of *The Final Days* in an overall positive light, he vociferously denied talking to anyone for the book. Shortly after publication of *The Final Days*, he cabled Nixon from Belgium, where he was serving as supreme commander of the North Atlantic Treaty Organization in Europe: "I . . . want to reassure you that I have not contributed in any way to the book." He also wrote a letter to a friend saying he was "depressed and appalled," and he then blamed the men around Nixon for talking, saying they "should have known better."

Haig also told columnist Victor Lasky that he hadn't spoken to anyone for the book, "despite repeated efforts by the author to get me to do so." According to Haig, Bob Woodward had flown to Brussels for an interview, but Haig had "declined to comment on the last days of the presidency of Richard Nixon." Another statement leaked by a Haig aide stated that Bob walked into Haig's office and said, "General, I can make you a hero or a bum. Which is it to be?"

These stories spread by Haig and his friends fail to ring true. Would Bob Woodward fly halfway around the world to meet with Al Haig unless he was certain an interview would occur? Would any smooth, experienced and intelligent interviewer open up with "I can make you a hero or a bum"? Not likely, particularly since Alexander Haig spoke to Bob just a few months later in an interview that led to a front-page story.[7]

Haig was anxious to disassociate himself from *The Final Days*. Near the end of the book was a scene that many readers interpreted as the president contemplating suicide:

> "You fellows, in your business," the President began, meaning the Army, which he always seemed to consider Haig's real business, "you have a way of handling problems like this. Somebody leaves a pistol in the drawer." Haig waited . . .

According to the *The Final Days*, Haig next directed that all sleeping pills and tranquilizers be taken away from Nixon. Since the president and Haig were alone for the gun-in-the-drawer conversation, and since the book described the "tone" of Nixon's voice, one must assume that either Haig provided the information or the authors lied, since Richard Nixon wasn't a source for the scene. As *Newsweek* noted on April 12, 1976, Haig's "thoughts about the last days are threaded through the work."

Other criticisms focused on the bounty of minute and, some felt, gratuitous details. The description of Nixon "gnawing" at a pill vial because he didn't have good motor control in his hands was one example. Nixon's sending back a wine he didn't like at a White House dinner was viewed by many as unnecessary.

The president's men also objected to the omniscience of the book. Henry Kissinger asked Ben Bradlee, "Just how did they know what I was thinking?" Combe said, "They put words into my mouth that I didn't say." The many "he thought" phrases would become a trademark of later Bob Woodward books. Said Evarts Graham, managing editor of the *St. Louis Post-Dispatch*, in a statement that appeared in the *New York Times*: "Don't try to read someone else's mind. That's an old bugaboo of mine."

Bob and Carl got a $300,000 advance from Simon and Schuster for *The Final Days*. Nearly thirty thousand words were excerpted in the *Post*-owned *Newsweek* magazine in exchange for the two authors receiving full salary while they took time off to research and to write the book.

But columnist Liz Smith beat *Newsweek* to the newsstands by publishing some of the juicier parts, including the allegations of Pat Nixon's afternoon drinking. Smith got the information from a New York journalist, Tony Schwartz, who had been given the information by Kitty Kelley, writer of unauthorized biographies. Kelley was Bob's friend and formerly worked in the *Post*'s library doing research. Carl sent Smith a congratulatory telegram on her "scoop."

The advance sale was 200,000 copies—and in the first five months 610,000 copies were sold. It also became the first volume to debut in the number one position on the *New York Times* bestseller list, topping it for twenty weeks. After the first week of release Simon and Schuster raised the price from $10.95 to $11.95 in order, explained Richard Snyder, to "get priority on the printing presses." David Obst told everyone that he was "going for the record" on the paperback advance. His aim was to surpass the $1.8 million that E. L. Doctorow had gotten for *Ragtime*. He didn't succeed, but the $1.55 million paid by Avon did create a new record for a nonfiction book, edging past the $1.5 million paid for *The Joy of Cooking*. Warner Books matched Avon's offer, but Avon got the deal because it put a $200,000 publicity and promotion budget into the contract. Robert Redford offered to buy the movie rights for a reported $1 million, but the negative publicity had gotten to Bob and Carl. In 1989 they would say they refused Redford's offer because they didn't want to appear to be "money grubbing." At the close of 1976, some year-end press assessments would say that the movie of *All the President's Men* and Bob and Carl's new book, *The Final Days*, helped Jimmy Carter win the White House from the Republicans.

Woodward and Bernstein certainly no longer needed to worry about where their next dollar was coming from. During the last week of December 1976, Simon and Schuster presented Bob and Carl with a check for $999,942 dollars, exactly $58 short of a million. The money, at least to Carl, seemed to be endless.

11

[Bob and Carl, 1976–79]

Love Stories

BEFORE BOB MARRIED Francie Barnard, she had been courted by Democratic senator Joe Biden of Delaware. Republican senator Charles "Mac" Mathias of Maryland had also been a suitor. "It was Bob or Biden," Sarah McClendon would tell friends later. "I told her to go for Woodward. It was a big mistake."

Bob told Francie that the fact that he had the number-one book in the country didn't mean anything to him. "I want to get married and raise a family," he said.

Following their wedding, Bob and Francie lived at her place briefly because the house Bob had discovered in the fall of 1974 wasn't yet ready. Shortly after they moved in, they adopted a black dog, part Labrador retriever, naming him after one of the characters in the novel Bob wrote at Yale. Outwardly, Bob and Francie were a picture of domestic tranquillity. Friends helped christen the house by planting a flock of plastic pink flamingos on the front lawn.

In 1975, Francie gave up her newspaper career and soon began taking art courses at the Corcoran School of Art in Washington. Francie Barnard would—a decade later—become an accomplished artist, with enough income from the sale of her abstract paintings to partly support herself. And Bob's desire for a family was fulfilled. Not quite two years after they were married, Francie gave birth to Mary Taliesin Woodward on November 10, 1976. They called her Tali, a shortening of the old Welsh name that had been in Francie's Texas family for years.

A few months after Tali was born, Bob and Francie moved

again, this time to Georgetown, close to Katharine Graham's. The house on Edmunds Street had lost its mystique. Ben Bradlee had moved out and had begun romancing his prize social reporter, Sally Quinn. Now separated, he was in the midst of divorce proceedings with his wife, Toni. General Haig left for Europe in January of 1975, a month after Bob had moved onto the twelve-house street. The General had been appointed by Gerald Ford to head NATO. The larger three-story, six-bedroom, six-thousand-square-foot Georgetown mansion, which had been built in 1858, was grand. There was a semicircular drive, a ten-by-twenty-seven-foot oval swimming pool bordered by a six-foot-four-inch brick wall in the back, and a large bathtub upstairs that sat eight people. Bob and Francie furnished the house modestly, with wicker furniture and a few Oriental rugs. The only extravagance was a stereo system piped through the house for Bob's classical music—the eventual cost for the sound system would run to more than $10,000.

Bob paid $255,000 for his new home. At first friends dubbed it The Castle. Later they would call it The Factory, a recognition of Bob's obsessive working habits.

There were no campy plastic flamingos for Nora and Carl. They were a shuttle couple, frequently commuting between New York and Washington on the Eastern Airlines flights that flew and landed every hour. They were such denizens of National and La Guardia airports that they began to write a novel together with a working tile of *The Eastern Shuttle*. Carl's ten-room Xanadu in Adams Morgan was a perfect place to entertain. Nora's New York address at 317 East Fifty-first Street was socially correct, but the apartment was too small.

So Carl and Nora used $240,000 of the Watergate money to buy a luxurious country estate on Sagaponack Road in Bridgehampton, a fashionable out-of-the-city address on Long Island. It was the kind of place that demanded a name. Carl and Nora called it Trees. There was a cottage to the rear of the large house, which they outfitted as Carl's office. He would leave the *Washington Post*, they decided, and become a "real" writer. He would compose his great book about the McCarthy era of the fifties and the effect it had on his parents. He called the work in progress *Progressive People*. Carl resigned from the *Post* at the end of 1976, but it would take him nearly a dozen years to complete his book. After a few months, Carl began to tell his friends he was "blocked"; they would nod in sympathy. He talked about submitting part of the manuscript to the *New Yorker* as a long article. Behind his back, however, the project became a running joke. Carl would never write that book alone, friends whispered.

Being married to an attractive, brilliant woman wasn't enough for Carl. His roving eye wouldn't and couldn't stop. Liz Smith remembered a party she gave on Long Island that both Carl and Nora attended. "Carl made a blatant pass at Lucie Arnaz, the actress. Nora was off somewhere and Carl talked to Lucie for a while and then said, 'I sure would like to see you again. When can we get together?' Lucie refused." Liz Smith said that she was shocked at Carl's behavior and told him so that evening.

Carl's escapades were now becoming legendary. One story that made its way around the social circuit concerned a young woman who woke up in Carl's bed. She immediately dialed a girlfriend from the nightstand phone. Sitting next to Carl, she announced, "Guess what, I've just fucked my second Pulitzer!"

Another tale that shocked the Hamptons concerned Carl's propositioning a sixteen-year-old girl at a dinner party. According to *New York* magazine, the teenager hadn't heard much about Watergate. "I was hardly born then," she said, and turned the graying Romeo down. She would also note, "A few years later he starting hitting on my mother."

Carl's recklessness expanded in other ways. There was the story, still told in New York literary circles, of Carl, Nora, writers Marie Brenner, Jesse Kornbluth and Liz Smith, all piling into a horse-drawn carriage after a Bring Your Worst Christmas Present party given by food writer Gael Greene in the back room of Le Cirque restaurant. In high spirits, Carl got in front and attempted to drive the coach. The carriage brake was on and the horse panicked, backing the wheels against the curb. All five occupants were thrown onto the sidewalk as the cab overturned. Brenner wound up on the bottom of the pile, bruised, shaken and angry. But she, like many of the women in Carl's life, quickly forgave him and remained his defender.

Carl did one major reportorial piece in 1977—his first year away from the *Post*—a twelve-thousand-word article for *Rolling Stone* titled "The CIA and the Media." In it Carl outlined the long relationship the press had enjoyed with the Central Intelligence

Agency. The principal allegations were that at least four-hundred journalists had worked directly or indirectly for the CIA from the 1950s to the present, and that in 1977, some seventy-five to ninety still had a working arrangement with the secretive Agency. Particularly controversial was the charge that the *New York Times*, CBS, and *Time* magazine allowed full-time agents to operate under the guise of reporters and issued them phony credentials. All three media giants denied Carl's allegations.

Among the sources for his story, Carl said, were thirty-five to forty CIA agents he had interviewed. The story made news for the rock-'n'-roll periodical in most major papers and newsmagazines, but Carl was attacked by many of his colleagues, particularly C. L. Sulzberger, the foreign columnist for the *Times*. As the *Times* noted in an article on the piece, "some foreign governments are using this situation as a weapon against the press." Even Ben Bradlee took Carl aside at a social gathering to tell him that the reporting was "flawed." That shook Carl's confidence, for he respected the editor's views.

The employees of *Rolling Stone* were also annoyed about Carl's writing for the magazine, but for different reasons. Carl, a star of Watergate and one of the two most famous journalists in America, was paid $27,000 for the article. Staffers at the magazine were said to be furious—the amount was more than most of them made in an entire year.

One of Bob's first attempts at a major post-Watergate story ended in frustration. He became a cog of an investigatory unit, later dubbed by some *Post* wags the "pussy posse." It was a long pursuit of several highly paid female congressional assistants who allegedly were paid for sexual favors instead of office work.

The *Post* unit—Bob (who at first looked only into financial dealings), Rudy Maxa and Marion Clark—spent months trying to uncover Ohio congressman Wayne Hays's sexual relationship with his nontyping assistant, Elizabeth Ray. The blond, thirty-three-year-old Ray admitted to sleeping with Hays in exchange for $14,000 in federal funds per year. But it was "Claxa" (Clark and Maxa—the conjunction was similar to the Woodstein nickname) who got the story in May of 1976. Ray contacted the two after she was thrown out of the congressman's office, hysterical, because he had married another woman and she hadn't been invited.

Three weeks later Bob tried to connect another Capitol twosome, Colleen Gardner and Texas congressman John Young. Gardner was a close friend of Elizabeth Ray's. Her salary was also nearly double that of her friend.

When Bob interviewed Gardner at her Alexandria, Virginia, apartment, his usually smooth interviewing techniques failed him. When he asked her point-blank if she was sleeping with her boss, Gardner answered by asking him if he was sleeping with his, implying Katharine Graham. Bob told her he had sources who knew she was making $25,800 a year and only had a high school diploma; therefore, she must be sleeping with someone. Gardner then got Bob to tell her his salary, which was $29,000 a year. She then retorted that she was just as valuable in her job as Bob Woodward was to his newspaper.

The irony was that Gardner later admitted she was indeed sleeping with the Texas congressman in exchange for her salary. But she was privately "put off" by Bob's directness and tough-guy techniques. She chose to give the story to the *New York Times* a few weeks later, thus allowing them to scoop both Bob and the *Post*.

Less than six months later Bob reversed the field and wrote three articles over a ten-day period on the Central Intelligence Agency's electronic bugging of natives in Micronesia. He said that the CIA was listening in so they could learn the islanders' strategy for gaining independence from the United States. Even though the series began on a Sunday in the coveted page-one, top-right-hand position, it drew more yawns than yelps. Micronesia drew a geographical blank for most Americans.

In the two follow-up stories, one implicated Henry Kissinger as approving the surveillance. The series was important, but it was no Watergate. A territory of 220 islands with just 110,000 people, though strategically located in the Pacific, between the Philippines and Hawaii, seemed too far away for readers or even the U.S. Congress to worry about. The Micronesians might as well have been on Mars.

Bob and Francie's marriage lasted three years. His workaholic habits overwhelmed her. After separating in February of 1978, Francie lived with Tali in the country house they'd bought on Gibson Island in southern Maryland. She filed for divorce in September. Bob had already begun seeing other women. One, Nancy Collins, an attractive, talented blonde, was considered the new "bombshell" reporter for the *Post*'s Style section and Sally

Quinn's heir apparent. She had scored a major coup for the paper, getting an early copy of H. R. Haldeman's Watergate memoirs, *The Ends of Power*, by doing some very good espionage work at the printer's plant in Pennsylvania. *Post* staffers named the caper Deep Book.

Joint custody of Tali was agreed upon early in Bob and Francie's negotiations, but the untangling of joint ownerships of two real estate properties, stocks, bonds, mutual funds, numerous tax-cutting limited partnerships and bank deposits took months. Francie had come into the marriage with a trust fund of her own. Her lawyer, Sharon Shanoff, said in a preliminary argument, "This case involves a large and diverse marital estate; the division of literally millions of dollars is at stake." Francie said that Bob earned "in excess of $840,000 in 1977" and asked for $5,000 a month temporary support.[1] Bob, in response, claimed he only cleared $1,600 a month from the *Post*, and even with the income from the stocks, bonds and a real estate mutual fund only had a total of $2,900 a month in income, or $35,000 a year. Bob listed his total assets as $1,057,000, but listed $501,800 in liabilities. According to his lawyer, Robert Liotta, he didn't seem to know where his next dollar was coming from: "Defendant admits that he earned substantial sums in 1977 but submits that this was one-time income from a successful venture. His regular income is $31,000 per year as a *Washington Post* reporter."[2] Then Bob, like his father had done nearly twenty-five years before with his own children, attempted to get custody of Tali by filing a counterclaim.

Bob asserted, "The counter-plaintiff [himself] is a fit and proper person to have the care, custody, and control of the child as sole custodian or on a joint custody basis which would maintain the regular, frequent, and substantial contact he has had with the child since her birth. The child's best interest would best be served by counter-plaintiff having sole or joint custody as he offers a stable home environment whereas Plaintiff [Francie], for all practical purposes, is living with another man and shuttling the child back and forth between her residence and that of her male friend. She has left the child for periods in excess of ten days with the counter-plaintiff in order to be with her male friend. One of these periods included the child's birthday."

Bob's attorney, who didn't mention that it was Tali's second birthday, said that Bob had put up 62.5 percent of both their houses and Francie had contributed just 37.5 percent. He had paid for everything else, Bob's lawyer claimed, and thus was to be awarded five-eighths of the real estate and all of everything else. No attorney's fees should be given to Francie, not even child support, except during the periods of the year the child resided with her.

This hardball counterclaim, made a day after their fourth anniversary, was unsettling. Bob did agree to pay temporary support and would later pay the mortgage on their Gibson Island home where Francie lived for a while with Tali. But the counterclaim forced a quick settlement, more to Bob's favor. Francie and Bob agreed to joint custody on March 26, 1979, and to a financial settlement with a division of property by the end of August.

A year after the divorce agreement, Francie said, "I felt I was a project. I had the right credentials . . . and he just wore me down."

Carl had told Nora about the book he wanted to write on their first date. And now he could write it. He had money—millions—a writing cottage behind his house in Bridgehampton and a supportive, attractive wife. Yet Carl did some research, wrote thirty pages and stopped. His creativity was soon channeled into an expensive redecoration of the Bridgehampton manse.

There were too many temptations in New York. The plays, the clubs, the restaurants. And everywhere they went, the paparazzi were there. The frequent flashbulbs' "pop-pop" lit their presence like fireflies of the city. They validated his success. He went to the literary dining salons such as Elaine's, where he could march to the front without a reservation. He would be recognized with a "This way, Mr. Bernstein." He was a literary lion now.

Carl and Nora lived as if the bestsellers would never end. But there hadn't been a bestseller in years and there was no prospect of a new one soon. Would a child solidify their marriage? Jacob Walker Bernstein was born on August 22, 1978. Nora wrote about her pregnancy a week before their first son's arrival for the *New York Times Magazine* (" 'How do you feel about your wife's body?' my husband was asked in our Lamaze class. 'I like it,' he said, 'but I won't be sorry when she gets her old one back.' ")

They were a family now. Carl, the family man, began an affair with Margaret Jay a few months later.

The "honorable" Margaret Jay was the daughter of Labor Party prime minister James Callaghan and was the wife of Peter Jay, the British ambassador to the United States. Peter Jay, was, in many ways, like Carl. He had been a journalist, and when he was named ambassador at the age of forty, there had been a protest. It was said he was too young, too inexperienced. Margaret Jay was a media person, too. She worked for the BBC's Washington bureau and produced a program for National Public Radio.

Margaret Jay and her husband loved to give intimate dinner parties—twenty-four guests was a typical number. When the Jays sent out invitations, they would specify in a separate note the evening's topic of conversation—Soviet relations with the West, for instance. At one of these parties, Carl Bernstein was presented to Margaret Jay.

Carl's affair with the wife of the United Kingdom's ambassador to the United States soon became another topic of conversation in upper-crust dining salons. Diana McLellan made it the first item in her "Ear" column when she switched from the *Star* to the *Post* and then embarrassed Carl further by announcing it on ABC's *Good Morning America* to David Hartman and a guffawing stage crew. When Nora found out about Carl's infidelity, she learned it was more than a one-night stand. Margaret and Carl were house-hunting together, she was told. Nora, who was in the seventh month of her second pregnancy at the time, put their year-old son, Jacob, under one arm, and the Washington apartment's best contemporary painting under the other. She caught the Eastern shuttle to New York. Three weeks later she went into labor, two months prematurely. She would blame Carl for the early delivery, which was performed by cesarean section.

Carl rushed to Mount Sinai hospital, perhaps hoping for a reconciliation and to be present for the baby's arrival. The hospital staff attempted to keep Carl out of the delivery room, but he blustered his way in. Nora and Carl's second son, Max Ephron Bernstein, born several pounds below normal weight, was kept in the hospital five weeks. During that time, Carl visited nearly every day, feeding and holding the child. After his hospital duties, he showed up at Elaine's and joked to the literati present that he was naming his son Early Bernstein. Carl Bernstein could always be counted on to show up and even provide dramatic eulogies at funerals. He now proved to be equally skilled in at least doing the right thing at the beginning of life.

When Nora got back to New York, she temporarily moved in with friends Bob Gottlieb (an Alfred A. Knopf editor and years later the editor of *The New Yorker*) and his wife, Maria Tucci. She next called Liz Smith. Nora poured out her troubles with Carl to the columnist for two hours by phone and demanded that the separation be announced in the syndicated column. One of her nicer pronouncements was that "Carl was a rat." Shortly after Nora's call, Carl was on the phone asking Liz Smith not to print the story, telling her that the marriage was still on. After Smith wrote the piece—and subsequent ones—about the former "literary couple," Carl called her and threated to sue, telling her she was "malicious." Smith was then forced to assemble every item she had written that included Carl's name and give them to her editor, Gil Spencer, at the *New York Daily News*. Spencer, according to Smith, told Carl, "Are you nuts? Don't be so pathological."[3]

Carl's allies didn't rush to defend him. One friend described him as "crazed." Richard Cohen took Nora's side. Ben Bradlee said that Carl had "shot himself in the foot." Only Bob, who had never liked Nora, seemed to support Carl. Carl was grateful. "I feel this bond with Bob," he said at the time. "We trust each other."

Carl returned to Margaret Jay, even though they were the focus of every tabloid and gossip columnist in the New York–Washington axis. Margaret and Peter Jay seemed to take it in stride. The diplomatic corps in Washington knew that Margaret and Peter had a "relaxed" relationship. Peter Jay was often seen in London escorting Elizabeth Spender, the daughter of British poet Stephen Spender, to parties. The Jays had three children to Nora and Carl's two and weren't about to split up over a fling. In the ways and customs of sophisticated international marriages, Carl Bernstein was in over his head. Still, they continued to see each other. Margaret was with him at an ABC Christmas party in Washington, a Kennedy Center gala and the Grammy Awards. Yet when the photographers snapped their pictures, Carl pretended to be puzzled and acted upset. "I never really understood until now why celebrities hate the press," he said, "They never leave you alone."

Nora adjusted. She spent a lot of time with her celebrity psychotherapist, Mildred Newman, coauthor of the bestselling book *How to Be Your Own Best Friend*. She began dating a Random House editor, Joe Fox, who was succeeded by real estate mogul and magazine publisher Mort Zuckerman. She went back to work, writing a movie script about the unwitting nuclear activist, Karen Silkwood for her friend Mike Nichols. A few years later, Nora would exact revenge—some would say pathological revenge—upon Carl in a novel titled *Heartburn*.

12

[Bob and Carl 1977–80]

Justices Denied

F<small>LOATING</small> AND floundering on a still vast, but shrinking sea of money, a somewhat humbled Carl approached Bob in 1979 with suggestions for a journalistic reunion. They could do a syndicated column together, Carl offered; it would be investigative journalism of the highest order. Perhaps remembering Carl's work habits, Bob jettisoned the idea. We'll go to Bradlee, Carl said next, and ask him to make us joint Metropolitan editors. Bob liked that idea. Bradlee didn't. He named Bob to the position of Metro editor without including Bernstein. Then Bradlee offered Carl his old job as a reporter. It would be a new start for the wayward writer. Carl, realizing that one can't go home again, passed. In mid-November of 1979, he would be named ABC television's Washington news bureau chief by its news division president, Roone Arledge.

Bob no longer needed Carl. He had already teamed up with Scott Armstrong. Scott was a blue-collar version of Bob whose curriculum vitae included Wheaton and Yale too, but the hard way. His father had been a paper salesman, not a lawyer or a judge. Scott and Bob had begun working on a book about the Supreme Court in 1977, shortly after the debate over the merits of *The Final Days* had subsided. The now established workaholic tendencies exhibited by Bob while working on this new book helped convince Francie Barnard to leave him in early 1978.

The genesis of the new project came during a cocktail party on April 10, 1977, at Katharine Graham's Georgetown house. Supreme Court justice Potter Stewart took Bob aside at the gathering and told him to call the next morning—he had something he wanted to talk about. Stewart was, like Bob, a Midwesterner, a proper son of Elihu Yale, and a Skull and Bones man—several steps above the Book and Snake pedigree of Robert Woodward. Stewart had an ax to grind, and the younger Yalie was to be his scribe.

Bob met with Stewart the next night, and over five hours Stewart told him of the complete antipathy he felt toward the court of Chief Justice Warren Burger. The dislike Potter Stewart felt for Burger seeped out of every pore. And it came across mixed with a little envy and superciliousness—the arrogance of a Yalie who had failed to rise above someone who had only gone to a cow college—Minnesota—and had somehow leapfrogged over him.

Stewart told Bob he would give him the details of the inner workings of the Supreme Court on the condition of complete anonymity: "Don't identify me in any form or shape." Stewart told Bob he would grease the way with the clerks, and with the justices who were his allies. He wanted to expose Burger as a bumbler, an aristocrat who didn't deserve the title, a man worthy only of disdain.

Stewart also despised Richard Nixon. This was part of the reason why he chose Bob Woodward for the mission against Burger. He told Bob he felt that his and Carl's reporting in the *Post* had been great for America. They had done the right thing by stopping Richard Nixon and his band of thugs.

Bob went home and typed out a fifteen-hundred-word memo on his evening with Potter Stewart. It would be the rough outline for his next book, *The Brethren*.

Stewart got four other justices—the ones on his side—to talk. He then persuaded more than a hundred clerks to speak with Bob Woodward and Scott Armstrong. Bob and Scott then deceived the clerks. They told them the book was about power, about decision-making in Washington, and the Supreme Court was just a part of that process. The clerks, thrown off by the subterfuge, said more than they would have ordinarily. In fact, they were dazzled. "I wanted to meet him," said one clerk. "I was flattered that he wanted to interview me." Some of the justices later said that their clerks "got conned."

"We each took four justices and both of us worked on Warren Burger," Bob told the *New York Times* in early 1980.[1] "Each of us wrote one of the book's seven sections. We redid each other's drafts, adding or subtracting . . . Afterwards we went out and did more interviews, got more documents, and more material, and finally turned in the first complete draft on Jan. 15, 1979.

Bob and Scott began with a $350,000 advance for *The Brethren*, budgeting $30,000 for research expenses. *Playboy* mitigated part of the expense budget by excerpting several thousand words in its October 1979 issue. Simon and Schuster expected *The Brethren* to do moderately well, but not become another number one bestseller. The publisher certainly did not expect bookstores to complain that they didn't get *enough* copies, griping that they were sold out before Christmas and left short. Even though the book hit the retail outlets just before the holidays, it became the seventh most popular title of 1979, sailing into 1980 at the top of most bestseller lists.

Perhaps the public expected to find the same kind of titillating gossip that had made *The Final Days* a phenomenon. If so, Bob and Scott delivered. Justice William O. Douglas was described as "incontinent" and "was overweight, smoked heavily and at times, drank too much." Justice Thurgood Marshall was made to sound like a character out of *Amos 'n' Andy*: "What's shakin', chiefy baby," was one remark allegedly given as a greeting to Burger. He was portrayed as a TV addict. Bob and Scott also quoted Marshall saying, "Yowza, yowza," to a group of tourists and impersonating an elevator operator. Marshall said later he had never spoken with the authors nor had he been asked to confirm any parts of the portrayal.

Another probably unnecessary episode that rankled many was a sequence describing the justices chuckling over an obscene and scatological cartoon. The drawing had all nine of them engaged in various sexual activities, including Justice Blackmun sodomizing a kangaroo and a nude Chief Justice Burger involved in fetishistic, sadomasochistic activities. Such juicy episodes certainly sold books. Potter Stewart and two of his allies, justices William Brennan and Lewis Powell, came out relatively well.

Former U.S. Attorney Griffin Bell immediately labeled the book "four hundred pages of gossip and trivia," and others were quick to point out the misuse of legal terminology.[2] Bob shrugged it off. "I suspect there are some errors in it," he told *People* magazine.

Scott Armstrong was now being confused with Carl Bernstein. He told an anecdote at book parties about a man who came up to him and said, "You must be Carl Bernstein." Scott answered, "No. If I were, I'd be having more fun."

At another book signing he was asked if he pronounced his name "steen or stine?" Scott said Strong, and, reportedly, when asked to sign the book, signed it "Carl Bernstrong."

At a *Washington Post* book luncheon for *The Brethren*, Carl, introducing his successor, Scott, and Bob, said, "Some people think Mr. Woodward is cold, distant and aloof. That's really not true. He's very personable—warmth itself. Once, during our [Watergate] investigation, when we were out at dinner, I said, 'Mr. Woodward, would you like a milk shake with your Big Mac?' He said, 'Call me Robert.' " Some publications began calling Bob and Scott, "Woodstrong."

Burger was certainly made to look like the incompetent fool Stewart wanted to portray. As *The New Republic* noted in its review of *The Brethren*, "The great debate among the clerks is whether the Chief is evil or stupid." It described the tome as "a poorly written adventure story for children or (much the same thing) a Leon Uris novel" and also called it a "trivial, vulgar, and stupid book." The attack was written by Graham Hughes, an author and professor of law at New York University.

Stewart, in what he told Bob and Scott, took pains to make Burger look bad. At one point, Potter Stewart was quoted in *The Brethren* as saying, "On ocean liners they used to have two captains. One for show, to take the women to dinner. The other to pilot the ship safely. The Chief [Burger] is the show captain. All we need now is a real captain."

The *Washington Post* ran excerpts from the book for eight consecutive days; an editor publicized it by telling *Time*, "The Supreme Court is the last secret institution in Washington. It's as secret as the CIA, but the process it goes through has never been examined." The Post corporation's subsidiary, *Newsweek*, did a cover story on the book. And *60 Minutes* aired a segment with Bob. But as the book received more attention and was read, more questions were asked than answers given. Bob and Scott came under fire for both the accuracy and the ethics of the reporting.

When asked in late 1979 why he had chosen to write about the Supreme Court, Bob had a ready one-word answer: "Curiosity." *The Brethren* was similar in tone to both *All the President's Men* and

The Final Days. It was written in the same breathy, anecdotal style and had no sources or bibliography listed. Trust me, Bob seemed to be asking. The critics, who had generally given a vote of no confidence for *The Final Days*, seemed to be answering, We don't. This created controversy, and as any publishing house knows, controversy can be a main ingredient in a successful book. Thus nearly three hundred mostly mixed or negative reviews, which might have reduced other writers to tears, helped earn Bob Woodward and Scott Armstrong hundreds of thousands of additional dollars in secondary rights and royalties fueling the book's rise to the top of the bestseller lists. There was even talk of a movie. One magazine speculated on Charles Bronson as Warren Burger and Burt Reynolds as Byron White.

The *Wall Street Journal*'s December 12, 1979, review was typical of many of the reviews: "We get only the standard clichés: Burger, pompous and devious; Douglas, arrogant and a fast worker; Marshall, lazy and unconcerned with legal doctrine; White [Justice Byron], pugnacious and insouciant, sincere but in over his head; Stewart moderate and patrician . . ." Potter Stewart's agenda was being carried out.

Although Bob knew all along that the book was to be only about the inner workings of the Supreme Court and told *Playboy* as much in a 1989 interview, he gave the *New York Times* a different version in 1980: "We started out on another subject, and when it didn't turn out, we broadened it to be a book on decision-making in Washington, including the White House and the Senate . . . then we narrowed it down from 1969 to 1976 because we didn't want to get involved in decisions pending before the court." Bob never mentioned Potter Stewart or the real genesis of the book in his *Times* interview. And when the *Times* brought up criticisms involving the "use of anonymous sources and subjective descriptions of the justices' thoughts," Bob was petulant:

"The legal establishment is not happy, obviously, because they think the courts and the law are their province. But the book speaks for itself, and anyone who's read it knows it's serious. It could be even called *The Making of the Law, 1969 to 1976*."

The criticisms of John G. Kester, a lawyer with the formidable Washington firm of Williams and Connolly and who used to be a law clerk for the late Supreme Court justice Hugo Black, were typical of what appeared in the media. Kester, writing in the *Washingtonian* magazine, said that he felt "soiled" reading Bob and

Scott's book. "To tell a good story, Woodward and Armstrong have taken liberties the scrupulous historian avoids," Kester wrote. He went on to enumerate the many "he felt" and "he must have thought" passages, questioning if the authors really knew that "Stewart's stomach knotted as he drove through Washington traffic. Without sources to check, who can say?"

Kester was particularly appalled by the characterization of the chief justice: "Warren Burger has not been beloved in this city the way Earl Warren was. That is no news to anyone in Washington who has followed the Court at all. Maybe Burger doesn't deserve to be.

"But can the chief justice really be as simple a character as *The Brethren* suggests? Or could it be a function of who talked and who kept silent and of the journalistic axiom that controversy is news while complexity is not?"

Kester had it nearly right, even without knowing that Potter Stewart was behind the character assassination of Burger. The attorney concluded, "*The Brethren* tries to convert the chief justice into a judicial Nixon, as Woodward saw Nixon—conspiratorial, secretive, self-indulgent, clumsy in the use of power, lacking in generous instincts. At one point, broadcasting to us from inside the chief justice's brain, the authors report that 'already he felt a kinship with these people, with Mitchell and Nixon.' One has the feeling of rereading *All the President's Men*, with the robed Burger a sort of Nixon in drag."[3]

Some of the most caustic comments came from Renata Adler in the *New York Times* and Anthony Lewis in the *New York Review of Books*. Bob and Scott adroitly managed to turn both reviews into incendiary debates, stoking the details into an even hotter issue in front of the public. Lewis wrote, "A journalistic challenge to institutional secrecy . . . depends upon credibility. In their reports for the *Washington Post* Woodward and Bernstein had freshness on their side . . . they succeeded in the end because they were believable and Richard Nixon was not." Then Lewis went on to describe his interview with a law clerk, Paul Hoeber, who claimed that at least one part of the book was false, fabricated and inaccurate. The disputed passage contended that Justice William J. Brennan voted against his own judgment in a landmark capital punishment case in order to curry favor with Justice Harry A. Blackmun. Hoeber said that he had spoken with twenty-nine of the thirty law clerks who had been present when the case about which Bob and Scott had written—*Moore vs. Illinois*—had been voted upon (the case involved the constitutionality of the death penalty). The twenty-nine clerks all backed Hoeber's contention that the passage was false.

Lewis's long essay on *The Brethren* took up five newspaper pages, nearly ten thousand words. It provoked a two-thousand-word, five-point rebuttal from Scott and Bob, which was followed by an even longer five-thousand-word reply by Lewis, who said he had interviewed most of the law clerks himself and stood by his original essay. Exhausted readers of the *New York Review of Books*, in order to correctly referee the debate, had to buy *The Brethren*—or at least borrow a copy.

Renata Adler, a *New Yorker* magazine writer, was assigned to review the book for the Sunday *New York Times Book Review*. She had just graduated from Yale Law School. She began by noting that any book offering "insights, or even secrets" over six terms of the U.S. Supreme Court was "an enormously ambitious undertaking." She then made an argument, a good one, on the widespread use of confidential and unknown sources. As Adler put it, "it makes stories almost impossible to verify. It suppresses a major element of almost every investigative story: Who wanted it known?" Then Adler asked, "Is there any tradition of reporting which requires that their *number* be protected as well? 'More than 200 people,' 'several justices,' 'more than 170 law clerks,' 'several dozen former employees.' How many?" asked Adler. "Two hundred and one people or 299? . . . What in the name of journalism would be compromised if we knew?"

Adler continued to pick away at Bob and Scott's book for several more columns, questioning the journalistic "weasel" words that they used to justify their research, such as *virtually* every instance and *at least one, usually two* and *often three, or four* sources. Vague, imprecise references such as these were meaningless, was Adler's point, particularly in a significant book about the inner workings of the high court.

She then found fault with Bob and Scott's declarative sentences that described justices as "furious" or "upset" or "disturbed" or "frightened" or "glad." She wrote that the authors used twenty-eight one-word or two-word phrases to describe the justices' seemingly manic-depressive states of mind. She said her favorite was "Marshall's clerks were miffed."

Adler then took the two authors to task for the many factual errors, such as the wrong year in which a case was said to have been decided or the inaccurate phrasing of legal language. She summarized her review by noting that *The Brethren* was an important work because of "who the authors are" and because of the ambitious subtitle of *Inside the Supreme Court*. She pronounced the book a failure and said that the only "scoop" there could be about the Supreme Court would be to reveal a crime or discover corruption. Since there were none, Adler concluded, a more analytical mind was needed to write about the court if a future book was to have meaning.

Bob and Scott would later claim that Adler's review had cost them $800,000 on the paperback sale to Avon, complaining that they had received "only" $880,000 because, as Bob said, "the *Times* controls the New York publishing scene." Scott Armstrong labeled it a "conspiracy." Still, there was enough money for Armstrong to buy a thirty-two-acre farm in Fauquier County, Virginia—horse country—some fifty miles from Washington.

The Adler review stung, and Bob said the critic was "ignorant and picky about points of law." Ten years later he would say that "she didn't understand how the court worked" and accuse the recent Yale Law School graduate of "infantile ignorance" because "she's not a practicing journalist."

There is little doubt that Warren Burger was not the most elegant or competent chief justice of the Supreme Court. And Bob Woodward and Scott Armstrong did carry out Potter Stewart's design of discrediting Burger in totality. Whether Stewart, his associates and the clerks gave Bob and Scott selective files and memorandums to buttress Stewart's case can only be speculated upon. Certainly the major sources had a bias against Burger; that slant was prevalent throughout *The Brethren*. So Potter Stewart accomplished his mission, with Bob Woodward and Scott Armstrong, in their role as conduits to the American public, aiding and abetting. A dozen years later Bob expressed satisfaction to investigative journalist Steven Weinberg in *Mother Jones* magazine that *The Brethren* was considered by scholars "a primary source" on certain cases that were argued before the court.

13

[Bob, 1979–81]

Janet's World

AFTER HIS second marriage ended, and following the negative and mixed reviews of *The Brethren*, Bob returned to the *Post* on a full-time basis, determined to succeed in management. He was named the assistant managing editor of Metro, the newspaper's section for local news, on May 1, 1979. The new job was viewed by both colleagues and critics as a first step toward Bob's replacing Ben Bradlee. It was an unspoken fantasy, a romantic scenario in which Jason Robards would hand over the reins to Robert Redford. But it existed as murmured gossip. In the newsroom, it was said that the vision of Bradlee passing the torch to Woodward had all the makings of a movie sequel.

Bradlee was nearly sixty now. He would probably hold the reins for five more years, ten years at the most. To many it may have seemed poetic that a former "knight adventurer," now an "archduke" (as new *Post* ombudsman Bill Green called the reporters and editors of the paper, comparing them to a medieval round table), might be handed the crown of an aging king of journalism. Sir Bob and Sir Carl had been first across the moat of the white castle on Pennsylvania Avenue, driving out King Richard. Sir Bob had helped to make the *Post* the finest newspaper kingdom in America.

But Bob was a loner who still came across as cold and haughty. He was not perceived as a "people" person. And now he was being asked to manage 108 news staffers. He was to be a disaster. His frailties and his surprising lack of communication with some of the staff were ignored by Bradlee and Simons. But who would have dared to ask the bravest knight of Watergate to step down so soon?

Stocked from first-rate aspirants that filled Ben Bradlee's in-box with hundreds of resumés each week, the *Post*, it seemed, could do no wrong. The paper drew talent—highly strung talent that threw tantrums when their stories were edited heavily or—God forbid—cut. There were tears and the throwing of computer keyboards by the new generation, which the less talented *Post* reporters dubbed "the brat pack." They were members of the new influx of writers and investigative reporters who aspired to work at the house of Woodstein. It was a newspaper Camelot, the place to be for any ambitious young journalist.

Jonathan Neumann was one of those, a *Philadelphia Inquirer* writer who had won a Pulitzer for a series of articles on police brutality. He had a secret source in the City of Brotherly Love's precincts who had been dubbed, à la Watergate, Deep Nightstick. But when Neumann came to the *Post* and dared to criticize Bob, he got a cold stare and was told, "Nobody talks to me that way." Other city reporters voiced anonymous complaints about Woodward's managerial skills. "He interferes" and (even more damning) "If Woodward would have been editor during Watergate, it would never have been reported" were two of the nicer remarks of *Post* staffers quoted anonymously in a *Washingtonian* article. The worst criticisms were on his waffling and indecision, causing frustration among other editors, from whose hands he sometimes rudely grabbed copy. Insensitive, he fired a reporter just before the reporter was about to have an operation.

"He gets excited about a story, then he loses interest," said one reporter. Another: "He flip-flops. He's a control freak." When someone dared to write an internal memo criticizing a story he had written, Bob was furious. "The next time you find an occasion for criticizing my work, you will consult with me in advance," Bob told the staffer with military briskness.

Bob knew what he did want. He held a meeting just after his promotion and told his staff that he wanted "holy shit stories." "If it's not a scandal or something that results in an indictment, he's not interested in it," concluded one staffer.

Bob tried to focus both on the newspaper and the writing of books. He retreated to his house in Georgetown, curtailing what little of his social life remained. He stopped dating. When Nina Hyde, the fashion editor, repeatedly introduced him to one of her assistants, hoping to make a match, Bob ended it by saying directly, "Nina, we've met."

He became driven to make the Metro section his fiefdom. He hired one of the researchers for *The Brethren*, Milton Benjamin, as his assistant. Benjamin, judged a snob by other reporters, exacerbated the problem with Bob's image. He lasted less than a year.

Assessments of Bob in the press were worse. He was compared to Nixon and called "insensitive" and "full of himself" by one magazine. Journalist Judy Bachrach rated him as being among Washington's lousiest lovers, calling him "pedantic" and "pompous." Another named him "the dark prince."

If all the attacks bothered him, Bob did not let on publicly. And he had his defenders. One left-handed compliment came from Richard Cohen. "He's a lot more concerned than he appears to be . . . he talks as if he read a book on how to be polite." Another friend: "He's not loathed. You just don't feel much warmth for him."

Toledo, Ohio, a large callus on the shores of Lake Erie, is noted for its bituminous coal shipping port. The city, midway between Cleveland and Detroit, is at the heart of the rust belt. In such an environment, Stratman Cooke's making it the hard way and getting a law degree was a black Horatio Alger tale. Becoming corporate secretary of the local electrical utility and the chairman of a city planning commission was icing on the cake. His wife, Loretta, who worked as an administrative assistant at the University of Toledo's continuing education program, was like-minded. She raised their two daughters—Janet and Nancy—to succeed in a dominant Caucasian society.

When Janet was five years old, Stratman Cooke gave her a typewriter. Later, a grade-school teacher would tell him his daughter wrote "beautiful poetry." A decade later, in 1968, Janet was one of those who would be among the first to integrate Maumee Valley Country Day School, an exclusive private academy. Nancy, the youngest child, would go to Brown, a New England Ivy League university, and would become a graphic artist. The Cooke family, with its exceptionally dark skin, lived as if it had always been part of the dominant white culture. Ben Bradlee would be quoted in Ellis Cose's, *The Press*, as saying "[Stratman Cooke] looked . . . in the mirror and . . . saw somebody who was white. He had paid an awful price to succeed in the white world, and his daughter had paid a price as well."

Janet didn't let her parents down. At Maumee Valley, she was a star student. But later she would say that her childhood, spent largely at the prep school were like "several years of intensive shock treatment." In the fall of 1972, Janet went off to Vassar College in Poughkeepsie, New York. The grades she earned there were good, but she was considered "high-strung" and unable to deal with the intense pressure of a highly competitive academic and social environment. Janet dropped out after her freshman year, coming home and enrolling at the University of Toledo. At the local level, Janet thrived. She made the honors list—one of one hundred and twenty in a school of four thousand. She also headed a petition drive that led to more courses about women. She did not become known for being associated with black causes.

Janet Cooke was remembered by her University of Toledo professors as a writer of "excellent poetry," a "beautiful writer." She was also viewed as one "who cut a lot of corners" and "who didn't face reality very squarely." Her bachelor's degree was in English literature.

Janet had worked on and off as an intern or trainee for the *Toledo Blade* newspaper since 1973. After a short stint at WGTE-TV, the local public television station, she rejoined the *Blade* in April of 1977 as a full-time reporter. Her first assignment was with *Living Today*, a Sunday lifestyle section.

One of Janet's first major stories—a series—was on the mental problems that college students faced away from home and the resulting suicides on campus. Most of the quotes came from her alma mater, the University of Toledo's counseling center. Several quotes could have described her Vassar experience. "Anxieties can develop because the student is away from home for the first time in a new and much larger setting, or under peer pressures," she quoted a counselor as saying.

Janet's writing rapidly evolved from the straightforward, pedestrian interview to a flashy, more assured style. Her bylines would sometimes appear on the same page as Sally Quinn's and Judith Martin's—two *Post* writers who were widely syndicated with the sub-byline "Washington Post–Los Angeles Times News Service."

If Janet had read Sally Quinn's 1975 memoir, *We're Going to*

Make You a Star, she might have believed that looks and style were two requisites needed to get one a job as a reporter at the *Post*. In her book, Sally described wearing "my nicest dress" to her interview with Ben Bradlee. Then when Ben had asked her to leave some things she had written, she told him she had never written anything. Another editor said, "Nobody's perfect," and Ben had said, "You're hired."

But Janet could write as well as look good. One could picture her as the black Sally Quinn.

When Janet wrote about routine subjects, such as her interview with the head of the Toledo Opera Association—the story was dull. But give her an opportunity to be creative and the story would be riveting. Her long piece titled "Memories of a Violent Marriage," about a battered wife, was brilliantly scripted and utterly untraceable. "But 31-year-old Beth Hill (not her real name)," Janet's story read in the second paragraph. The writing captivated the reader: "She is still attractive. The perfect teeth, long auburn hair, and youthful figure belie the trouble that the body has seen. Five years ago, perhaps she could have been a model." Reading further into the article, disturbing images emerged: "Like the teeth which fell out when her former husband threw a heavy trophy into her face. And the breasts that had to be reconstructed when tumors—which may have been a result of constant beatings—made two mastectomies necessary."

There were other, similar stories, which used the disclaimer "not their real names." One, on children of divorced parents, used composite characters and said so. Another piece by Janet was a spellbinding first-person account of her being trapped in a house alone while an unknown person outside tried to break in. The story was impossible to verify. The Toledo police force "happened" to be on strike at the time.

On July 12, 1979, Janet sent her resumé, six newspaper clippings of her writing and a letter to the *Post*, embellishing her background. The description now said that she had graduated from Vassar, magna cum laude, with a master's degree from the University of Toledo.

"Dear Mr. Bradlee," the letter read, "I have been a full-time reporter for *The Blade* for slightly more than two years, and I am now ready to tackle the challenge of working for a larger newspaper in a major city." Bradlee, stimulated by Cooke's claim of honors from Vassar, sent the resumé and clippings to Bob Woodward, who wrote a note to an assistant, saying he would interview Janet Cooke.

In late July, a few days after her twenty-fifth birthday, Janet entered the fifth-floor newsroom, bedazzling everyone with whom she spoke. Here was the prototype—the most-sought-after journalism recruit in America—a black woman who looked like a cross between Jayne Kennedy and Diana Ross. An honors student from an exceptional school and with a graduate degree as a bonus. Two years on a big-city daily. And she was well turned out—the designer clothes complemented her trim figure. Nobody thought to check her resumé, which, like the hairpiece she wore and the long plastic nails glued on her fingers, was false.

"We don't call colleges," managing editor Howard Simons said later. "You can't get college transcripts anyway."[1]

A summary of her interviews was prepared. It described her as being "high on everyone's list" and a "self-starter." Only one editor, an African American, dissented. "There's still a lot of Vassar in her," he said.

Two months later, Bob Woodward wrote a memo to the personnel department asking if he could go ahead and hire her. Many editors would remember no background checks of any kind ever being made, so bowled over was the newsroom with Janet Cooke's manner and poise. Others would say that *The Blade* was called.

Janet Cooke began working at the *Post* on January 3, 1980.[2] She was assigned to write for the District Weekly, a zoned edition that was distributed on Thursdays, but only within the District of Columbia. It was near the bottom of the newspaper's reportorial chain, one of the assignments that went to a beginner, or to older reporters at the end of their careers.

Janet Cooke made both an auspicious and appropriate debut. Her first bylined article, which ran two weeks after she was hired, took up nearly a third of a page just inside the section, structured as a column called "City Faces." It was about a black beauty contest—Miss Look of Radiance—sponsored by L'Oréal's black cosmetic line. It was an incisive, thoughtful piece.

Janet Cooke did much more than interview the contest winners. She wrote it as if it were a nuts-and-bolts business story, delving into how two giant cosmetics firms, L'Oréal and Revlon, were muscling into the black cosmetics business, using their power to push out a smaller, African-American-owned cosmetics company,

Johnson Products. There were good quotes from all three competitors, as well as the beauty contest winners.

Janet seemed to focus on black issues after that—people of color made up the bulk of the District Weekly's readership. There was an interview with a black prisoner at a penitentiary, serving fifteen years to life, who had just received a bachelor's degree and been named to *Who's Who Among Students in American Colleges and Universities*. "William Biggs never had time to finish junior high school," she wrote. "He was, as he explains it, 'too busy getting into trouble.' "

Her leads soon had the cadence and the new-journalism techniques of a Carl Bernstein. She began a lead front-page story on gifted black teenagers with "Closing her eyes, 17-year-old Kim Boyd polishes off a quadratic equation faster than a speeding abacus. Just like she said she could."

Later, Janet would get away with the kind of writing that might have been censored at other papers. A long story about the center of Washington's drug activity, Fourteenth and U streets, contained dialect and words that raised some readers' eyebrows:

> "You don't come talkin' about cleaning up no place where people was born and raised. These niggers ain't gonna stand for it. You see that corner out there? It's these people's CORNER. It's their life. It's these brothers' and sisters' life, they home. This is all we know."

Whether or not it was verbatim quoting, Janet Cooke's writing was believable street talk. And later in the article, when Janet described a person whose neck had been slashed as "screaming, blood flowing like burgundy from the open wound," it was effective enough to earn high marks from her editors.

But Janet Cooke's articles for the District Weekly section of the *Post* did not earn her raves from the newsroom's black reporters as it did from the white ones such as Bob Woodward. Janet dressed white, dated white men and roomed with a white *Post* reporter—Elsa Walsh.[3] She was white in every way except for the color of her skin. One black staffer called her "a physical fraud."

In Toledo, Janet had written as if color-blind. At the *Post*, she was encouraged to write about blacks and the "black experience." Bob Woodward asked for the "Hey, Martha, read this" piece—or the "holy shit" story—and Janet would deliver it.

In the summer of 1980, Janet told Milton Coleman, the thirty-four-year-old black city editor, about an eight-year-old heroin addict. Coleman was enthusiastic. "You find that kid," he said, "and it's a front-page story."

The *Post* protected its sources. Who knew who Deep Throat was? So after fifty-two bylines, Janet produced a typed outline about an eight-year-old heroin addict. It was based, she said, on 145 pages of notes. Her first draft was thirteen and a half pages long, about thirty-five hundred words. Milton Coleman thought it was near perfect. He suggested a few changes, asked that it be cut slightly, and told her to rearrange the content. Coleman said that the story should be composed like modern jazz, particularly like the music of saxophonist John Coltrane.

As for the "not-his-real-name" identity, the *Post* had a policy. An editor could ask the name of a source; if a reporter wouldn't reveal it, the editor had the right to reject the story. Milton Coleman believed in Janet Cooke. He didn't ask who her sources were. Neither did Howard Simons. Neither did Bob Woodward. Janet said she was worried. The boyfriend of the young addict's mother had threatened to kill her with a knife if she breached the confidentiality of the boy's name. Enough said.[4]

The story on the child addict, now titled "Jimmy's World," was scheduled to run on September 28, 1980. Janet had outdone herself. There were lines that would make many suburbanites wince and turn away from the newspaper—"The needle slides into the boy's soft skin like a straw pushed into the center of a freshly baked cake"—then tentatively turn back for another voyeuristic morsel. The edited article came in at 2,256-words and was illustrated sensationally with a drawing of a hypodermic needle being injected into the arm of a smiling black child. It was suggested that the drawing, so powerful in its impact, run inside the nearly nine hundred thousand copies of the *Post* because subscribers could be "eating breakfast" while reading the paper.

Bob read the story for libel. It passed. Since all parties had fake names, nobody could be libeled, was Bob's reasoning. Then he called Janet into his office to give him an oral version of her story. Months later, he would say she was "a terrific actress."

Ben Bradlee read it. He said it was a "helluva job," a page-one story. The feature was set in type and the presses of the *Washington Post* began to grind out copies. Through the Washington Post–Los Angeles Times News Service it was made available to an additional three hundred papers. The newsmagazine *U.S. News and World Report* ran the account the next week in totality.

The story struck a nerve. Hundreds of letters were sent to the newspaper. Surprisingly, the public reaction's focus was not on the scourge of drugs, but on the plight of the eight-year-old child. How could a reporter watch such a crime and not do anything? readers wanted to know. Why wasn't the child's name given to the police? Where did a story end and the protection of a human life begin?

Washington's city government reacted. At first Mayor Marion Barry spent thousands of police man-hours searching for "Jimmy." When the police hunt was exhausted, city officials began to make noises that spread doubt on the child's existence. The mayor said that no drug dealer would let a reporter watch him "shoot up a child." *Post* attorney Edward Bennett Williams thought the story was a "phony." Alyce Gullattee, a professor at Howard University, and director of the school's drug research program, had been interviewed by Janet. She thought the story was false as well. When she called Bob Woodward to tell him so, she was told he was busy and transferred to an assistant.

Bob Woodward knew perhaps better than anyone that controversy sells. He promoted Janet Cooke from her role as a starlet for the District Weekly to full-fledged star working directly under him in Metro. If Janet Cooke had been noticed previously, now one couldn't miss her. When she strutted through the newsroom, all heads turned. But for all her outer confidence and posing, inside she was a nervous wreck. A bottle of Maalox stayed on her desk, a permanent monument to her insecurities. She overspent, bounced checks and dodged bill collectors. She continued buying designer clothes and began driving a new Datsun 280Z sports car.

There were plenty of doubters at the *Washington Post*, too, particularly among the black editors and reporters. Courtland Milloy had Janet take him to Jimmy's house and concluded that she didn't even know her way around the neighborhood. Vivian Aplin-Brownlee, Janet's editor at the District Weekly, hadn't believed the story from the start. "In her eagerness to make a name she would write further than the truth would allow," she said later. Janet's roommate, Elsa Walsh, also was doubtful. She told others that Janet wasn't brave enough to go into such a dangerous setting. Bob Woodward was among the few who still had faith. He attributed the skepticism to "professional jealousy." When he moved Janet onto his staff, he called it a "battlefield promotion." Later he would say, "I believed the story."

Janet began to believe it as much as Bob. In November, a month after "Jimmy's World" ran, she promised another front-page revelation. This time, she said, it was about a precocious fourteen-year-old prostitute and her twenty-year-old pimp. She had just spent time with them in a Georgetown restaurant.

The black editors insisted someone else go with Janet to meet the young "lady of the night." Janet was unable to produce her. Warning bells went off in some editors' heads, but Bob was untroubled, attaching "no particular significance" to the failed follow-up to "Jimmy."

Public officials, still unable to find the fictitious "Jimmy," began to criticize the *Post* and Janet Cooke. Bob's reaction was to "go into our Watergate mode—protect the source and back the reporter."

With these warning signs, an editor might have either put a tighter rein on Janet Cooke or let her quietly fade into at least temporary anonymity among the nearly five hundred reporters at the paper. Bob did neither. When Milton Coleman wrote a memo to Bob suggesting "Jimmy's World" be nominated for a Pulitzer, Bob agreed. He also entered it in the Maryland-D.C. press association's annual contest where it won second prize. But before the *Post* nominated Janet Cook's story for the Pulitzer Prize, several editors came to Bob and expressed their doubts again. They felt it could "disgrace" the paper. Bob's reaction to the onslaught of staff criticism was a shrugged "in for a dime, in for a dollar."

Like many successes in life, Janet Cooke's Pulitzer Prize was a result of fortuitous chance. Entered for a Pulitzer Prize under the local-reporting category, "Jimmy's World" lost out to a small Washington State newspaper for its coverage of the Mount St. Helen's volcanic eruption. The Pulitzer board, led by Roger Wilkins, who had once been an opinion-page editor at the *Post* and now worked for the crosstown rival *Star*, overruled the feature-story committee. Wilkins told the Pulitzer board he could find child addicts within ten blocks of Columbia University, where the awards were being judged. The feature committee had already decided on a story by *Village Voice* writer Teresa Carpenter, who had written about the murder of *Playboy* centerfold model Dorothy Stratten. The feature committee, led by film critic Judith Crist, had spent weeks reviewing 160 stories. The group was furious at being overruled; they had never seen Janet Cooke's story and during the judging process had decided to avoid, according to Crist, "anything dealing with anonymous people, composite characters." But in the interest of being seen as team players they remained silent while the Pulitzer board gave out its annual awards.

When the *Post* was notified, Janet Cooke was at Bob's alma mater, Yale University in New Haven, Connecticut, investigating the John Hinckley–Jodie Foster connection.[5] Later a *Post* editor would say that even the quotes used in Janet Cooke's New Haven story seemed to be fabricated. The *Post* newsroom staff celebrated without her. Donald Graham, who had recently become publisher of the *Post*, succeeding his mother, wrote Janet a laudatory letter. He noted that the recognition for "Woodward, Milton, Stan, Vivian . . . feels mighty like vindication." He then referred to the "abuse" the editors had been getting about the authenticity of the story. He also said that Janet was the "kind of journalist the *Post* needs for its future."

Janet came home from Yale. She posed for a picture that ran with a repeat of "Jimmy's World" on page six of the Metro section the next day. The photo was taken on the roof of the newspaper's building. Janet was shot in half-profile, her arms crossed, the city skyline in the background. A small gust of wind seemed to have made her hairpiece billow. If she had known where to look, she would have been able to see Bob's first apartment, where he had allegedly moved the flowerpot to arrange middle-of-the-night meetings with an invented Deep Throat.

The *Post* then transmitted a copy of the "Jimmy's World" article to the hundreds of newspapers that subscribed to its news service. Included was an updated personnel form that Janet had just filled out. One of the recipients of Janet's newest resumé was *The Blade*.

The ante had been upped with Janet's new data. She had added a year of study at the Sorbonne in Paris to her academic credits. She said she spoke French, Spanish, Portuguese and Italian. There were six journalism awards from two different Ohio press associations. And she listed playing piano as an additional accomplishment. Nobody at the *Post* had checked it against her original application and resumé.

The first to notice the discrepancies in Janet's biography was her former newspaper employer, *The Blade*. An editor called the Associated Press and suggested that the AP correct itself. The AP Toledo correspondent, Michael Holmes, called Vassar, the Sorbonne and the University of Toledo. Then he called the *Post*. He got Janet Cooke. She stuck to her story. An assistant to the president of Vassar phoned Ben Bradlee. At the same time, another AP editor called Howard Simons. Milton Coleman was also called, who in turned called Bob Woodward.

Now Bob Woodward told Janet, "I don't believe you on the 'Jimmy' story." Ben Bradlee, who spoke fluent French, tested her on languages. She failed. Then Bradlee and Woodward sent Janet and Coleman out to find "Jimmy's" house, which Janet insisted she could still find. A few hours later, Coleman called in. Janet couldn't find it.

Bob and other editors began to interrogate Janet upon her return from her fruitless search for the house. Ben Bradlee said, "You're like Richard Nixon. You're trying to cover up." Janet stuck to the accuracy of her story. Bob and three other editors intensified the questioning. After nine hours, shortly past midnight, Janet Cooke admitted that the story and resumé were false. She handwrote a confession, admitting, "I never encountered or interviewed an eight-year-old heroin addict." A month later she said she didn't think she would be caught because managing editor Howard Simons had told her he wasn't going to make her reveal the boy's name, his mother or the address.

Bob said he still admired "Jimmy's World." According to him, "it is a brilliant story—fake and fraud that it is."

Bob wasn't there. The rumor circulating among the Wheaton Community High's class of '61 was that Bob, the hero of Watergate, was indeed coming to the reunion. Near midnight, one of the women, who had had a little too much to drink decided to telephone Washington. Surprisingly, Bob answered.

"Guess who this is?" It was a fourteen year-old's dating opener. Her girlfriends gather near the phone, giggling. Bob listened, politely guarded, distant, as the woman asked him why he hadn't come to the twenty-year reunion. The woman hung up the phone without identifying herself. Bob, she told her friends, didn't seem pleased about being called.

Early the next morning, less than a day after receiving the first warning bells from Vassar and the Associated Press, the *Post* informed the Pulitzer board that it was returning the prize, telling them that "Jimmy's World" had been fabricated. It was the first admission of a fraudulent entry in the history of the awards.

Roger Wilkins, who had said there were child addicts near 116th Street and Broadway—the site of Columbia University, where the Pulitzers are annually awarded—was silent, but the other judges weren't. Robert Maynard, editor of the *Oakland Tribune*, was angry. "I find it frustrating and dismaying that five very busy editors spent three days reviewing one hundred and sixty-four submissions only to have the feature-story award given to a submission the jury never reviewed."

Judith Crist blamed Janet's newspaper: "The primary fault lies with the *Washington Post*, not that poor girl." But John Finnegan, executive editor of the *St. Paul Dispatch* and a member of the local-reporting committee, said there was no reason to doubt the story. He told reporters he assumed the *Post* had checked it out. "It was a beautiful piece of writing," he said.

Janet Cooke's mother, Loretta, immediately flew to Washington to be with her daughter. They secluded themselves at Janet's apartment. Later Janet told a national television show, "I did not want to fail." She complained of the *Post*'s "competitiveness. The need to be first, to be flashiest, to be sensational."

The newspaper's embarrassment continued. A civil suit was filed against Bob Woodward, Ben Bradlee, and three other editors by three District of Columbia civil activists on behalf of the Board of Education. The four-count suit charged the editors with publishing a hoax and that the District had suffered "financial loss." One plaintiff claimed that he had been afraid to send his children to District schools because they "might be subjected to the elements of 'Jimmy's World.'" The total amount came to $4.2 million. The lawsuit was dismissed.

Bob Woodward was clearly chagrined. His friends tried to console him. When he attended the symphony shortly after the *Post* returned the Pulitzer, his friend and fellow Watergate book author Jim Doyle told him, "It's not a big deal." "Oh, yes," Bob said, "It's a very big deal."

Bob tried to smooth over his growing differences with the newsroom, inviting staffers to his Georgetown house to "air out the matter," as one reporter described it. The crowded meeting turned ugly. His reporters voiced their darkest thoughts and even a copy aide shouted at him.

For the most part, Janet Cooke was treated as a leper by the publishing industry after the scandal. A year later she wrote a story for the *Washingtonian* magazine about matchmakers. It was an unfortunate choice of subject matter. Titled "Searching for Someone Special," the piece began, "We'll call her Samantha." The article described women who had "sea-blue eyes." Samantha and the others in the story were not the "real names."

Janet went on *Donahue*. There was said to be a contract to write for *Cosmopolitan*. It never materialized. She was hired to work as a reporter for the *Wilmington* (Del.) *News-Journal*, but the newsroom protested and Janet Cooke was never given a chance to redeem herself in newspapers.

A pop song about the scandal by a woman named "Phranc" who referred to herself as an "American Jewish lesbian folk-singer" got plenty of national airtime on alternative radio stations. The lyrics named "Ben Bradlee of Watergate fame" and ended up with the phrase "pack of lies." A play inspired by the scandal was written and given a 1984 summer run in Williamstown, Massachusetts. It starred Bianca Jagger, whose name, coincidentally, would be one of many linked romantically with Carl Bernstein during the 1980s.

Janet Cooke eventually drifted away from journalism, married a lawyer, moved to Paris and finally learned French. In 1992 she was reported to be writing fiction in France.

For the first time Bob became the butt of popular jokes. "I know where Jimmy lives," began one. "He lives next to Deep Throat." An ice-cream parlor a few blocks from Bob's house announced a Jimmy's World sundae. The ingredients were not named. "Trust us to make it up," the ice-cream shop's sign read. When other publications questioned Bob Woodward's writing after the Cooke scandal, they would invariably insert the "trust me" phrase and a mention of Janet Cooke as part of his resumé. It was, Bob would tell friends later, the nadir of his newspaper career. He contemplated leaving journalism.

Typical of the scathing criticism from his colleagues in the press was British journalist Henry Fairlie. Fairlie would write in *The Washingtonian* in 1983: "I once watched a party of high school students being escorted around the newsroom of the *Post* . . . Just as the children exclaim, 'Ooh!' when one of them detects the panda, lying curled up in a corner, so they exclaimed, 'Ooh!' when they at last spotted Woodward, chewing a bean sprout, and no doubt ruminating on the brilliance of the Janet Cooke story, which the *Post* was, under his direction and with his extravagant praise, about to run."

A few months after the Janet Cooke affair, Bob Woodward was quietly removed from his assistant managing editor's position in the Metro section and made head of a much smaller eight-man investigative unit, soon called the "swat team." Donald Graham took him to dinner and told him that he was a valued employee of the *Washington Post* and that he wanted him to stay. He also told him he would never have Ben Bradlee's job. Bob began telling friends he would focus on writing books. "Books," he said, "get remembered."

14

[*Carl and Bob, 1979–86*]

The ABCs of Heartburn

BY THE END of the seventies, Carl had begun affecting a sort of arrogance that was off-putting, at least to strangers. To those who did know him, it was almost charming, a suit of armor for his vulnerability. His insecurity may have been intensified by fears that maybe the critics were right, maybe he wasn't that good, and maybe he'd never write anything of consequence again.

"I went to see him for a book I was writing," said Washington author Tom Kelly, who was more than two decades older than Carl. "It was at the Madison Hotel coffee shop. He thought he was Walter Lippmann. I couldn't get a question in. He just talked about the state of journalism for an hour."

Roone Arledge, the head of ABC news, was already privately admitting that Carl's hiring as Washington bureau chief had been an error. Later he would confide to Liz Smith, "It was the biggest mistake of my television career."

Shortly after he became the chief of the Washington bureau, Carl's hiring was joked about by the on-air performers at ABC. "It's the Peter Principle gone mad," Ted Koppel told *New York* magazine. Another observed, "Roone hired Carl because he couldn't get Ed Asner."[1]

Carl had set himself up for the ridicule. Many ABC staffers whispered that he had partied his way into the job in the Hamptons during the summer of 1979. At first he was to do a profile of Henry Kissinger for the network. But Roone Arledge, dubbed "the great star-fucker" by an unhappy former employee, was intrigued by the impact the hiring of a hero of Watergate heading up his news team would have in the nation's capital.

Even before Carl began, there were rumblings of unhappiness among the ABC bureaucracy. Carl was filling shoes that, if not big, were beloved. His predecessor, George Watson, had joined the network in 1962. He had been at the helm of the Washington headquarters since 1976 and had a corps of loyalists throughout the office, even after his departure. Faced with being kicked upstairs to a faceless job and an impressive title, but little else, Watson left town for the fledging Cable News Network (CNN) in Atlanta.[2] His allies were among the first to complain about Carl while pronouncing Watson's work "magnificent." Carl's $150,000 salary plus expenses were said to be "out of line."

Making friends and cultivating a few potential defenders might have helped Carl in his new position. He did neither. He attempted to rewrite Sam Donaldson's news scripts just before airtime, and once he telephoned him at three in the morning to tell him he'd be joining him to question White House foreign affairs expert Zbigniew Brzezinski on *Issues and Answers*, ABC's version of *Meet the Press*. Brzezinski refused to let Carl make the last-minute change. Carl looked over *World News Tonight* anchor Frank Reynolds's shoulder when he was writing news copy and offered comments.[3] Carl might have gotten away with his presumptions had he shown a stronger work ethic. But he wasn't there every day to lead his staff.

"You just didn't know where he was half the time," said one ABC employee later about Carl's tenure at the network. The day Ronald Reagan was shot by John Hinckley—March 30, 1981—Carl came in during the afternoon and asked, "What's happening?" Staffers claimed that coverage was already decided and Carl "just got in the way."

Still, Carl was the second syllable of Woodstein, and his phone calls were usually answered. But Carl was burning bridges in those quarters as well. He used a friendship chit at the Treasury with public affairs deputy chief Joseph Laitin to get the secretary— G. William Miller—to a closed-circuit hook-up of ABC affiliates that was to extol the network's programming. A light interview with Miller and Ted Koppel was planned. When the time for the Koppel spot came, the interview didn't. Miller was left under hot studio lights for more than a half hour while Hollywood entertainers first regaled the stations with songs and patter. The secretary of the Treasury was finally brought on and then was unceremoniously grilled by Koppel, who asked tough questions and then interrupted his answers. Laitin, the public affairs man responsible for Miller's embarrassment was furious with Carl.

Carl's love life was, as usual, frenetic. Nora was filing for divorce in New York, Margaret Jay had gone to London, and Carl's name was now being linked with fashion designer Mary McFadden and also with Brooke Hayward, whose theatrical family and background could be said to be a WASP version of Nora Ephron's. Hayward had written, like Nora, a sizzling tell-all memoir, *Haywire*, about her family, incorporating suicides, mental breakdowns and show business gossip. It was a major bestseller in 1977, becoming a made-for-TV movie in 1981. In a small world, Hayward's editor at Alfred A. Knopf was Bob Gottlieb, with whom (and his wife) Nora had stayed after leaving Carl.

There were, however, a few bright spots for Carl Bernstein at ABC. He always had an idea for an angle or a lead, while letting others do the legwork. Some became major pieces on the network's half-hour evening news. But the self-generated stories were few in totality. After several months on the job, the Washington staff provided the final insult. He was simply ignored, the ABC foot soldiers working around him.

Only Bob was loyal. "Carl's going to come out of this on top," he said in early 1980. "Whether it's two or five years from now, people will say he was a brilliant choice."

It didn't take Nora long to file for divorce. She first sued in New York on June 16, 1980, asking for an uncontested judgment and at least temporary custody of their two sons. At the time, the relationship was amicable enough for Nora and Carl to exchange separate net-worth statements. The big question other than child support and visitation rights seemed to be the Bridgehampton house. It was in Nora's name and Carl wanted it. That hurdle was crossed when Carl got a bank loan in May of 1982, gave Nora $165,000 and assumed the mortgage payments. All seemed well, and attorneys for both sides envisioned a friendly split.

But that was all before Nora's novel *Heartburn*. The book, which might well have been titled *Nora's Revenge*, gave a detailed, first-person account of Carl and Nora's marriage told in chatty, fictional form. It was published by Alfred A. Knopf with a strong first printing of forty thousand. Then it was sold to the Literary Guild book club for a hefty amount. The paperback auction started in the "six figures" according to her editor, Bob Gottlieb. Pocket Books' bid was highest. An excerpt was published in the first issue of the newly revitalized *Vanity Fair*, and "everyone," it was said in Hollywood, wanted to do the movie.

In the book, Carl was made a newspaper columnist and Nora, an author of cookbooks. There were "best friends" roles written in for a fictionalized Richard Cohen and his wife. Margaret Jay, who could be described physically as coltish or lanky, was destroyed in one paragraph by Nora, who wrote that the character Thelma (based on Margaret) was "a fairly tall person with a neck as long as an arm and a nose as long as a thumb and you should see her legs, never mind her feet, which are sort of splayed."

With Thelma/Margaret demolished, Nora went after Carl. Her most famous quote, and one that will stay with Carl Bernstein for the balance of his life, described the unfaithful columnist husband as a "man capable of having sex with a Venetian blind." A few years later, *Playboy* would ask Carl, in jest, if such an act was possible.

Heartburn was as close to a carbon of Carl and Nora's life together as a book could have been and still escape litigation. Nora's character had two sons, one born prematurely after the Rachel/Nora character went into labor while trying to spy on Mark/Carl who was making love with Thelma/Margaret inside her house. Nora wrote that her husband was a "Jewish prince" who wouldn't lift a finger to get a stick of butter from the refrigerator but expected his wife to act as a servant.

Perhaps Nora's worst blow in *Heartburn* was recycling Carl's story about washing the carbon paper while wearing his white suit the first day of his newspaper career. It had been Carl's favorite "pickup" opener, the one he often used in bars to endear himself and gain sympathy from women. Carl was reportedly mortified— the carbon-paper tale had to go into his dead file of seduction stories.

Carl reacted condescendingly to the book. He told *New York* the novel was "very clever" when the magazine asked for his comment. He told *Playboy* it was "a clever piece of gossip," and he wrote a letter to Nora telling her the book was "clever."

Inside, it is likely that Carl Bernstein bled. He had been embarrassed, humiliated. And although he continued to bluster through the days and nights with a comes-with-the-territory bravado, Carl was beginning to fall apart, drinking too much, womanizing and still spending money as if he were a newly crowned heavyweight champion.

Ted Koppel tried to set Carl straight. He told him he was about to fall flat on his face. He said that network reporters weren't "interested in covering the news. They want to get on the air, and they don't care too much what it is they put on the air as long as they're on the air. They don't want a week off while they report the story, because then they're not on the air and somebody else will get their job and then they're *really* not on the air." Carl still didn't get it. And office politics was his weak point.

Executives whom Carl should have befriended became enemies. He had a screaming match with Jeff Gralnick, the producer of *ABC World News Tonight*, saying that Gralnick was trying to "impede him." He jumped on top of a desk in Washington, attempting to assert his authority, but ended up looking foolish, yelling at a group of lower-level employees. A newsman who bolted from ABC to join CNN left with some sneering comments aimed at Carl. "Maybe he was hired for the cocktail circuit" was one of the nicer remarks.

By the fall of 1980, after less than a year on the job, rumors were already circulating about Carl's shaky status with the network. He was on his way out, they said. The only real question was who would replace him and what would ABC do about its embarrassment. A report in the *Washington Post* said that Carl "hasn't made a lot of friends" since arriving at the network. Carl may not have been aware of the imminent coup. He spent most of November touring South Africa and picking up much-needed speaking fees.

Roone Arledge announced Carl's ouster on April 13, 1981, demoting him to correspondent and replacing him with an eleven-year veteran of the network, Bill Knowles. Carl's rich $150,000-per-year contract remained intact. The network smoothed over his departure by saying he had contributed to the "Iran [hostage] and presidential inauguration stories." Carl said he was "pleased."

The now former head of the network's Washington offices described his new assignment as "a new ABC News reporting effort. The job will be to establish and run a special reporting operation that will do in-depth reporting for all ABC News entities. I will be the principal on-air correspondent."

The assignment as a blown-dry, stand-up television news reporter, while not creating the same fiasco that had imperiled his year as bureau chief, was still far less than an unqualified success. Although some reviewers gave Carl solid points for covering such subjects as the Falkland Islands War or the Beirut bombings on *20/20*, others weren't so sure. One taped Falklands report later made its way through a snickering foreign-correspondents circuit. The out-take showed an angry Carl, cursing at the camera, wiping his brow with a full roll of toilet paper and in the end hurling it at the camera. It was one of the lowest points of his ABC career.

Yet he was still Carl Bernstein, *the* Carl Bernstein. He and Bob were given a half hour of star treatment by Ted Koppel on *Nightline* during the tenth anniversary of the Watergate break-in, June 17, 1982. One of Koppel's questions cut right to the heart of the matter when he asked Carl, "You know that there are a lot of people . . . who say to this day, 'There never was a Deep Throat; you guys made it all up.' Or it was a composite of a number of people."

Carl's answer: "If you read the book, [*All the President's Men*] very carefully, you can see how it's not a composite, as a matter of fact; that it is one person. We have been absolutely scrupulous in describing the events involving that person, and I mean, again, I come back to this thing about who we are and who we were. We are reporters. We were reporters then. We wrote a book, it was about how we reported. I got to tell you, we're not clever enough to make it up."

Bob put in a good word for his former neighbor. "And you go back and look at the data," he told Koppel, "and you see that the lawyers and Al Haig at the time certainly knew that Nixon was lying and covering up."

The next year, in 1983, Carl fell apart as dramatically as his marriage had four years earlier. There were two separate police scrapes on July 14th within twelve hours. The first, for drunk driving; the second, for an auto accident that led to a lawsuit. Carl would check into a hospital; Nora said it may have been a nervous breakdown. Nearly broke, Carl failed to make child support payments for eight months in succession. He borrowed $16,000 from Bob, eventually repaying him. His separation from Nora drifted into another year without resolution.

Nearly fourteen months later, the divorce still not adjudicated, Carl reversed the playing field. He filed as plaintiff in the District of Columbia, without notifying Nora. She claimed that his reason for choosing Washington, giving him the "home" advantage, was because *Heartburn* was about to become a motion picture. Nora said that since *Heartburn* would make her a lot of money, Carl was going to invoke the District of Columbia's equitable distribution law in order to acquire interest in the "book, film, and other assets." In New York, he would, according to Nora's attorneys, qualify for neither. Carl, Nora's attorneys said, was "forum shopping."

Carl won. The venue was moved to Washington.

But the reason for having "Woodstein" attorney Robert Liotta move Nora to Carl's home ground was not just to leech money out of *Heartburn*. It was Carl's intent to legally make sure that Nora didn't ridicule him in any other literary efforts she might have in mind, to "chill" *Heartburn* as a film by forcing changes in the script, to make sure no other ancillary *Heartburn* rights were sold and to stop Nora from talking about him in the press. Carl based much of his arguments on the need to protect their two sons.

Nora capitulated. In a separate six-page agreement signed by her on May 2, 1985, Nora pledged to "do everything within my power to see that no harm is caused to our children as the result of either the publication of the Book or a movie based on the Book." She protested that "the production of a movie will probably have little effect upon the children, given their young ages. It is . . . unlikely to cause them any harm." Nevertheless, Nora promised "every reasonable effort . . . to avoid any detrimental effect of harm to our children." Nora also agreed to portray the father, Mark/Carl, as a "caring, loving, and conscientious father." She agreed not to portray Carl's parents in the movie and not to discuss her life with Carl in any interview.

There was more. She agreed never to write about Carl in the future, never to use the children for publicity purposes and to put aside 5 percent of all proceeds she got from *Heartburn* in trust for the education of their two sons. She also agreed that Carl would get to see a copy of her finished script prior to shooting.

When Carl got Nora's shooting script, the same one she had given to the film's director, Mike Nichols, he blew up. In an emotional fourteen-page letter to Nora on July 18, he claimed that Nora had broken their agreement and was not, according to Nora's script, portraying him as a loving husband. In the letter, he said, he was going to get a contempt-of-court citation against Nora and was going to stop the making of the movie version of *Heartburn*.[4]

Carl accused Nora of continuing to "exploit" him and their two sons and of conducting a "public circus of false information, insinuation and assumption about the circumstances of our marriage, separation, and divorce."

Then Carl went into a long diatribe on the script. He said that Nora's script had the youngest child, Sophie (the gender of both children was changed for the film), held by the mother or a maid repeatedly but not by the father. According to Carl, the script showed the father as being "passive, indifferent . . . oblivious." He called Nora's script "self-serving" and a "cheap docu-drama." Carl continued to make the point that care should be taken to see that "nothing would ever make Max or Jacob feel ashamed or contemptuous."

Carl next offered Nora some assistance on rewriting the script, suggesting that it be written without causing any damage to their family. Carl then launched into a rambling account of why their marriage had gone awry, suggesting that they both were to blame and talking about "reaching for the illusory brass ring instead of touching real life."

Carl began to enumerate each page of the script he found offensive with an explanation. Pages twenty-nine through thirty-three all concerned the children, and Carl objected to each page. He went on for several more pages like this, at times even objecting to the name Nora had given the housekeeper, taunting her by suggesting it was the first name of a famous black pop singer then identifying the celebrity (Della Reese) as if it were wrong to use it in a script. On another page of the script he suggested Nora use Judy Collins on the sound track as a singer for the children's nursery rhymes (the producers used Carly Simon, a close approximation). Carl said after finishing the screenplay he felt just as he had when he read *Heartburn*. "You're very clever," he wrote Nora, but told her he wouldn't "play dead." Carl said that anyone who read the script, "including [he threatened] the judge," would find the film "shamefully exploitive." Then in all capital letters, he typed, "I FELL IN LOVE WITH SOMEONE ELSE. IF OUR MARRIAGE HAD BEEN WORKING, THAT COULD HAVE NEVER HAPPENED." Although Carl never specified why the marriage wasn't working in the lengthy polemic, he clearly portrayed himself as a victim, driven to infidelity by a wife who didn't know how to deal with a man such as himself, who wanted to change him.

All through the long letter, Carl expressed concern about their two sons and how the boys would react when they saw the film at an older stage in life. But reading his typed communication, one might get the impression that Carl was at least partly concerned with how *he* was portrayed on-screen as well as what his two sons might view. Carl seemed to be blurring the line between fiction with reality in his letter when he wrote that "the implication is . . . I was with Thelma/Margaret while you . . . were lying in the hospital . . . it never happened."

The letter continued, "I'm a terrific father. . . ." Carl's emotional state came through on paper, as he called Nora's movie script the "seventh year of your long march" and Nora someone who "keeps up this kind of drumbeat" and alleged "not too many mothers have ever pulled this stunt . . . keeping their families in a three-ring public circus."

Carl closed with, "Maybe *I'll* [his emphasis] write about it . . . I'm a pretty good reporter. And I tell the truth."

If Carl's tough letter was intended to take the chutzpah out of Nora's witty tale of infidelity translated to film, it did the trick. Carl Feldman was soon Anglicized to Foreman, the sex of both children was changed to female, and the husband was then given enough kitchy-koos with the children to be suspected of studying the parenting style of a TV sitcom dad. The script was flattened, the juice drawn out, leaving Mike Nichols with a leveled shell with which to work and knowing that an angry Carl Bernstein was figuratively looking over his shoulder during every day of the filming.

Meryl Streep was chosen to play Rachel/Nora. Jack Nicholson was Mark/Carl, thus forever enshrining Carl Bernstein as the man whose life was portrayed on-screen by two of the most important motion picture leading men of the century.[5] The veteran character actors Richard Masur and Stockard Channing played the Siegels/Cohens; Karen Akers, a Broadway actress and singer, was given the part of Thelma/Margaret. Fearing Carl's wrath, her on-screen presence was cut to thirty seconds by the producers, and a major fantasy scene in which Rachel/Nora imagined catching Mark/Carl in bed with a black-negligee-wearing Akers was deleted from the film even though it had been shot and edited. Nicholson's line to Streep was to be, "Honey, I can explain everything."

When *Heartburn* opened in July of 1986, it was apparent to everyone that something had gone wrong. Carl was still firing away, saying publicly, "I hear it's a slight film," and alternately, "a little film." Years later, he would call the movie *Howard the Duck, Part Two.*[6] Still, Paramount felt that the watts generated by Streep and Nicholson would draw enough people into the theaters on its opening weekend of July 25.

But the reviews important to a light comedy aimed at a mature audience of adults, thirty years and older, were mixed. The *New York Times* said that Nicholson's "part is barely there" and that Streep seemed "to be fighting the script." The spunky Rita Kempley destroyed it in the *Washington Post*'s Weekend section in a few paragraphs. She said the film had been "so waspified you'd think Nora Ephron had married Woodward instead of Bernstein." She labeled it "tame . . . ironically because of a litigious Carl Bernstein." *Newsweek* headlined its review, "Where Has All the Passion Gone?" and concluded, "It's less a slice of life than a slice of lifestyle."

If Carl's goal was, as reported, to have Nora's film "sink like a stone," he was successful. *Heartburn*, a film as flat as the forty-eight-foot screens upon which it was shown, slid out of most theaters after three weeks, grossing a disappointing $28 million during its brief run.

A final divorce settlement was reached before the film opened. Carl agreed to pay $1180 per month child support and 50 percent of the cost of their two boys' summer camps and private schools. Each agreed to contribute a portion of any further creative works into a college trust fund. The divorce agreement ran eighteen legal-length pages. Nora's "seven-year-long march" was over.

[Carl and Bob, 1983–87]

Hitting Bottom

THE BROWN five-speed 1977 Toyota Corolla was shifted into ban-zai by Carl Bernstein. He led Washington, D.C., police officer Kenneth Adams on a giddy chase through the hilly, narrow streets of the Adams Morgan section of the city. At three-fifteen A.M., July 14, 1983, the Hispanic district was so quiet one could occasionally hear the roar of an animal from the National Zoo nearby. It was a hot sticky night.

Adams, Badge 45 of the 2nd Precinct, and his partner, I. R. Mararac, counted the violations. The Toyota was clocked at twen-ty to twenty-five miles an hour over the normal twenty-five mile per hour speed limit. The car had no running lights. It had gone through a red light. It had turned left at a no-left-turn intersection. That made four charges. The fifth—the big one—looked like a DWI. They pulled the Japanese compact over.

Mararac gave the driver a quick field Breathalyzer test for alco-hol. It showed .12, enough to take the driver in—a reading of .10 was the dividing point used by D.C. police. Above .10, one was considered intoxicated. According to the test, the car's owner was drunk.

At headquarters, the thirty-nine-year-old driver of the Toyota was given a second Breathalyzer test at three-fifty that morning. It read .11, still in the intoxicated range. After another half hour, a third test was given. It was identical.[1]

"You are under arrest," Officer Adams said to Carl Bernstein. "I am now advising you of your rights under the D.C. Implied

Consent Act of October twenty-first, 1972, as amended by Public Law 4-213, September twenty-fifth, 1982."

The police officer read Carl five required sentences. Carl was told he could refuse to have chemical tests, blood tests or urine tests performed. Carl was also told that a refusal to take these tests would result in an automatic one-year revocation of his license. It would also weigh heavily against him in a court of law, an officer said.

After reading the required boilerplate to Carl, the police officer added, "Have you read or had read to you the warning as to your rights under the District of Columbia Implied Consent Act?"

Carl refused to answer.

"Have you read or had read to you the warning as to the consequences of what will happen to you, if you refuse?"

Carl refused to answer.

"Do you understand these rights and consequences?"

Carl refused to answer.

"Do you consent to take two chemical tests?"

Carl refused to answer.[2]

Carl Bernstein could go home now, but he didn't have the $500 bail money. He used his telephone call and dialed Bob, who arrived soon after to save Carl the indignity of a night in jail.

"Are you all right, Carl?" Bob asked.

"No," was Carl's answer.

Carl was behind schedule. He had gone home and slept after his arrest, awoke late and had then met with one of his producers, Betsy West, at ABC-TV. Carl, the superb writer of the printed page, seduced by the glitz and glamour of television news, was now a glorified street reporter. Roone Arledge had wooed him and Carl had succumbed. What else was there? The book he was writing was going nowhere. So one year with Roone, the celebrity fawner, and then out. Now, Carl was a reporter again—a $150,000 (plus perks) per year TV correspondent. The networks preferred the term *correspondent* to *reporter* for the men and women who did stand-ups in front of government buildings and airline crashes.

Before the arrest he had been scheduled to be on a *Nightline* special—a ninety-minute show on journalistic ethics. He had insisted on appearing on the show, and Ted Koppel had told the staff, "Well, we've got to add one more." Now, less than twenty-four hours later, Koppel was rearranging the deck chairs on Carl's *Titanic*, saying "Well, we've got to take one out."

Correspondent Bernstein was late for an appointment at the Cuban Interests section. The Cubans were located inside the Czechoslovakian embassy near Sixteenth Street and Kalorama Road, Northwest. He would meet with Ramon Sanchez Parodi to talk about a visit to the Communist island nation, a visit that Carl likely knew, assuming he got the requisite Castro interview, would give him a choice of *20/20*, *Nightline*, or a network news slot.

Hurrying to the appointment in the ninety-degree heat, Carl overshot his turn as he headed south down Sixteenth Street. The major four-lane artery connected the District of Columbia's northwestern border and the White House at the heart of the capital city. Realizing his error, he slammed on the brakes in front of an embassy and across from the recently renamed Malcolm X Park. Carl shifted his Toyota into reverse and floored it, the tires burning a film of rubber into the baked, black asphalt. He drove backward on Sixteenth Street at thirty miles an hour, not seeing the light-colored Mercedes-Benz 300 diesel sedan that was turning onto Kalorama Road.

The loud sound of metal on metal that followed skidding tires ricocheted off the embassies and apartment buildings on Sixteenth Street. Carl had backed into the driver's side of the Mercedes and had pushed in its door. He got out of his Toyota and stood there, nervously rocking back and forth. Waves of heat rose invisibly from the blistered pavement. The driver of the Mercedes, Franklyn Musgrave, M.D., was trying to open his door, but it was jammed shut from the collision. Alone in the luxury car, he slid over and got out on the passenger side.

Carl stumbled toward the doctor. "I'm sorry, I'm sorry, it's my fault. Don't call the police."

Dr. Musgrave—who would later testify under oath that there was "an odor of alcohol on his breath" and who would say that Carl's "speech was slurred" and "his eyes were bloodshot and watering" and "his gait was wobbling, swaying"—tried to walk out onto Sixteenth Street in search of a policeman.

Carl then repeated over and over, "I want to leave and get a Coke. I want to leave and get a Coke. I want to leave and get a Coke."

A cop was flagged down, but he was a U.S. park policeman, an officer who couldn't charge people with traffic violations. After asking Carl and the doctor if they were both all right, he told them to exchange insurance information and driver's licenses.

Carl had neither. He asked the park policeman if he could leave and get the information. "You ought not to leave the scene of an accident," the park policeman told him. But Carl asked again and got the okay to leave. As he departed, someone in the crowd of onlookers yelled, "Don't let him get away."

When Carl returned, he was with an attractive young woman, Georgeanne Thanos, his secretary at ABC Television. Georgeanne, taking in the scene, which was now lined with late-afternoon loiterers, said, "Oh, poor Carl." She gave Dr. Musgrave her ABC business card. "Don't call his insurance company," Georgeanne said. "When you have your car repaired, just come here to this office and I will give you a check."

Musgrave gave Carl's secretary his card.

"Oh," Georgeanne said, "you are a doctor."

The "doctor," a gynecologist who had grown up on the tiny British West Indies island of St. Kitts, did not form a favorable opinion of Carl. He would say later that he sensed "an arrogance to the man. The insensitivity was most pronounced."

Two other witnesses at the scene would later give depositions that sided with the doctor. One, a former Norfolk State University basketball player by the name of Major Lewter, described Carl at the scene of the accident this way: "I noticed his eyes was blood-shot and it appeared he had one too many drinks. I didn't lean over to smell the alcohol, but as he started walking back from the scene, he stopped and the gentleman from the Mercedes-Benz was getting out of his car slowly, and I went up to him and asked him was he all right, and he said he didn't know. He just stood there as if to be in shock." Lewter then said, "I noticed he [Carl] was walking in a swervelike manner like he had too much to drink. That is why I stopped arguing with him because I could see he had too much to drink."

Lewter continued to pound nails into Carl's coffin with his testimony: "I noticed about the color of his eyes and about the way he was bouncing. He was rocking back and forth and he began to walk away from the scene. I couldn't smell his breath because he didn't say any words to me. Being six nine [fifteen inches taller than Carl], I didn't want to lean over and smell his breath, but just by being a police officer and having that experience I could tell by my observation he had been drinking."

That was the clincher, Lewter's disclosure that he had been a member of the Metro Special Police, the force of the D.C. Transit Department. He was considered an expert—a "dream witness"— by a litigating attorney, and together with the doctor and a third witness, a Mr. Tyrone Exton, he created daunting evidence.

The deposition of the witnesses wasn't to establish who would pay the $2,500 worth of damage to Dr. Musgrave's Mercedes or the smaller $533.32 invoice for the repair of Carl's car, which was presented by the Calvert Toyota dealership of Arlington, Virginia. It was because Dr. Musgrave would later be diagnosed with damage to two lower spinal disks by a long list of medical experts and would claim not only a loss of revenue from his medical practice but a new inability to dance, play tennis or perform amorous acts with his wife.[3] He asked the courts to award him $1 million in compensatory damages and $1 million in punitive damages. When Carl and ABC Television (whom the doctor sued jointly) didn't immediately settle, he raised the amount to $3 million on each count.

Carl, who was first slated to depose on July 31, 1985, changed that date because of schedule conflicts. He showed up one hour late for the second disposition on November 20, 1985. It was cut short and a third date was set. When Carl was finally deposed, he had a different view of the afternoon's events.

It was Franklyn Musgrave who was driving improperly, Carl answered in a legal interrogatory. It was the doctor who was the sole cause of the accident and was negligent. Neither, Carl said, had he been drinking nor taking any drugs or medicines prior to the accident. Musgrave was litigious, Carl's attorneys claimed, and had filed the suit only after learning of Carl's celebrity.[4]

Bob, knowing about both of the traffic incidents, grew worried about Carl's mental and physical state. Bob was working on his fourth book, interviewing people about the life of John Belushi, the television and motion picture comic who had been deep into a world of alcohol and drugs. Bob might have thought that Carl could be in trouble.[5]

"Woodstein" was now a ten-year-old franchise. The name was as valuable to the *Washington Post* as Cheerios or a Disney character would be to their parent corporations. And to the *Post*, it was synonymous with the enhancement of its reputation in the early seventies. Woodstein was a great part of the legacy that helped to make the *Post* a national newspaper. Damage to Carl's reputation could rub off on Bob and destroy the Woodstein legend. But their relationship was more than that. Bob loved Carl in spite of his faults—they had seen too much, done too much, shared too many secrets. They would always be linked, inexorably, by the public and to each other forever.

Bob Woodward was not one to let matters get out of hand. He went to Ben Bradlee and Howard Simons and talked to them about Carl, expressing his concerns. Bradlee, too, was fond of Carl. He also knew that further erosion of Carl's image could harm the *Washington Post*.

Ben and Howard played it just as Bob and Carl had done with the CREEP "grunts" a decade earlier. Without telephoning first, the two *Post* editors drove over to Carl's ten-room apartment on Ontario Road the same afternoon they talked with Bob. Carl, they told him, you have to see a psychiatrist. Maybe you should check yourself into a hospital for observation for a few days. Surprisingly, Carl readily agreed. Bob drove Carl to Sibley Hospital, a top medical institution in the far northwest quadrant of the District of Columbia. Carl was admitted for depression, exhaustion and "severe migraine headaches." One of the tests the hospital performed was a CAT scan. Later he also began seeing a prominent Connecticut Avenue psychotherapist. The therapist would tell Carl he had observable problems that Carl would have to address.

Bob visited Carl at Sibley on the evening of July 27, 1983. It was the tenth anniversary of the start of the Watergate Senate hearings. The Washington PBS outlet, WETA Television, broadcast a special program, "Summer of Judgment," to mark the tenth anniversary of the Senate committee's role in Watergate. It was narrated in soft, southern tones by Charles McDowell of the *Richmond News Leader*.

In the hospital, Carl and Bob watched the program's two-minute opening montage. There were flashes of *Washington Post* headlines. WATERGATE PANEL AIMS AT DEEPER CAMPAIGN PROBE, a page-one story began. The narrator's voice rose, unveiling tragic drama: "The darkest passage in American history . . . to place the president above the law . . . [and describing seventy-six-year-old U.S. senator Sam Ervin] a senator who sprang out of Southern folklore; as wily a country boy who ever came out of North Carolina."

Then a younger, unblemished Woodstein was on the screen. "Particularly the work of Bob Woodward and Carl Bernstein of the *Washington Post*," the narrator said, and the camera flashed on a clip of Carl and Bob's story. . . . Denies fund was to buy silence read the headline, with their old nemesis, former attorney general John Mitchell's picture next to it. Then . . . there was Scott Armstrong. Scott who had danced at Bob's first wedding, the one to Kathy. Best man at the second. Scott, who had cooled off with Bob during hot summers at the Northside Park pool in Wheaton. Scott, who had helped write (even more than Carl) *The Final Days*, and who had coauthored *The Brethren* with Bob; there indeed was Scott Armstrong, almost part three of a triangle that could have been called Scott Woodstein, in the role of staffer and favorite "leaker" to the press for the Senate Watergate panel.

Then another player, Sam Dash, the counsel to the Senate panel: ". . . bringing all America into the democratic process."

Jeb Magruder, Richard Nixon's former assistant, was making a cameo. John Mitchell authorized the break-in, he told the senators (what, the attorney general did it?) and G. Gordon Liddy masterminded it. Magruder justified the break-in citing a speech of William Sloan Coffin's that urged "the burning of draft cards and mass disobedience," a very un-Republican remembrance.

Now Mitchell: "On hindsight, it was a grievous error," he told the panel.

Next onstage, the star of the show, John Dean was brought on with fanfare by the narrator. He was introduced as "a young man in a hurry," venerated in the camera's backshots by his wife Maureen's ethereal glow—completing the joint portrait of perfect piety.

Bob and Carl watched Dean recite his best lines: "I told him how much it would cost. I told him it could be as much as a million dollars. He told me that would be no problem. . . . I began by telling the president there was a cancer growing on the presidency. And if the cancer was not removed, he could be killed by it."

Not to be outdone by Dean's reach for enshrinement in *Bartlett's Familiar Quotations*, Tennessee senator Howard Baker was saying next, "What did the president know and when did he know it?" The speeches of the participants became modern Shakespeare.

Bombshell time: "All of his conversations are recorded," Alexander Butterfield, the former assistant to H. R. Haldeman told the panel, sending wire reporters racing for the pay phones.

"Not since the administration of Thomas Jefferson had a subpoena been served on a president of the United States," the narrator intoned.

A babble of Senate voices: "Executive privilege . . . no precedent for litigation . . . determine whether the president is above the law."

Then the pugnacious, argumentative John Ehrlichman was being pummeled by Lowell Weicker, a Republican senator from Connecticut. "Do you mean to tell me," Weicker was asking in high dudgeon, "that you consider private investigations going into sexual habits, drinking habits, domestic problems, personal and social activities a proper subject during the course of a political campaign? Do you really want to bring the political system down to this level?"

Ehrlichman's better White House half, H. R. Haldeman: the two had been described by various unflattering appellations, one of which was Nixon's "two German shepherds."

"Every president has his SOB and I'm Richard Nixon's," Haldeman told the senators, reinforcing that image.

The narrator, burnishing Haldeman's public visage, then called him "a contemporary Prussian."

Bit players flashed by. Donald Segretti and Robert Benz. Who played Segretti in the movie? And who was Robert Benz? It was so hard to remember after ten years.

"Talk of impeachment was in the air," the voice-over continued, bridging the gap between witnesses.

The cameras cut away from the senators to Peter Rodino, a congressman from New Jersey: ". . . should recommend whether the House of Representatives . . . articles calling for the impeachment of Richard M. Nixon."

"This was an occasion when obscure politicians rose above themselves," said the unseen narrator.

"We are here to make this constitution a vital document and to end the abuse of power," said Paul Sarbanes, the Democratic senator from Maryland.

Bob and Carl had been responsible for this congressional carnival.[6] Bob Woodward and Carl Bernstein had played the lead roles of a vigilant press in forcing a president of the United States to resign from office. They should have been able to revel with their families in their triumph, watching the televised flashbacks. Didn't Jimmy Breslin write a column demanding that high schools be named after them? Woodstein High, he had suggested, at a point midway between Washington and Wheaton. But ten years later Carl was in a hospital being examined for a possible nervous breakdown and Bob was here, comforting him. There were no wives. Bob had just celebrated his fortieth birthday, Carl was still thirty-nine. Four divorce proceedings had taken place. Bob's second marriage had lasted less than five years. Carl's second was approaching a fifth year in the courts. The fame, and the resulting fortune, had happened too fast and they hadn't handled it well.

There had been a time in 1976 when Bob and Carl had been riding in the back of a limousine to yet another speaking engagement (and yet another $5,000 fee). They were on top of three top-ten lists. They had had the number one bestselling hardcover and the leading paperback. Their story was made into the number one grossing movie in America. They were being confused with Robert Redford and Dustin Hoffman. Carl tried to get a grip on it all. He had told *Esquire*, "We have to sit down and think about what this could do to us. How we control it. And how we decide what we're going to do next."

Watching the PBS television show now, it seemed as if it had been a dream. Bob didn't wait for the credits of the Watergate TV show. He said goodnight to Carl before "The Summer of Judgment" was over.

Carl got out of the hospital a day later. Unrepentant, he soon showed up in the Hamptons with Margaret Jay, making the rounds of summer literary parties. Ms. Jay let it be known that she had joined Carl direct from Martha's Vineyard where she had been a houseguest of Katharine Graham's.

16

[Bob 1979–87]

Blues for Belushi

Midway through the 1980s, Bob seemed to be going in several different directions at once. He tried television scripts, cowriting one of the final episodes of the NBC series *Hill Street Blues*.[1] He was reported to be cowriting a miniseries based on William Shirer's book about Germany in the thirties, *The Nightmare Years*. And he headed a team of four writers penning a three-hour, made-for-TV movie, *Under Siege*.

The film, which didn't get aired until 1986, may have stalled Bob's television scriptwriting career. It was panned by critics and got poor ratings. Confusing to most viewers, it concerned terrorist attacks in an America of the future. Warned Tom Shales in a review: "Face the facts of the terrorist age or risk having to sit through more films like this. Woe is we." The *Post* criticism was headlined "Foolish Foray."

That Bob was seriously considering a career in television after the Janet Cooke disaster had been revealed in 1982. CBS News began a full-press attempt at seducing him to the network, offering "several hundred thousand dollars" per year to head an investigative unit.[2] News anchor Dan Rather took him to lunch. Commentator Bill Moyers and CBS News president Ed Joyce flattered and promised ego gratifying regular on-air appearances. The *Wall Street Journal* suggested on April 5, 1982, that Bob was using the CBS offer as "leverage" to make a final effort to succeed Ben Bradlee. One *Post* staffer was quoted by the *Journal* as saying Bob was "playing a tricky game."

Donald Graham took Bob to dinner. He liked his star reporter and wanted him to stay. But this time he told him that managing was not his *forte* and reiterated that Bradlee's job was no longer part of his future at the *Washington Post*. Ben Bradlee then wrote him a personal note telling him that he was part of the "soul" of the newspaper. But Bob was now always to be a knight, never a king at the *Post*. He stayed.

Bob Woodward developed new passions. After the Janet Cooke debacle, he purchased a forty-five-foot ketch he named *Timeless*. He learned to sail and soon set forth on a five-and-a-half-day cruise to Bermuda that became known as "Bob's death sail" because of the distance and inexperience of the crew. Bob took four *Post* colleagues and a lawyer, former Watergate prosecutor Carl Feldbaum, on the trip.

During the days at sea, the six men wiled away the hours by concocting a spy novel, which they tentatively titled *Tilt*. Each took turns dictating a chapter. By the end of the voyage, a rough draft had been produced, which Bob said ran "three to four hundred" pages. It was presented informally to Simon and Schuster but never published.

Bob's predilection for practical jokes, evident at Yale, began to surface again. At Don Graham's house he shocked a quiet party for a departing *Post* employee by hiring a belly dancer. The majority was said to be "grossed out" by his gaffe. Friends soon began to wreak revenge. Someone claiming to be a personal assistant to Adnan Khashoggi, the Middle East arms merchant, called him and arranged an appointment. Bob cooled his heels in a hotel for nearly an hour before he realized that it was April 1 and the name written in his calendar was a Mr. Aperill Folsday.

There was another negative aftershock from Bob's two-year stint as an editor of Metro. He pressed one of his investigative reporters, Pat Tyler, to follow through on a story he himself had begun in 1976, abandoning it to write *The Brethren*. The story was complex in its twists and turns, but the principal allegation was that the president of Mobil Oil, William P. Tavoulareas, had created a shipping business for his son, Peter, and then funneled millions of dollars of contracts in the name of Mobil Oil to him, resulting in a bounty of riches for his son. The front-page, four-thousand-word story, which ran on November 30, 1979, was headlined "Mobil Chief Sets Up Son in Venture."

The genesis of the piece was Bob's handling his 1976 file to Tyler and telling him "it smelled." Tyler then joined with a free-lance reporter, Sandy Golden, who had graduated from Carl Bernstein's high school, Montgomery Blair, a year after Carl and who wanted to follow in his footsteps. Golden had uncovered a source, a disgruntled former son-in-law of Tavoulareas who wanted to tell everything he knew about the father-son business relationship.

Using the interview from the former in-law, Mobil Oil informers, a government source and Bob's files, the story was "lawyered" and okayed by Bob and two other *Post* editors. The president of Mobil Oil was not amused. A four-page rebuttal was issued, accusing the *Post* of "innuendo and inaccurate statements of what is in fact an open, straightforward, well-known business relationship."

A follow-up story ran on December 1, 1979, printing part of the rebuttal but also saying that Tavoulareas "may have given false and misleading statements under oath" and that he misused corporate assets to enrich his son.

Despite the possibly defamatory and malicious allegations, neither Bob nor Pat Tyler had informed Mobil that a story was being written or had read the corporation the story and asked for comments. (Such comments had been a mark of Bob and Carl's Watergate stories—the *Post* would always insert a White House denial.) Bob professed shock. "I can't believe that. I find it incredible that he hasn't contacted you," Bob told a spokesman for Mobil.

A third story was written, using some clarifying information given by Tavoulareas to Ben Bradlee. The *Post* executive editor, quoting Walter Lippmann, claimed that the story was not a retraction but where "the truth emerges."

Although Bob and two other editors thought the series was great, other staffers disagreed. Managing editor Howard Simons reportedly called it a "cheap shot." A copy editor, referring to the column length of the story, called it "a withered peanut in an eighty-four-inch gilded shell." Tavoulareas also disagreed. After several requests for a full retraction, he sued for defamatory libel in the amount of $50 million. The suit named Bob, the *Post*, Ben Bradlee, Katharine Graham, Pat Tyler and Sandy Golden. Tavoulareas also sued his former son-in-law for $20 million.

This time the *Post* and its employees were pitted against a larger, more formidable opponent. The newspaper certainly had millions of dollars and the law firm of Williams and Connolly to defend it. But Mobil Oil had billions and seemed willing to spend whatever was needed to win.

Before the Tavoulareas suit reached the courts three incidents occurred that buttressed the Mobil Oil president's case of a "systems failure" on the part of the *Washington Post*. The first was the Janet Cooke affair. Tavoulareas's lawyers suggested that Bob's reporter Pat Tyler was another Janet Cooke.

The second, entered as a court document by Tavoulareas, was a Style section story by Ben Bradlee's wife, Sally Quinn. Sally reported that during an interview, the presidential national security adviser Zbigniew Brzezinski had begun to flirt with a female reporter and unzipped his fly. Supposedly a photographer had snapped a photo of the incident, which Brzezinski had then autographed and sent to Quinn. But the anecdote was phony. The paper had to retract the story saying, "Brzezinski did not commit such an act, and there is no picture of him doing so. The *Washington Post* sincerely regrets the error."

Ben Bradlee—in a quote similar to Bob's "brilliant story" line after Janet Cooke had been disgraced—told *Time* that it had been "a son of a bitch of a good story." Tavoulareas's lawyers then said that it showed that the paper was "more interested in a *good* story than in a *true* story."

Another piece upon which Mobil Oil gleefully jumped was an item in a *Post* gossip column that claimed President Jimmy Carter had electronically eavesdropped on Ronald and Nancy Reagan when they stayed at Blair House, the guest quarters across the street from the White House, before Reagan's inauguration. When the rumor proved not to be true, the *Post* said it was still an acceptable story because the item was in a gossip column and it was acceptable to report rumors in that part of the paper.

Before the trial, the *Post* conducted a private survey in an attempt to measure its standing in the community. The poll concluded that the paper was still thought of as the force that had made Richard Nixon resign. That was thought to be a positive inside a liberal District of Columbia. The *Post*'s lawyers then asked for a jury trial instead of a judge. Bob suggested the attorneys bring out his Watergate reporting record right away. "No," said one of the lawyers, "we're going to let the jury discover that you're Robert Redford."

The three-week trial was a circus, with Tavoulareas swaying the jury by carrying a Bible to court and reading it during lulls. He wept several times when he was put on the stand.

Bob tried to put the best face on the case, saying in court that the story was a "model of digging, thinking, and being fair." Ben Bradlee called it "a textbook case of how a responsible paper should behave."

Tavoulareas's lawyers' main point, which seemed to win over the six-person jury, was that the major sources for the *Post* story all had a bias against the Mobil Oil head. After three days of deliberation, the jury voted in favor of Mobil, awarding the Tavoulareas family more than $2 million. The judgment was upheld in one higher court, but was eventually reversed in 1987. The Supreme court of the United States then refused to hear it, ending the case after nearly eight years. Both sides claimed a victory of sorts. Tavoulareas said that nothing any judge decided could take away his initial unanimous jury decision. Ben Bradlee said, "It's good to get it behind us with the knowledge that we were right on the facts." A jubilant staffer placed a sign on his door that said, "it's not over until the fat lady sings."

The case was considered a landmark decision, with the Supreme Court's refusal to reverse the appeal ruling called a boost for investigative journalism. Libel lawyers said that the nonruling would make it "less likely that public figures will sue when they feel a story is wrong." Still, the story cost the newspaper nearly $2 million in legal fees and some of the luster of its once unsullied post-Watergate reputation.[3]

While most of the consequences of the Janet Cooke affair were negative for Bob, there was one positive result. Elsa Walsh, Janet's roommate, was "noticed" by Bob, and the two soon became romantically involved.

Walsh, a Metro reporter, had joined the *Post* just after Janet Cooke, after graduating from the University of California at Berkeley. Her first bylined story ran on July 16, 1980. Most of her early articles had been routine pieces gathered on the Maryland and Virginia beat. Resourceful, she soon hit the front page with a feature story titled "Bringing Up Superbabies."

Elsa Walsh was soon noticed in other ways. An attractive buxom woman who grew up in a large northern-California family, she sat at a desk near the end of the Metro section, next to the sports department. Her late visits from the suburbs to file a story were particularly welcomed by the night sports reporters. The predominately male scribes became happily distracted by her habit of wearing revealing tank tops—more than one male writer would make unscheduled strolls past her desk. Once, when "too much cleavage" was revealed, Bob was asked to "talk to her."

If Elsa Walsh in the early 1980s was being admired by the male members of the newsroom, Bob, too, was attempting to cultivate a newer, more gentle image. He tried to be friendlier, less distant—a new role for him. He would purchase and bring in several tubs of Baskin-Robbins ice cream for the night staff, complete with syrups and toppings. But the efforts were clumsy. He would leave the cartons on a vacant desk and retreat to his office, sometimes without saying a word.

At first Bob and Elsa attempted to keep their budding romance a secret. After all, he was her boss, and nearly a decade and a half older. Secrecy would be difficult in any workplace—impossible in a newsroom of aggressive reporters. The relationship became known to *Post* staffers by 1982, and soon after that Bob and Elsa began living together at The Factory, Bob's Georgetown house.

The house quickly began filling up. After Colorado senator Gary Hart separated from his wife, Lee, he stayed at Bob's residence for several months. But after Hart began spending more time at another woman's apartment, Bob called Hart's staff and said he would "tell the truth" if asked about it. Hart moved out shortly afterward. Other newly separated reporters who worked at the *Post* also moved in for short stays. One male journalist called it a "halfway house" for separated fathers. Bob seemed not to notice. He was involved in a big story again, another book that would "get remembered."

A reader of *Rolling Stone* magazine once had a letter to the editor published which claimed that asking Bob Woodward to write about John Belushi was like having the heavy-metal rock group Twisted Sister play at your parents' fiftieth wedding anniversary. Bob Woodward, as soberly straight-arrow as they come, was an unlikely person to choose to write compassionately about a comic who helped revolutionize late-night television and movie comedies. Anyone who followed the Janet Cooke fiasco would have sensed that a decidedly less than street-smart Bob was the last person to understand the murky world of addictive drugs.

It wasn't that Bob couldn't dig up facts or get his phone calls returned. But Bob Woodward, who listened to classical music—not rock—and who preferred foreign art films to the antics of a movie like *Animal House*, couldn't have possibly understood John

Belushi. Judy Belushi, who contacted Bob Woodward through her sister and asked him to write about her late husband, would appear to have gotten through to the wrong syllable of Woodstein. Carl Bernstein would have been a more likely choice.

After John Belushi died on March 5, 1982, Judy felt she wasn't getting the straight story from the Los Angeles police department. She wanted to convince a writer to uncover what she felt was a mystery. She telephoned the *Chicago Sun-Times* columnist Mike Royko and asked him to look into her husband's death. Belushi had played a character loosely modeled on Royko in the movie *Continental Divide*. But Royko declined, apologizing, saying investigative reporting was not his "sort of thing."

John Belushi's widow next thought of Bob Woodward. She knew that Bob, like her and John, was from Wheaton. Judy felt that they should have a lot in common. John and Bob had been on the football team—they even shared the same coach, Belushi some six years after Woodward.[4] And Bob had been chairman of the Tiger Turnout Committee, as had Judy. Judy had never read any of Bob's books, but that was all right. John had read some of the best parts of *All the President's Men* aloud to her.

Judy's sister, Pam, a lawyer, met with Bob. She reported to Judy that Bob didn't just want to write about the Los Angeles police matter—he wanted to write about John's life. Judy declined; she had a book of her own in mind.[5]

But two and a half months after John Belushi died, an article about his death, written by Cheryl Lavin, appeared in the *Chicago Tribune* magazine. The piece was harsh, describing Belushi as dying "naked and alone in a rented Hollywood bungalow with half a dozen needle marks up and down each arm with both cocaine and heroin in his blood. . . . [He] had an old man's body . . . with the hardened arteries and swollen, bloated organs."

The story, appearing in a powerful Midwest newspaper so close to Wheaton, disturbed Judy Belushi. And when she heard that Lavin was using the article as a springboard to get a book contract for an unauthorized biography of John, she decided to speak with Bob Woodward again.

Judy Belushi, who now describes Bob Woodward as a "seductive chameleon," was impressed by him. She noted that he spoke softly, "something I've noticed many lawyers do." He was "signaling important thoughts with a slight hesitation . . . then an emphasis on key words."

Bob professed an affinity with John Belushi. He said he knew what it was to have an early success and told her that *All the President's Men* had been his *Animal House*. Pushing all the right buttons, Bob said he wanted to do a series of articles. He told her he saw himself not unlike the reporter in *Citizen Kane*, searching for the meaning of "Rosebud." Judy Belushi liked that comparison. Later he would compliment her writings, by saying, about his staff at the *Post* "I wish I had people with your perception."

Judy called her friends and asked them to cooperate with him. After Jim Belushi, John's brother, was interviewed by Bob, he told his sister-in-law, "Boy, he really hates Wheaton." Jim told Judy, according to her memoir, *Samarai Widow* that Bob asked him, "What is it about Wheaton that fucked us all up?" Later Bob would write in *Wired* that there was pressure "to succeed" if one grew up in Wheaton.

Shortly after agreeing to look into the circumstances surrounding John Belushi's death, Bob went to Los Angeles for interviews. He talked with Belushi intimates actor Dan Aykroyd and director John Landis. Judy soon got a call from John Belushi's former manager, Bernie Brillstein. She was told that Bob Woodward was writing a book, not a series of articles. When Judy called Bob, he told her he was not doing a book "at this time" but a series of articles for the *Washington Post*. He told her it was important that they trust each other.

In fact, Bob Woodward signed a contract with Simon and Schuster in 1982 for a "book with photos" less than two months after he began talking to Judy Belushi. The advance was $600,000. In 1984 Bob would claim it didn't become a book about John Belushi until a later, unspecified date.

But Judy Belushi continued to trust Bob. She gave him family photos, which Bob said "offer such insight.' She read him parts of her diary. She sat through twenty-one separate interviews with him. And she opened doors and finessed access to reclusive and suspicious Hollywood celebrities.

In January of 1984, *People* magazine ran an item saying Bob Woodward was coming out with a new book about the life of John Belushi titled *Wired*. To Judy Belushi, the title meant "fucked up on drugs." She called Bob. He admitted that the newspaper series was now a book, but he said he thought the title was multidimensional. According to Bob, it meant "wired into the system" or "energized." He then said he hadn't liked the title of *All the*

President's Men at first, either. Judy Belushi was alarmed. Bob didn't get Judy's demonstrated concern for her husband's reputation.

A lunch was planned at the Four Seasons restaurant in New York with Judy, her sister, Pam, John's brother, Jim, and Bob, who came with his editor, Alice Mayhew. At the lunch, Bob told Pam that *Wired* was still not the final title and that he wouldn't use any of the photos Judy had loaned him. Judy wasn't worried about the photos; she was knowledgeable enough to know that Bob needed a signed release to use any of them in a book. Other titles were still being considered—*John* and *A Portrait of a Star* were two that Judy and he had discussed earlier. There were others: *A Casualty Along the Way* and *Death of a Star*. A week later, Bob told Judy the title would definitely be *Wired*. Judy began disassociating herself from the book and asked that all photos and documents be returned. Bob promised they would be sent back to her.

On May 16, 1984, Bob wrote Judy Belushi a letter on *Washington Post* stationery, enclosing five photos she had given him and saying "unfortunately they were used in the book." He apologized, but offered neither remuneration nor any promise that the pictures would be removed from later editions of the book.

Judy Belushi called her lawyer and asked him if she had a case for a lawsuit. Her attorney, George Galloway, said she did. "Sue his ass," Judy told him, and he did, asking for $100,000 for use of the photographs and asking that distribution of the book be halted.

Simon and Schuster was delighted. Judy Belushi's frequent interviews in magazines, newspapers and on television were terrific publicity for *Wired*. Sorry, said Simon and Schuster's attorneys to Judy Belushi's lawyer two weeks later, we shipped 135,000 copies of *Wired* on May 18, we've already got reorders for 2,000 copies, the excerpt in the July issue of *Playboy* is on the newsstand, the Literary Guild, the book club for which it is the main selection, has mailed their June catalog, it's been serialized in the *Post* and fifty other papers, some reviews have been printed, and Bob's been booked for the *Today* show, the *Merv Griffin Show* and *Donahue*. A restraining order was not granted. Simon and Schuster ordered another 100,000 copies printed, without Judy's photos.

When Judy Belushi's legal fees passed $15,000, she told her attorney to settle. She got $35,000 from the publisher. It was, one could cynically say, the most efficient promotion budget ever spent pushing a book at Simon and Schuster.

Wired may have been one of Bob Woodward's better books. It was the only one with source notes and a list of interviews and since Bob was given access to Judy and John Belushi's correspondence, financial records and friends, it was brutally accurate. But Bob failed to grasp the essence of the actor-comedian, treating his life as if it were one long true-life cops-and-drugs drama.

The reviews for *Wired* were mixed, but the best since *All the President's Men*, though some were left-handed compliments. The *Chicago Tribune* gave it a "brilliant" and the *Los Angeles Times* said it "doesn't spare us the squalid details." The *Philadelphia Inquirer* called it "fascinating, in a perverse, *National Enquirer* kind of way." One critic said that Bob's style read like a "coroner's report." Pocket Books, Simon and Schuster's subsidiary, liked the *Inquirer*'s quote so much it was used in one of the paperback editions. But *Kirkus Reviews*, an important trade publication, summarized it as "pointless docudrama" and *Time* called it "long on details but short on insight."

Besides Judy Belushi's lawsuit, Bob got into trouble elsewhere after the book was out. First, he told Diane Sawyer on *CBS Morning News* on June 7, 1984, that he had heard that "probably forty people" were regular cocaine users at the *Post*. Ben Bradlee was, to put it mildly, angered: "I don't know what the hell Bob is talking about. Cocaine is illegal, and if I hear of anyone using it . . . it's out the door, goodbye."

Diane Sawyer said after the interview that forty people "seemed a lot to me, even as gossip." Bob said that Diane Sawyer set him up.

Post staffers had a field day smirking about Bob's comment. The rock-'n'-roll critic, Richard Harrington, walked around the newsroom with a tightly rolled dollar bill stuffed up his nose. Another *Post* employee told the *Washingtonian* magazine, "I tried coke once, but I almost drowned." Carl and Bob's friend, the quotable Richard Cohen, said, "I assume the *Post* is no different from an insurance company. We have the statistically correct number of bisexuals, homosexuals, pederasts, and coke heads. I don't know any of the pedarasts and I don't know any of the coke heads."

And there were more lawsuits. A Beverly Hills doctor, Robert J. Feder, sued Bob for $20 million for implying in *Wired* that he gave

John Belushi and other performers amphetamines to get them "up" for live performances. Bob countersued for $500,000. The matter became moot after the celebrity ear, nose and throat specialist suffered a stroke and became speechless. Both sides dropped their charges.

The Chateau Marmont, the hotel in which John died, sued Bob and his publisher for $18 million because it was called "seedy" on the book's dust jacket. The owner said, "He made it sound like a downtown bus station where drug deals are made." Simon and Schuster deleted the remark in future printings, explaining that Bob was referring to Belushi's mess and not the hotel. "I'd enjoy staying there myself," claimed Bob. The hotel withdrew the suit upon getting two favorable pages of publicity in *People* magazine, the retraction and the apology.

John Belushi's parents were distraught over the portrayal of their son. John's father said he had a shotgun in his closet and would use it on Bob if he ever came back to Wheaton. Mrs. Belushi, John's mother, after learning that Bob had a daughter, said that she hoped "something like this happens to her so he can know how it feels."

Hollywood allies of Judy Belushi spent a lot of time trashing the book and subsequently helping sales. Jack Nicholson, soon to play Carl Bernstein in *Heartburn*, called Bob "a ghoul and an exploiter of emotionally disturbed widows." Nicholson had smoked marijuana in Bob's presence and Bob had written that Nicholson used it regularly. Bob himself admitted to an interviewer during the book tour that he himself had smoked the drug "before Watergate."

Dan Aykroyd called *Wired* "pulp trash" and a "sleaze book." Aykroyd said it showed "none of John's warmth, none of his humor." He stopped talking to the print media for several years because of the book.

Tim Kazurinsky, a friend of Judy's and a regular on *Saturday Night Live*, said he'd spit in Bob's eye if he saw him, bemoaning that many people would believe *Wired*. Said Kazurinsky, "After all, Bob Woodward wrote it. He's God. He's . . . Watergate."

Even *Playboy* jumped back into the fray, publishing an acid-laced parody of the book, calling it *Tired*. There was a full-page lampoon of the book's cover with Bob as John Belushi. The satire's aim was to send up Bob's dullness.

Bob soon got fed up with the attacks. "I don't have to apologize for doing this book," he told an interviewer. Then repeating what he had told Judy Belushi, he added, "It's like the search for Rosebud in *Citizen Kane*. It becomes 'tell me about a person I never saw.' "

More damaging to Bob Woodward's literary reputation was a long, searing article by Lynn Hirschberg in the September 27, 1984 issue of *Rolling Stone*, two months after the book was released. While unkind to Judy Belushi, it was tougher on Bob:

> Woodward stops to look for another document. He's like a kid searching for a toy. There is something childlike about him—he has very bright eyes and an open face—and during the last hour he's been fidgeting like a ten-year-old, playing with a penknife, tapping his desk rhythmically with a ruler. This all belies the fact that Woodward is quite serious. His mind is uncannily focused.

Bob was angered by Lynn Hirschberg's piece. The twenty-five-year-old Hirschberg later telephoned him, saying that Judy Belushi had been allowed to rewrite some of her quotes. Bob took notes during their telephone conversation and then typed out a six-page letter to *Rolling Stone* founder Jann Wenner, rebutting and protesting the article and using his notes to quote—and embarrass—the young magazine writer.

17

[Bob, 1981–88]

Spy vs. Spy?

Although he never turns down an invitation to speak to groups of employees at CIA or FBI headquarters ("a chance to hand out my business card in case anybody wants to call me") Woodward says he rarely gives lectures.

—*Yale Alumni Magazine*
May 1988

IF BOB WOODWARD owed Alexander Haig anything, he paid him back severalfold at the beginning of the Reagan years. In early 1981, when Haig's nomination for secretary of state promised to get tied up by the Congress, Bob came to the rescue.

The problem arose when Massachusetts senator Paul Tsongas wanted the audiotaped conversations between Haig and Richard Nixon released to the confirmation committee. Haig fought the process. Then Bob weighed in with his first-ever signed opinion opposite the editorial page, saying it wasn't necessary to release the tapes. The column, published on January 15, argued that there should be limits in reviewing one's fitness for a cabinet position. Bob implied that the tapes were beyond those limits. He also said that, besides, "the audio quality is terrible," and "the transcribing would be a nightmare," making the transcriptions "as maddening as the man [Nixon] himself."

Bob balanced the piece by writing in the last two paragraphs that he didn't agree with Watergate prosecutor Leon Jaworski's assessment that Haig was "heroic." Bob said that Haig was a "shameless self-promoter," but he had kept "a rickety and criminal ship of state afloat and helped ease Nixon out of office." Haig was approved handily the day after the column ran. Bob has since explained that *Post* editorial-page chief Meg Greenfield asked him to write the column.

Two months later, after the assassination attempt on President Ronald Reagan, Alexander Haig came under fire in the press. The controversy was sparked both by the much quoted "I am in control here" comment he made at a press conference following the shooting and by his arrogant, autocratic manner with associates. When rumors began to circulate that Haig was on his way out, Bob obtained notes of senior staff meetings that recorded Haig's thoughts and actions. Bob presented them under his byline in glowing detail on the front page of the *Post*, on February 19, 1982.

"The notes show Haig as a man who is knowledgeable and deeply concerned about foreign affairs," Bob wrote, adding that the secretary of state wanted "continuity in American foreign policy with adherence to previous commitments." Bob went on to report in the long story that the notes showed "Haig's admiration for Reagan's ability to charm and influence others."

When Haig did resign from the Reagan cabinet on June 25, 1982—many insiders said he was fired—Bob's assistant, Milton Benjamin, who had edited and rewritten drafts of *The Brethren*, wrote a news story the day after Haig's departure comparing him with Gen. Douglas MacArthur. Benjamin, too, said Haig had held the White House together during Richard Nixon's battle to avoid impeachment. The piece gave Haig positive reviews of his role in Europe as commander of the North Atlantic Treaty Organization (NATO) and used Haig's own comparison of himself with MacArthur to paint him as "a dying breed" who could "operate with a degree of independence no longer acceptable."

Nearly a week later, Bob wrote another front-page piece saying unnamed sources had told him that Haig had been "set up" by White House rivals. Bob quoted a Haig deputy as saying, "There was a master plan to get rid of him." Bob reported that the Haig associate named George Bush, James A. Baker, Michael Deaver and Richard Darman as the four White House insiders responsible for his ouster. The Haig ally, Bob wrote, believed the general was ousted as a result of personality and policy differences with the White House staff. He added that George Bush considered Haig a future rival for the presidency and was "no friend."

Bob Woodward was granted an interview with William Joseph Casey, the director of the U.S. Central Intelligence Agency, on September 28, 1983. Although he had refused several reporters, including Mike Wallace of *60 Minutes*, Casey gave Bob an interview on the condition "that I never see anything in print," meaning that the interview was for background only. Bob met with the CIA director at the Old Executive Office Building next to the White House.

That William Casey would choose Bob Woodward as a conduit of information might appear curious. Bob represented the *Washington Post*, a paper with which Casey was constantly in conflict. William Safire of the *New York Times* was a good friend and a much more logical choice. Bill Buckley, an ex-CIA man himself, would also have made sense. But if Casey had checked Bob's background, he may have discovered records that named Bob a contributor to an intelligence organization or "the company" itself, as employees or informants often call the Langley, Virginia, headquarters. It could then be easily understood.

Casey, a New Yorker, had unswervingly backed Richard Nixon over Nelson Rockefeller in 1960 for the Republican presidential nomination. He had raised millions of dollars from friends on Wall Street (where he had made his fortune) for Nixon in 1967, helping him to defeat Hubert Humphrey. Nixon had then appointed him to several posts, including chairman of the Securities and Exchange Commission, member of the Arms Control Commission, undersecretary of state and president of the government-sponsored Export-Import Bank. And he remained loyal to Richard Nixon until the end. In mid-1973 he wrote to the president, saying, "All of us who view you as a national asset with a historic mission, and the general public, want to put all the political shenanigans behind us and get on with the vital things to be done."

Bob Woodward, the man most responsible for the demise of one of Casey's mentors, as the window for William Casey's views? It seems unlikely that Casey would select Bob Woodward, a man who was perhaps the most responsible for the fall of Richard Nixon. Nevertheless, he did.

A month later, on October 27, 1983, William Casey invited Bob Woodward to his home for dinner after Bob requested a second interview. Casey told his chief of public affairs, George Lauder, about the impending dinner and asked him to attend. Lauder, alarmed by the growing relationship, and afraid Casey was being too forthcoming refused, asking for an account of the meeting later.

Bob met with Casey at the new house he had recently purchased in northwest Washington. The property had once been part of a large estate owned by Nelson Rockefeller, a man Casey had despised. The CIA director's wife, Sophia, was in Florida; his daughter, Bernadette, played hostess and prepared the meal. They discussed recent news events that were already public knowledge: the U.S. invasion of Grenada, the bombing of the Marine barracks in Beirut and the shooting down of Korean Airlines flight 007, which had killed several Americans, including conservative U.S. congressman Larry McDonald.

Except for this and two other meetings, all of Bob's contacts with William Casey were attended by George Lauder. According to CIA records, Bob Woodward had thirteen contacts of substance with William J. Casey.

Bob used his interviews with Casey, some visits to the Middle East in 1984 and information from his sources in the intelligence community as the basis for his 1987 book, *Veil: The Secret Wars of the CIA 1981–1987*. The book was listed in Simon and Schuster's fall catalog as "Untitled, The Secret Wars . . ." The word that was to be the book's title was said to be so explosive that it couldn't be revealed before publication, but that was pure P. T. Barnum bombast. *Veil* was simply a code name for a disinformation campaign against Libya.

As he had done in *All the President's Men*, Bob embellished and fabricated—this time about the depth of his relationship with William Casey—in order to make the book seem even more important than it was, an unnecessary device. In "A Note to the Readers," Bob wrote that he had had "more than four dozen interviews or substantive discussions" with the director of the CIA between 1983 and 1987. On CBS's *60 Minutes*, just after the book was released, Bob referred to "four dozen interviews over three years." Then on ABC's *Nightline*, it became "more than fifty." Bob told *Washingtonian* writer Barbara Matusow that he had had "frequent dinner meetings" with Casey even though there had been but one.

Certainly Bob had some informative, substantive meetings with William J. Casey. And there was the single dinner and two breakfasts—one in the CIA dining room and another at Casey's home—but both of the breakfast meetings had several others present. Bob thought he was indeed close to Casey. In 1990 he would describe him to Yale classmates at a twenty-fifty reunion as a "second father."

The total of thirteen contacts—not fifty or four dozen—is borne out by a 1987 Freedom of Information Act inquiry made by the media watchdog group Accuracy in Media. AIM asked the CIA for a record of *all* contacts between William Casey and Bob Woodward (see Appendix B). Information and privacy coordinator John H. Wright said that the contacts between Bob and Casey were counted using the CIA director's appointment and telephone logs, and from the agency's Office of Public Affairs. There may indeed have been brief exchanges between Bob and Casey at public functions that may have been counted by Bob as some of his four dozen plus contacts, but such conversations would likely have been of dubious relevance. And since the CIA director was accompanied everywhere by security, it's improbable that there were additional interviews that would have gone unnoticed.

Still, there was a lot of news and gossip in Bob's new book. The book said that Casey thought President Reagan was lazy, that the Moslem king of Saudi Arabia was a heavy drinker, that former president of Egypt Anwar Sadat abused drugs, that Libyan president Muammar Qaddafi often went around "in drag" and that Casey had ordered the CIA to assassinate Mideast splinter-party leader Sheikh Mohammed Hussein Fadlallah (it was a failed attempt, but eight innocent people were killed in the process).

According to Bob's CIA saga, Casey had gotten money for the intelligence agency from the Saudi Arabian ambassador to the United States, Prince Bandar bin Sultan, and used it to fund counterterrorist operations and to provide arms for the contras in Nicaragua. Bob also maintained that Casey approved diverting profits from Iranian arms sales to the contras.

But Jeane Kirkpatrick, a former UN ambassador and a close friend of Casey's, said that the CIA director—after getting to know Bob Woodward—didn't trust him. Kirkpatrick said Casey felt that any book by Bob Woodward would be negative. This may have been the reason why the Central Intelligence Agency listed the final contact between Bob and William Casey as May 3, 1985 (there seems to have been a quarrel between the two according to the FOIA inquiry at that point). That leaves a two-and-a-half-year gap between the last contact and the book's release in the fall of 1987.

Alexander Haig—about to make a 1988 run for the presidency—

certainly came out well in *Veil*. Bob, reading Nancy Reagan's mind, wrote, "She thought Haig had star quality—he was handsome, forceful, had military bearing, was charming and warm." He also read William Casey's mind: "Haig understood foreign policy, Casey thought." Bob also had a spin on Haig's famous remark—"I am in control here"—after the 1981 shooting of President Reagan. He wrote that press spokesman Larry Speakes's "shaky performance" in briefing the press after the assassination attempt had forced Haig to act and "misread the Constitution."

The big controversy in *Veil*, of course, came out of the final chapter. The last four pages claimed that after Casey suffered a seizure as a result of brain cancer in mid-December 1986, Bob visited him at Georgetown Hospital in Washington, supposedly getting a confession of sorts from him. The account of the visit had Casey acknowledging he knew that profits from Iranian arms sales had gone directly to the Nicaraguan contras.

Casey had a cancerous growth removed from the left side of his brain on December 18, 1986. The surgery created a paralysis on the right side of his face (including his tongue) and in his right arm and leg, similar to what people experience after a massive stroke. Casey's resulting speech impediment caused his words to be slurred or garbled. It was hard for people to understand him. His wife, Sophia, communicated with her husband by having him use a kind of primitive sign language or by nodding and shaking his head.

According to the biography *Casey*, by Joseph Persico, Secretary of the Treasury Donald Regan and Edwin Meese III, Ronald Reagan's chief of staff, visited Casey in the hospital on the morning of January 29, 1987, to suggest he resign. They told others his voice was unintelligible. The then CIA deputy director, Robert Gates, brought him the resignation letter to sign later that day. Casey scratched out a barely legible signature with his left hand. An old friend from World War II, Bert Jolis, said that he was "not able to understand a single word he said." Casey's secretary, Betty Murphy, said that he could "no more communicate than the man in the moon." One of Casey's doctors was quoted as saying, "I never heard him make a coherent verbal response." Former Nixon aide Chuck Colson, a friend of Casey's and an old nemesis of Bob's from Watergate days, said he had been hospitalized in the room below Casey's at the time and had visited Casey a day after Bob's alleged visit, but the CIA director had "only been able to squeeze my hand." The one man who said he understood some words was the man who would eventually replace him, Robert Gates. But later he asked out loud, "Was I reading words into Casey's noises?"

In order to leave his bed, the CIA director had to be lifted and settled into a chair where he sat slumped. This was done from time to time in order to prevent bedsores.

Only Bob Woodward claimed to understand an entire five-minute interview that he supposedly had with the dying William J. Casey. Only Bob Woodward remembered having a conversation with Casey, who sat (according to Bob's description to a *Newsweek* artist) bolt upright in a chair.

Sophia Casey was interviewed twice by phone by the author; four Central Intelligence Agency employees who had knowledge of the security were questioned; as was one former member of the hospital's security staff. The author visited Casey's sixth-floor hospital suite on several occasions. He fails to see how Bob's account of the Georgetown hospital visit and interview was possible.

To understand the impossibility of Bob's version of the visit, one has to know the layout of the sixth floor of Georgetown Hospital where Casey's two-room suite was located. The suite was situated directly next to the main nurses' station, where five to seven nurses are usually on duty. The station was so close, it was nearly possible to lean from its waist-high partition and touch Casey's suite number on the wall—C6316. So if Bob had somehow finessed his way past CIA security, hospital security and the Casey family—all of whom had an interest in protecting the CIA director from unwanted visitors—he would still likely have been seen by one or more of the nurses, who were also on alert.

The CIA security force had two men on Casey's detail. One sat by Casey's door, and the other sat next to one of the two elevator entrances that were located on different parts of the floor. The man by the elevator had a view of the corridor that led to Casey's suite. There were three rotating shifts for each twenty-four-hour period. When anyone approached Casey's suite, two forms of identification were required to be shown. This included Casey's doctors, even though they had been there many times before. Only Casey's immediate family was exempt. Bob did approach the suite on one occasion—January 22, 1987—and got close enough, according to the CIA security people, to see the number and probably Casey's alias, "Lacey," which was marked on a clipboard to the right of the door. But the security detail didn't just ask him to leave, as was reported in *Veil*. According to one of the author's sources, Bob was walked to the elevator door and then "pushed, physically, into the elevator."

The chief of hospital security assigned one man to guard Casey as a courtesy. Such protection was often extended to celebrities or top government officials. The nurses were also extra-watchful in those situations.

Sophia Casey's routine was unwavering. She arrived each evening during the dinner hour and stayed until breakfast was served, not leaving until their adult daughter, Bernadette, arrived. The suite had a small bathroom, so there was no need to leave C6316. Mrs. Casey spent each night in a comfortable armchair, dozing sporadically, but getting most of her sleep in the day after returning home.

During his publicity appearance on *Nightline* Bob claimed he had help getting in the suite (he called it a room). Former CIA director Adm. Stansfield Turner, Bob's friend since 1966, said on *Good Morning America* on September 30, 1987, that Bob told him that he had walked by the room and Casey had waved him in. But that wouldn't have been possible since the suite had a small anteroom outside the main room and, from the site where the bed is fixed, a waving hand would not have been visible. The author, who walked by C6316 several times, could only see the current occupant's toes.

The stories continued to change. Bob told a Knight-Ridder syndicate news reporter, Ryan Murphy, that he had showed a press pass to get in. That story was repeated by Bob to *Washingtonian* magazine.[1] Bob told television talk-show host Larry King that he just "walked in."

Earlier in *Veil*, Bob described his single dinner with Casey and Casey's home furnishings in lavish detail, mentioning the "rich Oriental rugs" and "the fine fabrics on the chairs and sofas." Even the color of the house's exterior was described. But he included no descriptions of the hospital room, Casey's dress or other details in the final deathbed interview. The seven-foot-high picture window, with its view of the Georgetown University track-and-field stadium was not mentioned. Casey's blue terry cloth robe, which he wore while awake, wasn't noted. The only phrase that offered a clue to being there was the line "scars from the craniotomy were still healing."

According to Sophia Casey and her daughter, Bernadette, the craniotomy was done through the top of the head. Unlike the large horseshoe-shaped line of stitches common in neurosurgery patients, a small incision requiring no stitches was made on Casey. At first Casey kept it hidden by wearing a cap, but after it began to heal he dispensed with the cap as it was barely notice-able. For Bob to note "the craniotomy scars" in late January he would have had to walk up to Casey, stare down and discern that the small iodine-tinted dot was indeed a scar and not a small birthmark. It was the last element one would have noticed during a visit.

Sophia Casey, appearing on *60 Minutes* on September 27, 1987, said that Bob's story was an "outright lie" and an "invented story." Her daughter agreed.

The controversy—like the controversy so prevalent in all of Bob's books—with the exception of *All The President's Men*—quick-ly helped *Veil* vault to the top of the *New York Times* bestseller list. Bob boasted to *60 Minutes* that "CIA security is nothing difficult to get around" and said that a "senior person" at the agency had told him, "Look, after all this is over we have to talk about security. Obviously yours is better than ours."

But on *Nightline* four days later, Ted Koppel got tough, forcing him to keep repeating that he wouldn't go "beyond what was in the book."

Said Koppel, "Well, the reason that I draw your attention and the viewers' attention to it is precisely because in almost every other respect, you are a very descriptive writer, but when it comes to that particular scene, which after all, is a very dramatic scene, and the one with which you close your book, there is no descrip-tion at all, none—none about the way he looked, really, none about where he was—was he in bed, was he in a chair?—no description of the room at all. It is almost devoid of anything other than this brief dialogue that you held, a dialogue in which body language plays almost as much a role as what was said. Why did you leave out any kind of description?"

Bob's response was that Casey's nineteen words, one nod and a half-smile were what was important. When Koppel asked more questions, Bob said he wouldn't go beyond the book because he needed to protect people who helped him get in the room.

Sophia Casey, too, attacked Bob on *Nightline* that evening, saying Bob's book was an "invention of his imagination."

Two days after the Koppel interview Bob seemed to back away, saying, "I cannot describe Casey as completely lucid."

But when Koppel pressed more on the visit, Bob snapped, "Use common sense. He was in the hospital three months. Did they go to the bathroom? Did they go to lunch? Did they go to sleep? The second time in the hospital I talked to him. No one from the family was there."

The controversy continued to be a book publisher's wildest dream. Ronald Reagan denounced *Veil* as "fiction about a man unable to communicate." The same day he admitted to signing a secret order authorizing terrorism in Lebanon, one of the book's allegations.

Lawrence Casey, the nephew of the CIA director, called it "Woodwardgate" and criticized *The Final Days*, *The Brethren*, *Wired* and Janet Cooke. "Perhaps it is time for someone . . . to do an investigative piece on Bob Woodward," Lawrence Casey concluded.

George Bush offered "to certify that Bill was not in any condition to have a conversation" based on a visit he made where Casey was only able "to squeeze my hand." Ed Meese called it "necrojournalism." Nancy Reagan wrote in her book, *My Turn*, that, when she was in the hospital for surgery, she spoke out in her sleep, saying, "Please don't let Bob Woodward in my room." Even President Napoleon Duarte of El Salvador joined the chorus. Bob said Duarte was a secret CIA informant. Duarte said Bob "makes me laugh" and that he "writes some things that appear not to be true—that he had gone to talk to Casey when he was sick and dying."

Between September 15 and October 15 of 1987 news about *Veil* and the ongoing controversy was in many major newspapers on virtually a daily basis. And many syndicated columnists backed Bob's view of the CIA. William Safire said, surprisingly, that the issue of whether or not Bob had visited Casey didn't matter. What did matter, said Safire, was that it was an important and revealing book.

Richard Reeves wrote "who cares" what Casey said in the hospital. He wrote—tongue in cheek—that Arthur Schlesinger, a former OSS associate of Casey's in World War II assumed Casey was saying, "Please leave, please leave." The point, Reeves wrote, is that *Veil* "is true and everybody knows it. This is a telling book about secret government and the subversion of democracy."

Jack Anderson said in his column that "we have reason to believe Woodward" because his people had met with Casey as well. His conclusion was that Casey was the same man whom Bob had portrayed.

Bob's ability to gather facts and gossip but not to provide insight provided most of the grist for the book's critics. Wrote William Blum, himself a CIA book author, in the *San Francisco Chronicle*, "It is certainly entertaining, but by no means exhaustive or analytical enough." Blum said, "Too much is not challenged by Woodward for us to learn what intellectual and moral substance lay behind the fanatical anticommunism of Casey, a man who has been accused of running an alternative foreign policy, a man called a 'shadow secretary of state.' Instead, Woodward offers us everyone's favorite banality in describing Casey's inner thoughts during World War II, when he visited Dachau a few days after it was liberated: 'People had done this to people?' "

Some revealing observations come from smaller journals. A former OSS officer, Dan Pinck, writing in *Foreign Intelligence Literary Scene*, said, "There is a veil of reality over his latest book. . . . Recombinant fabrications of fiction mixed with unsurprising fact have become a new form of writing contemporary history. Woodward, in *Veil*, demonstrates this art form in pristine purity."

But the all-important Sunday *New York Times Book Review* praised *Veil*. Wrote David C. Martin: "Woodward has gotten into the belly of the beast. It's all here. . . . This is real-time intelligence."[2]

Simon and Schuster picked up the remarks made by Adm. Bobby Inman on the long *Nightline* program—it ran well over the normal half-hour—as a blurb for the paperback: "I take my hat off to Bob Woodward as one of the great investigative reporters we've seen in modern times." On the same program, Inman, the former deputy director of the CIA, added a comment Simon and Schuster didn't use: "I'm not prepared to concede to him that he knows more about intelligence sources than I do." Bob's response: "First, I'd want to concede to Admiral Inman that I do not know more about methods and sources than he. I was not saying that. I was saying I took great care with sources in government, in the intelligence agencies, and going through and making those decisions."

Casey, Inman and Turner were three transparent sources for *Veil* (Turner has publicly admitted being a source) though Bob claimed he interviewed more than two hundred and fifty people for the book. He did not give an exact number. As in each of his previous efforts except for *Wired*, there was neither a bibliography nor source notes.

Bob hired a young red-haired 1982 Berkeley graduate, Barbara Feinman, as his researcher for *Veil*. One report said he gave Feinman a $50,000 bonus for working with him. Feinman denied the amount of the bonus to the author, noting, "But it [the report] did help me get a lot of dates."

Bob dedicated *Veil* "to Elsa," an indication that he was becoming serious about Elsa Walsh, his housemate of six years. In *Wired*, he had acknowledged her with "my esteem and affection for direction, advice, an editor's sharp pencil and a friend's gentle encouragement."

But there was evidence that she had become much more than a companion, friend or another book acknowledgment. A framed photo of the two kissing was now on prominent display in The Factory's living room. He often had flowers delivered to her while she was at her desk, belying his cold image. He even went with her on an assigned stakeout—she was covering Washington's cocaine-using mayor Marion Barry—shivering at dawn in an attempt to determine whether or not the mayor was attending his Alcoholics Anonymous meetings. Walsh, for her part, seemed to be in a state of euphoric bliss. "He loves to hug and kiss. He makes you feel important. He's very affectionate. He's very physical," was her rave review of Bob to writer Barbara Matusow in 1987. She gave him a very out-of-character dog, a tiny Tibetan Lhasa apso they named Pym. She began writing a biographical film script about him. Later it evolved into a fictional whodunit featuring both Bob and Elsa. Mary Tyler Moore's television film company was said to be interested.

Simon and Schuster's first printing of *Veil* totaled 601,000 copies. Bob's advance was an even million dollars. It was selected by the Book-of-the-Month Club. CBS Television optioned it for a miniseries. The *Post* syndicated it to forty-six other papers for nearly

$75,000; Bob had sold the excerpts to the *Post* for a dollar, but had stayed on full salary while writing the book—the same deal as with *The Brethren* and his other books. But the normally stodgy *U.S. News and World Report* scooped the syndicate release by printing key excerpts, acquiring the manuscript with the help of two former *Newsweek* staffers who had defected to the magazine.

For the first time, Simon and Schuster miscalculated the demand for a Bob Woodward book. *Veil* sold briskly for the first two weeks, then died. In 1991 there would be more than two hundred thousand returned copies in a Simon and Schuster warehouse.

18

[Carl and Bob, 1983–89]

Love and Movies

THERE CAME a point in the 1980s, a Manhattan moment captured by the ink of New York tabloids, when Carl Bernstein became the fallback item, the East Side fool of gossip columnists. If Carl realized that he had become a walking joke, it certainly didn't stop him. The parade of high-voltage women in his life continued.

There were the literary women. After Brooke Hayward, he was reported to be in a relationship with Kathleen Tynan, the widow of London drama critic Kenneth Tynan. Carl had helped her with a book about her late husband. Tynan said her relationship with Carl wasn't romantic. There was also a friendship with the much praised essayist Joan Didion. Didion wouldn't comment when asked about the friendship.

But Carl's best-known liaison was with an actress a dozen years his elder, Elizabeth Taylor. The Taylor romance reached a crescendo of sorts when she and Carl rented an unheated house in Sag Harbor, a fashionable Long Island summer community popular with writers and celebrities. Residents, unused to having a Hollywood icon in their presence, joked about installing bleacher seats across the street from the house. The most dramatic remembrance was when Taylor, said to be chilly in the unheated house, sent Carl scurrying to a K Mart late at night to fetch electric blankets.

Some print gossips speculated on whether or not Taylor and Carl were engaged. They certainly had their lovers' quarrels. After one battle at a very proper New York City dinner party, Carl went to the host's piano and surprised the guests by performing "Why Do Fools Fall in Love." Other public ignominies endured by Carl because of the Taylor affair included a loud dispute over her favors with cosmetics executive Dennis Stein. When Carl and Stein appeared to be squaring off, they were said to resemble "two aging, rutting rams at the peak of mating season."

Carl's carousing low point was reached in 1988. The satirical magazine *Spy*, devoted to poking fun at celebrities, declared Carl its first runner-up in what they termed a Pro-Am Ironman Nightlife Decathlon (the winner was author Anthony Haden-Guest). The magazine's reporters shadowed Carl on Monday, April 18, 1988, as he made his way to one party and two bars, finally repairing to a woman's apartment an hour after midnight. *Spy* noted that Carl was still working on his book, which they said was now titled *Disloyal*.

In 1987 and 1988, Bob was working closely on the $13.5-million film version of *Wired*. He would be played the way he had described his vision of himself to Judy Belushi, that of the reporter in *Citizen Kane* searching for Rosebud. In the movie version of *Wired*, which some began referring to as *Weird* because of the leaked plot, John Belushi returned to life, awakening at the morgue, and then received a tour of his career by a Puerto Rican taxi driver played by actor Ray Sharkey. An omniscient Bob Woodward hovered nearby taking notes and at times engaging in dialogues with Belushi, played by look-alike Michael Chiklis. Bob was portrayed by a morose character actor, J. T. Walsh, who bore a close resemblance to Bob, though with slightly less hair.[1]

An article in the *New York Times* described Walsh's Woodward character as being "unnecessarily pompous and intrusive." That was probably accurate, but replacing Walsh with another actor wouldn't have saved the movie. Said the *Times:* "It makes all the wrong decisions, though for the best of reasons. . . . *Wired* never manages to convince its audience that Belushi was a great talent, or that his story is the story of America, as is said more than once." The *Times* was being kind. If *Wired* was not the worst major film of the 1980s, it certainly had a lock at being placed among the bottom ten.

Somehow Alexander Haig's presence managed to make an obligatory Hitchcockian cameo in Bob's first scene of the film. Bob Woodward is shown in his office talking with Judy Belushi on the phone when an editor bursts in and asks, "You hear about Haig?"

The Woodward character says, "This is John Belushi's widow on the phone. I'll get right to the Haig story."

Belushi, Bob and the taxi man discuss Belushi's life as they revisit various of its venues. At one point Belushi says to the cabdriver, "Bob Woodward—I used to do that guy." Says the cabbie, "Now he's doing you. He's going to be your biographer. He's going to do for you what he did for Nixon." "I'm fucked," Belushi says, and later begins referring to Bob as "Bob 'Pulitzer' Woodward."

One even more surreal scene included a "conehead" Nixon speaking with Bob Woodward as played by Belushi in the person of Chiklis. A bad joke about Deep Throat was thrown in gratuitously.

There was also a return to Wheaton to a house said to be the Belushis' but which looked amazingly like Bob's first house on Cross Street.

With the Woodward character on-screen almost as much as Belushi, the film could be seen as being nearly as much a profile of Bob Woodward and his reportorial techniques as the life of John Belushi. One early moment in the film has Bob speaking with an unnamed Ben Bradlee impersonator. Bradlee mused, "Wheaton . . . Billy Graham, Red Grange, you and John Belushi," then pausing to weigh the significance.

Possibly the worst moment of the film is when a choking, gagging Belushi, in the throes of dying of a drug overdose, turns to a stolid, passive Woodward and gasps to his soon-to-be biographer, "Breathe for me, Woodward." Bob's rejoinder is to calmly ask him why he shot himself up with needles.

There were other scenes which exceeded that but fortunately they wound up on the cutting room floor. One had Bob Woodward in a "Saturday Night Live" skit with John Belushi and an unnamed Gilda Radner. Bob played himself while Belushi was impersonating Henry Kissinger. The "Gilda Radner" actress was the love interest fought over by John/Henry and Bob.

Bob Woodward, who served as technical adviser for *Wired*, supported the movie to the end. When it was screened at the Cannes Film Festival in May of 1989, the closing credits were greeted by hisses, boos and loud whistles. But Bob bravely appeared at a Cannes press conference for the film and took the critics' blows. When one Canadian journalist rose and said he "almost choked on my *petit déjeuner,*" complaining of the Bob Woodward character's "extraordinary intrusion," Bob stuffily defended the movie.

"It's an adaption, and in my estimation, an exceptional one. Ordinarily, authors don't like what they see in movies. . . . This one renders, with unusual clarity, the themes of the book. I think the movie is very effective. I accept the choices they made. It's one way to unravel the story."

The producer, Edward Feldman, suggested that Bob "was supporting the film without remuneration, at least temporarily: "[Bob] is one of the most loyal book authors we have ever dealt with. We didn't have the money to pick up the book. Bob carried us for a long time. His presence here is an indication of that support."

Said Bob revealingly, "[The movie] reflects my view of Hollywood and Hollywood's view of me—a cold, compulsive, workaholic fact-gatherer. I plead guilty."

Bob Woodward and the film version of *Wired* had no friends in Hollywood after the Cannes showing. In a case of overkill, the powerful Creative Artists Agency, headed by Michael Ovitz, was reported to take steps to chill the film by using its influence to prevent its release. Michael Chiklis, who had portrayed Belushi, was fired from a production that starred Dan Aykroyd, as was the Bob Woodward look-alike, J. T. Walsh. Aykroyd, in an interview with rock cable network MTV, let his feelings be known. "I have witches working now to jinx the thing. I hope it never gets seen and I'm going to hurl all the negative energy I can against it." In August of 1989 he would tell *CBS This Morning*'s Harry Smith, "These people are exploiting my dead friend. Of course I'm going to take a position."

Although CAA's Ovitz denied trying to stop the film, his clients included Aykroyd, Bill Murray, Jim Belushi, John Landis and (at the time of his death) John Belushi. Landis threatened to sue the motion picture's producers for invasion of privacy because a person playing a producer resembled him, although only the Aykroyd character was named in the movie. Producer Feldman claimed Ovitz telephoned him in preproduction and asked him not to make the motion picture.

When Taurus Entertainment, a tiny distribution unit of United Artists, took on the distribution of *Wired*, some theaters balked at booking the movie, including the Loew's chain, owned by Columbia Pictures. Columbia, and it's sister studio TriStar, had strong working relationships with Ovitz and the Creative Artists Agency.

Ovitz needn't have bothered. Wrote the *Post's* veteran cinema critic, Rita Kempley, "It is an overproduced, inconclusive, superficial and somewhat boring attempt at explaining Belushi's self-destruction. And it tells us that this slovenly grouch's story—'It's Not Such a Wonderful Life'—is somehow also America's story."

Michael Wilmington's critical essay in the *Los Angeles Times* was also mixed. He described the film as a "whacked-out . . . *Citizen Kane* squeezed through *Saturday Night Live* and blasted with *National Lampoon* blood and bile." While praising much of the acting, Wilmington implied that the movie was at least better than the book by saying, "Belushi was trapped in the terse, white sidewalks of Woodward's prose, the police-blotter flatness and austerity. . . . Woodward projected little or zero simpatico for his subject."

A macabre coincidence didn't help the film and led to even more last-minute cancellations by theater chains. Jose Menendez, who five days before *Wired* opened had purchased the video distribution rights to the film for $4 million, was found dead—his body riddled with bullets—in mid-August, 1989 shortly before the film's release.

Wired opened on August 25, 1989, and disappeared faster than a mouthful of popcorn. The opening weekend was the worst debut of any major film that year, with a gross of $681,000 in just 680 theaters, an average of less than twenty-five tickets per screening. By the end of 1989, it was forgotten, flickering back into public attention briefly by being considered for nearly every motion picture critic's annual worst-film list.

Another docudrama based on a Bob Woodward-Carl Bernstein book was filmed in 1989, the three-hour, made-for-TV version of *The Final Days.* As was becoming the norm with any project involving Bob and Carl, a brouhaha erupted from its filming.

At first the filmmakers kept the project secret, perhaps expecting controversy. When a researcher from the production company, Green Street Productions, wrote to the Pentagon's broadcast branch in January, she attempted to deceive them, claiming a film was being produced about Richard Nixon called *E.O.B.* (Executive

Office Building). She explained it was about Watergate from Richard Nixon's point of view. The Green Street employee then requested footage of the White House; the presidential yacht, *Sequoia*; Nixon's compound at Key Biscayne; and shots of Nixon during foreign trips. The film company also contacted Nixon administration members for help, but did not tell them the project was *The Final Days*.

There began the controversy. When friends of Richard Nixon learned that a movie was being made of *The Final Days*, they shifted into high gear, urging that no help be given to the film-makers and accusing them of "covering up the true nature of the project."

Bob, who worked closely with Green Street—the director was a Yale classmate, Richard Pearce—said the Nixon loyalists were engaging in "classic enemies-list mentality. Don't they ever learn?"

An aide to Richard Nixon, John Taylor, then wrote to Bob, attacking his "enemies-list" remark, asserting that because his friend Carl Bernstein had done everything in his power to soften and create "a commercial failure" out of the movie version of *Heartburn*, then surely there was no inconsistency "in protecting the Nixon family from unfair assaults."

Wrote Taylor: "I guess we *haven't* learned. I assume that you will not believe RN has 'learned' until he rolls over and plays dead in the face of outrages such as an ABC Entertainment dramatization of *The Final Days*. You may be assured that this will never happen."

Taylor speculated that if ABC had its way, Nixon would be played by Pee-wee Herman and Pat Nixon by Madeline Kahn. And, said Taylor, if the movie was as distorted as the book, the public would tune in to "watch 'Battle of the Soap Opera Stars' on another network instead."

Taylor then wrote a blanket memo to all of Richard Nixon's friends warning them of what he felt was the deception being practiced by the movie people and said they, meaning Bob and the film crew, were "covering up." Alluding to Pat Nixon's stroke after she read *The Final Days*, Taylor reminded them that the book had "had near-tragic consequences in the Nixon family when it was first released." Taylor called the project "singularly odious and vicious."

If the film's producers thought that the controversy would blow over before the three-hour movie aired, they were to be disappointed. When Richard Nixon learned that AT&T was sponsoring the $7-million project, he publicly switched both his home and office phones to competitor MCI and suggested his friends follow his example. Taylor then wrote a letter to AT&T chairman Robert E. Allen, saying, "Perhaps you should change your corporate slogan to 'reach out and smear someone!' "[2] Friends of the film's opponents attended the 1989 stockholders meeting of Capital Cities/ABC, the corporate parent of ABC television, and spoke out loudly against the expected distortions in the docudrama.

Of particular concern was one of the film's final moments, the prayer scene between Richard Nixon and Henry Kissinger. When Bob and Carl had written about the final days of Nixon's presidency, they had described Nixon as remaining on his knees after the prayer, sobbing, then beating his fists on the floor and moaning, "What have I done? What has happened?" The scene had been included in both Richard Nixon's and Henry Kissinger's memoirs, and because it was, Bob and Carl often pointed to it as an example of *The Final Days* standing the test of time.

But while it was true that both Kissinger and Nixon had written about the scene, admitting they had prayed together, and that Nixon had wept, both denied the carpet pounding and the quotations. Bob and Carl had attributed Nixon's words to Kissinger's describing the incident to Nixon aides Brent Scowcroft and Lawrence Eagleburger. Both Scowcroft and Eagleburger denied Kissinger had related such a description. In the ABC television version, Bob and Carl's scene was repeated and even amplified, with a stern Kissinger played by Theodore Bikel and Nixon played by actor Lane Smith. This time, however, Nixon was shown curled into a fetal position after his sobs. Smith was not a neutral observer. At a press conference he told one about his personal remembrance of Nixon's firing of Bob Haldeman and John Ehrlichman: "I just knew the guy was lying. And I remember seeing his last speech to his staff, and I thought it was the most bizarre thing I had ever seen in my life." But Smith tempered that statement by saying he approached the role "from a place of compassion."

Smith said that Nixon's final speech to his staff showed "someone who was vulnerable and showing great pain, right on the edge of breaking down. We had no idea that this Richard Nixon even existed."

Executive producer Stu Samuels said he believed Richard Nixon had been a battered child. "I don't want to get into particulars, but, yes, there is foundation for the belief that he got bashed around," Samuels told an interviewer.

Bob and Carl both helped to publicize the film, appearing at press conferences and giving interviews. At one joint question-and-answer session with *TV Guide*, Bob called Nixon "a criminal . . . you never can feel he wasn't guilty" and mused about Nixon's "sense that you could order sandwiches or nuclear war and people would obey."

Carl said in the same October 28, 1989 edition, "Neither of us had ever been conventionally anti-Nixon." A day later he would tell another interviewer, "It's empathetic to the whole family, including Richard Nixon." But, said Carl in the next breath, "there's no question about the criminality, about the venality, about the self-pity, about his putting his own interests in front of the presidency."

Carl, who needed money a lot more than Bob, told the *Chicago Tribune* how he regretted turning down a million dollars in 1976 for film rights to *The Final Days*, saying, "I get a stomachache when I think about this." He blamed William Safire, who wrote a 1976 column implying that Carl and Bob were "crass and commercial" for their reluctance to sell the book to the movies.

The film aired on Sunday, October 29, kicking off the important network "sweeps" fall-ratings period. A combination of the campaign against the film and an episode of CBS's popular *Murder, She Wrote* followed by a made-for-television movie starring Donna Mills as an amnesia victim may have turned the public's attention away from the real-life soap opera of the Nixon family. The fluff was even lighter on NBC, where comedienne Jackee, according to one TV listing, was "impersonating her twin sister in a deadly game of financial intrigue."

The Final Days finished a dismal fifty-eighth out of seventy-seven rated programs. It received a 17 percent share of the audience, the worst showing of any ABC Sunday movie that season. Among networks, ABC finished fourth, behind Fox.

The opponents of the film didn't let up after the showing. The day after it was aired, one of Richard Nixon's lawyers during Watergate, Leonard Garment, weighed in with a *New York Times* opinion piece saying he found his portrayal "offensive" and the docudrama "a cartoon." He reiterated that there had been no collapse by Nixon and no beating of fists on the carpet (a TV crew member had called it "the rug deal with Kissinger"). Garment said

The Final Days was "littered with false pictures, false sequences, and words that were not spoken by the people who speak them." The next day, the *Times* ran an editorial headlined "Fiction Blurs Fact," which cautioned that "viewers of *The Final Days* needed forceful warnings about the varied authenticity of its source materials." And a few days later, *Times* critic Walter Goodman lambasted the docudrama, saying, "There must be men and women in the network news divisions who are appalled by what is being purveyed under the implied aegis of their craft." Added Theo Lippman in the *Baltimore Sun*, "They [the audience] were served up a concoction of facts and, where the facts didn't 'work,' of dramatic invention."

Tom Shales of the *Washington Post* admired the film version of *The Final Days*. He compared the production to *Citizen Kane*, *The Godfather* and *Aida* all in the same sentence. Continuing the *Kane* analogy (which undoubtedly pleased Bob), he wrote that actor Richard Kiley's J. Fred Buzhardt "functions the way the reporter did in *Citizen Kane*." But he described the scene where Nixon struggled with an aspirin bottle while one of the Watergate tapes played in the background as "probably apocryphal. Yet the imagery is so pungent it has the punch of truth."

On Thanksgiving weekend, November 25, 1989, three months after the *Wired* disaster, and just weeks after the airing of *The Final Days* Bob married Elsa Walsh after an eight-year relationship. This time it was more than a quick, simple ceremony. Bob's father flew in from Wheaton and presided over the vows. Bob's daughter, Tali, now a teenager, was the maid of honor. The sprinkling of notables among the two hundred guests who attended the wedding and dinner at the posh Grand Hotel near his Georgetown house included spy-novel author Tom Clancy; mentors Richard Snyder and Alice Mayhew from Simon and Schuster; Katharine Graham, who still had the "final say" in *Post* financial matters and who also lived just around the corner from Bob; White House budget chief Richard Darman; and, of course, Carl Bernstein, who was said to have made an eloquent speech. Elsa Walsh looked radiant in a brown velvet dress.

Elsa was in the midst of covering the trial of a local cocaine kingpin, so the two said they would be honeymooning in Italy only after the verdict.[3] Elsa said the marriage was "her only, his last."

[Carl and Bob, 1984–91]

Carl's Comeback, Bob's War

WOMEN HAD been behind the ascendency of Carl Bernstein from newspaper reporter to a popular target for *paparrazi*. They had been behind his descent to becoming journalism's court jester. And it was the lure of women, famous women, that had helped keep him in the tabloids—providing him with lucrative speaking fees—and away from the typewriter for nearly a decade. Thus one might have predicted that a woman would impel him to pick up the manuscript he had neglected since the seventies and eventually complete his nearly forgotten book about his childhood.

The Jockey Club, inside the Ritz Carlton hotel was the consummate insiders' dining choice of *haute* Washington in 1984. The front room of the restaurant, was where Nancy Reagan and Republican cabinet wives lunched and where powerful politicians and celebrities dined at night. It served almost as a private club to influential residents of the capital city, much as the "21" Club serves New York City.

After his arrest for drunk driving in 1983, Carl had continued in a freefall toward the lowest point of his professional life as a journalist. But on this April, 1984 evening, there was no sign that he had hit bottom. He seemed nearly carefree in the company of his friend, writer Joan Didion. Midway through the expensive dinner he passed her the manuscript he'd begun in 1977. He had completed only fifty pages. He asked her as casually as he could if she would read it.

Of course she would, Didion told him. Right away, that very night.

"It knocked me out," Didion would say later. She urged Carl to go back to his book and finish it. Carl agreed. Suddenly, after hearing these words from Didion, it became all he wanted to do. Still, Carl needed discipline—a trait he had never possessed—with the possible exception of the Watergate years.

"It had become his *Answered Prayers*," a friend said, referring to Truman Capote's unfinished project.

Carl couldn't continue his book in New York, with all its plea-surable distractions. He tried, but in 1986 fled to Bob's George-town house—a place where, he knew, the American work ethic was present in spades. Carl settled in on the third floor. The room was the one in which Gary Hart had lived after separating from his wife, Lee.

When Carl moved in, Bob was working on *Veil* and was writing daily, not leaving his word processor until at least ten pages were embedded into a memory disc. In a way, it became like the early days of their partnership, the two trading pages, reviewing each other's work. Barbara Feinman, Bob's researcher, hovered nearby, playing policeman while Bob frequently shouted encouragement and commands: "Work!" "All day!"

Though Carl's book would have embellishments, errors and at least one major fabrication, it was also a heartfelt outpouring of his emotions, some of which explained his hatred of Richard Nixon. To Carl, Nixon's surveillance of his staff and the dirty tricks carried out by CREEP were all just a continuation of the same kind of government harassment that had forced his father to go from being a well-paid union organizer to the owner of a Laundromat in a poor black neighborhood. That was what was behind *Loyalties*, the book Carl eventually produced through enormous effort and a push over the edge by friends.

There were times when Carl would drive around in a car with Bob Woodward in tow and a tape recorder running. Carl would pour out memories while Bob interrogated him. One tumultuous moment occurred while Carl was talking about a fight he got into as a child when another kid called his mother a communist. Carl broke into tears. They stopped the tape recorder and pulled the car over to the side of the road until Carl recovered his composure. Then Bob calmly asked, "what did you think of communism?"

Carl included some of these exchanges with Bob in *Loyalties*. In the book, he referred to Bob only as Woodward, never using the first name, assuming the reader would know that it could only be *the* Woodward—a conceit revisited from their first book together.

After the jump start at Bob's house, Carl returned to New York where he finished *Loyalties* on an Apple computer in his $4,500-per-month rented town house on East Sixty-second Street. Carl eventually turned in the manuscript to Simon and Schuster in early 1988. He would then help orchestrate anticipation over the course of the year leading up to his book's publication.

Bob was among the first to speak out: "This is a great comeback for Carl. It's a spectacular book."

Joan Didion agreed: "It's a terrific book. [Carl] tends to look for conspiracy. It's not beyond his imagination . . . as it is most people."

Marie Brenner said it was "brave." Even Nora Ephron called it "wonderful."

Carl was, for the moment, on top again, at least as far as publicity went. There were positive pieces in *New York*, *Vanity Fair*, *Fame*, *Vogue*, *Rolling Stone* and the *Washington Post Magazine* well before the book was in the stores. Carl himself may have ingeniously sucker-punched *Fame* publisher Steve Greenberg. Meeting Greenberg in a bar, Carl asked him to kill a story about him in the magazine. Though no story had been planned, Greenberg quickly scheduled a profile.

Richard Snyder at Simon and Schuster was reported to have paid Carl an advance of $900,000 in 1986 for *Loyalties* and a second, later effort as part of a two-book contract. After Carl delivered the manuscript in mid-January of 1988, Simon and Schuster began to plan a major advertising and publicity push for the book's spring 1989 release. Book-of-the-Month club chose the book as an alternate selection. Movie deals were rumored. The attention, after years of drifting, came none too soon. Katharine Graham had not invited Carl to her gala seventieth birthday celebration in 1987; Bob had attended as had Nora Ephron and even Margaret Jay. The slight had hurt—it was one further indication Carl had been left behind in the literary and journalistic parade.

Not surprisingly, the people who didn't want to see *Loyalties* published were Carl's parents. Al and Sylvia Bernstein were embarrassed by the manuscript. Sylvia still worked behind a counter at Garfinckel's, an old-line, expensive clothing and specialty store that has since gone out of business. Al didn't want his Communist past rehashed in a heavily promoted book. He had a professional job again, raising funds for the National Conference of Christians and Jews. Carl's own two sisters didn't want to be interviewed by Carl.

But Carl had to finish and publish the book. *Loyalties* had become a way for him to explain his tumultuous life thus far. As he wrote in the slim volume, "it is my father for whom I write, whose judgment I most respect, whose approval I still seek." The 2,500 documents he had received from the FBI in a Freedom of Information inquiry about his parents encircled his work area on the second floor of his Upper East Side town house, consuming him. To Carl, it may have seemed that the government's persecution of his parents had continued through the Nixon administration. And it was Carl who had then exposed Nixon, stopping evil in its tracks.

Still, Carl took time in the book to acknowledge and thank many of the women in his life for their help. He dedicated it to Kathleen Tynan, Bob Woodward and his two sons. On another page he recognized Joan Didion, Lillian Hellman, Alice Mayhew, Nora Ephron, Margaret Jay, Elizabeth Taylor and Barbara Feinman, as well as a list of less well-known women friends, then added motion picture actress Shirley MacLaine, publishing executive Joni Evans, and his agent, Lynn Nesbit.

Carl had huge hopes for *Loyalties*. But, smartly, he underplayed it. "I wrote it for me and a few of my friends," he modestly told *Fame* of his twelve-year ordeal. "Obviously I hope it sells, because I could use the money. Who I am is what's in the book."

Kirkus Reviews was one of the first to pass judgment, calling it "an effective and affecting evocation of a Kafkaesque period in U.S. history . . . while self-indulgent and disjointed . . . the result of his devotion presents a moving and human record of activists who showed grace under intolerance."

The *New York Times* reviewed it twice, once in the Sunday *Book Review* and a day later in a regular daily review by Christopher Lehmann-Haupt, who was less congratulatory than *Kirkus Reviews*, saying, "He digs and digs. But he ends up drowning. . . .

What might have been a fascinating psychological journey turns out in the end to have been just flat and dull."

The rest of the notices were more like those in the *New York Times* than *Kirkus Reviews*. Even the *Washington Post* complained about Carl's "inability to separate wheat from chaff." The *Los Angeles Times* said, "*Loyalties* is not likely to restore Bernstein's literary reputation," the *Atlanta Journal* saw it as a "love-hate letter to his parents" and the *Boston Globe* called it "more head-spinning than gripping."

Faced with stacks of *Loyalties* in bookstores across the country, each volume a loiterer, Simon and Schuster took out full-page ads in major papers. The ads reprinted words of praise not from newspaper or magazine reviews but from Carl's friends. This who's who of literary and media names included Gay Talese, Studs Terkel, David Halberstam, Ted Koppel, Bruce J. Friedman and Roger Rosenblatt. The only blurb from a print journal was from *Kirkus Reviews*.

The book still languished in bookstores in spite of the ads, and Carl's appearances on everything from *Good Morning America* to *Larry King Live* didn't seem to help. On King's show, Carl was again challenged by the abrasive conservative columnist John Lofton on the accuracy of what critics called a "major revelation"—a 1978 interview with Washington insider Clark Clifford. Clifford supposedly had revealed to Carl that President Truman had manufactured a loyalty problem in order to gain reelection in 1948. Lofton claimed he had just spoken to Clark Clifford and that Clifford had not only denied it, but, according to Lofton, "doesn't even remember you interviewing him."

Carl replied by recalling the Nixon-Kissinger prayer scene and saying that nobody believed that at the time. He said that "John Lofton has a kind of agenda" and "I don't think John . . . has any trouble with the truth." The author, who sent the *Larry King Live* transcript and Carl's chapter on Clifford's view to Clifford himself, received a call from the famed Washington attorney on the morning of January 7, 1993. Clifford called Carl's chapter "garbled . . . dumb . . . totally untrue." He could not remember the interview (see Appendix C).

Loyalties would become the first book by either Carl or Bob *not* to make a bestseller list, not even to be a modest commercial success. By the end of 1989, *Loyalties* filled the remainder bins of discount stores, many of the copies already autographed by the author.

Before beginning on his new project, a book originally slated to be an examination of leadership in the U.S. military, Bob endured another wide burst of criticism by other newspapers; for a *Post* story he wrote on March 2, 1989.

When Texas senator John Tower appeared before a Senate committee for his confirmation as secretary of defense in the Bush administration, Bob wrote a front-page story that implied Tower was a drunk and a womanizer. The story was headlined: "Incidents at Defense Base Cited; Drunkenness, Harassment of Women Alleged."

The story revealed that Bob Jackson, a retired Air Force sergeant, had told the FBI he had observed Tower drunkenly fondling two women at an Air Force base near Austin, Texas at unspecified dates between 1976 and 1978. Bob's article reported that Jackson told the FBI other people had observed the incident and that the FBI also had independent corroboration of Jackson's account. Bob quoted the sergeant as saying Tower had touched the breasts of one woman and patted the buttocks of another. The sergeant told Bob if it had been his daughter, he would have been "sent to Leavenworth," implying he would have physically assaulted Tower and been willing to go to prison for the deed.

The Air Force sergeant was Bob's only named witness to the incident. At other points in the piece he referred to "informed sources" and "a source" and "the source." It was impossible to determine how many sources Bob had used for the article or if he had ever spoken with any of the corroborating witnesses.

The following day, the veracity of Bob's piece became questionable when an Air Force document showed that Jackson had been released from the service because of mental problems. It also suggested that Sergeant Jackson hadn't been on the Air Force base when the purported event occurred.

Though the *Post* never offered a formal retraction, Bob immediately co-wrote another story that included the history of Jackson's psychiatric problems. And Tower had other problems. He was not approved by the Senate for secretary of defense, losing 53–47.

Later, Tower would write in his memoirs, *Consequences*, that "Bob Woodward's byline on the story gave it an extra dimension. Because Woodward is half of the Watergate reporting duo, his name always attracts interest and gives his subject matter a tinge of scandal."

Bob began his sixth book in 1989, after the Tower affair. His formula for writing had become predictable. A suggestion from another person was usually the genesis of his books. His now-perfected style often put him inside the minds of the nonfictional characters who populated his books. This made sometimes dry reality read like thrilling fiction, yet the public was still reading factual accounts. Bob, with seeming omniscience would describe a person's feelings and thoughts whether or not he had interviewed that person. A Bob Woodward book often punctuated an important point with a dramatic, one-sentence paragraph before going on to the next sequence of thoughts. Each of his books was much longer on detail and facts than insight, analysis or explanation of motivation. Every book, after the first two Watergate volumes, used a single main source, usually fewer than five secondary sources and then a lot of filler—detail provided by hundreds of interviews. Each volume, with the exception of *Wired*, had no bibliography, end notes or other source listings normally found at the end of nonfiction books of the genre Bob had written. And each volume, after *All the President's Men*, would generate controversy, happily hyped by Simon and Schuster and aided by Bob Woodward. The result was six bestsellers, all reaching the coveted number one position on the *New York Times Book Review*'s weekly bestseller list.

When Bob had cowritten *The Final Days*, Max Lerner had described the book as "hot history" in the *Saturday Review*. A decade and a half later, the term had been refined by others into "instant history." Bob Woodward had now become a defined industry.

His new effort, *The Commanders*, would follow Bob's pretested pattern. It was referred to by some critics as a "ticktock" book—meaning that it was a step-by-step countdown of actions leading to an event. Bob's main source was Gen. Colin Powell, chairman of the Joint Chiefs of Staff, who managed to find time to be interviewed by Bob some forty times for the book, spending hundreds of hours with him answering questions. The secondary sources were presidential adviser for national security Brent Scowcroft; Defense Secretary Richard Cheney; Bob's friend, White House legal counsel and neighbor, C. Boyden Gray; White House budget director Richard Darman; and probably fellow Yalie and Book and Snaker, Congressman Les Aspin of Wisconsin. *The Commanders* was suggested by Richard Snyder, Bob's longtime patron at Simon and Schuster.[1]

The likely reason Cheney, Powell and others talked to Bob in such depth was because the book was originally intended to be a study of the inner workings of the Pentagon. After it was begun, historic events—the war in Panama and the nation's Desert Storm offensive against Iraq—changed the nature of the project, helping to make it an even bigger bestseller. Jealous journalists would call it "Woodward's luck."

For *The Commanders*, Bob created a new wrinkle in his writing style. Besides putting quotation marks around what he wished people to believe was said, even though he had no direct confirmation of the conversation, he now created conversations in which characters spoke without quotation marks. Bob explained this was "when sources were unsure about exact wording."

Bob also used one of his own recreational habits—high-stakes poker games—as a metaphor to describe General Powell's thoughts: "Poker. It was high stakes. . . . Craps. The country was at the table and the dice had been thrown. This was the moment of waiting, the dice in midair. Soon they would hit the cloth and arrive at the far end."[2]

The dramatics were also transported to the battlefield. U.S. Special Forces troops were described as possessing "enough firepower to make any battle seem like a nonnuclear version of World War Three." Military aircraft on the way to Panama became "a lot of aluminum flying through the air."

Alexander Haig, who had been one of the first to drop out of the 1988 presidential race and who had left public life to write his memoirs for a reported $2.5 million went without praise in a Woodward book for the first time.[3] Bob reported that Pentagon leaders wanted to avoid a "Haig syndrome" with Colin Powell. According to Bob, the military had resented Haig's rapid advancement at the White House.

As with *Veil*, questions were raised as to whether or not a reporter had the right to harbor important information. Should it have been printed on the pages of the *Washington Post* before the book was printed? Paraphrasing Sen. Howard Baker, Jon Weiner, a history professor at the University of California, questioned in *The Nation*: "What did Woodward know and when did he know it? When Woodward found out the Chair of the Joint Chiefs of Staff opposed war and favored sanctions—assuming that Powell disclosed this before January 15—why wasn't that headline news in the *Washington Post*? Why did that information become private property, which Simon and Schuster would sell to the public months later for $24.95? The information Woodward possessed would have been a powerful weapon for the antiwar movement."

Bob, while not responding directly to *The Nation*, explained that he had pledged not to write about the information given to him except in book form. The antiwar movement and the effect on the country were less important than his word of honor, he seemed to be saying.

Because of Iraq's military actions, Bob worked on the final portions *The Commanders* until the middle of March 1991. The book was released in mid-May, and, as usual, *Newsweek*, the *Post* subsidiary, gave it front-cover treatment and published excerpts. The *Washington Post* gave it 317 column inches and 27 photos over four days, distributing excerpts to its syndicate of newspapers. In the lead review of the May 5 *Post* book review supplement, Clay Blair effused that *The Commanders* "contains so many startling revelations, it is difficult to know where to begin and how to convey them in a brief review." He also called Bob "the fourth estate's premier investigative journalist." Quipped *The New Republic* about Blair's praise, "On the negative side, the book fails to outline a cure for cancer."

Yet overall, *The Commanders* may have been among the best received of Bob's books. Journalists marveled at his access to the decision makers in Washington. And while many still questioned his reportorial techniques, few queried the overall accuracy of the book. Not having the same relationship with men like Colin Powell or Richard Darman, they couldn't.

Michael Massing in the *New York Review of Books* called *The Commanders* "a vivid glimpse into Colin Powell's mind" and said "for the most part his reporting has stood up over time." But he, too, questioned Bob's reluctance to reveal newsbreaking matters in the *Post* rather than in the book, printing verbatim part of an interview broadcaster Bob Edwards had conducted for National Public Radio:

Edwards: You work for a daily newspaper, and I know . . . you probably have some feelings about sitting on information, but there has to be a lag time between the time you learned all this and the time it appears in a hardback book.

Woodward: That's right, but there isn't much lag time. If you look, the war only ended two months ago, and if there was something that was so crucial that I felt that this has to be in the newspaper right away, I would have gone to the sources I have—and said that. Happily, that really did not occur.

Edwards: But if you could have published this stuff at the time you learned it, it has much more impact—it's like your Watergate reporting—every new element that you published produced a turn in the story.

Woodward: Well, in Watergate we're talking about crimes. In this case, we're talking about no crimes. There's no portrait in here of somebody with their hands in the cookie jar or doing something illegal. There's a lot of emotion and there's a lot of debate and . . . anxiety, uncertainty.

Summed up Massing: "This is not convincing. The Gulf crisis did not involve illegal acts, but it did involve matters of war and peace. What could be more consequential than that?"

As usual, a book by Bob Woodward was a media event. Virtually every publication or broadcasting outlet covered *The Commanders*. *Business Week* compared Bob with Kitty Kelley. The *New York Times*'s Christopher Lehmann-Haupt—who had reviewed many of Bob's and Carl's books—declared it "unsatisfying" but a "superior sort of quickie book." *USA Today* complained that the book "canonizes Powell . . . so much is told from Powell's point of view that that is the effect." The questions and criticisms didn't matter in terms of commercial success. *The Commanders* quickly rose to the top of nearly every bestseller compilation, largely because in May 1991 one couldn't pick up a newspaper or magazine without reading something about it.

Though the book clearly put General Powell in a favorable light, it earned him the reputation of a gossip, particularly among the Capitol Hill congressional members with whom he was expected to play politics. After the Gulf War, George Bush renominated him to the chairmanship of the Joint Chiefs of Staff five months before his term was to end. But Powell did not sail through the reconfirmation process, even though he was clearly one of the heroes of the Iraqi conflict. *The Commanders* was of concern to the U.S. Senate.

Georgia Democratic leader Sam Nunn accused him of revealing secrets. "There are things in the book that are clearly classified," the senator lectured.

Virginia's John Warner was concerned about Powell's unburdening himself to Bob, particularly the revelation that Powell favored sanctions rather than a military strike. "Often, people who want to express opinions divergent from other leaders' will allow a decent interval of time," Warner said.

Chided Sen. Trent Lott of Mississippi, "The time you wasted . . . talking to that author."

General Powell, who called Bob "a friend" admitted to the senators he had conversed with him frequently in 1989 and 1990. But he told the senate committee, in offering his own review of *The Commanders*, "The result is a book that is interesting and that should be read for what it is—a combination of fact, of fiction, of accurate quotations, and in some cases not-so-accurate quotations."

Bob responded to press questions that Powell had never suggested to him the book contained fiction and expressed surprise. Powell was then renominated the next day unanimously to a second term.

Still, the marriage with Elsa Walsh was working out. At the end of *The Commanders'* acknowledgments, he wrote that she had brought "balance to my life."

20

[Bob and Carl, 1990–92]

Reunions and Secrets

THE MYTH of Bob Woodward is that he is a creator of books, a masterful investigative journalist and a collector of information supplied by secret sources.

But all of Bob Woodward's books, except for one, have been someone else's idea. Investigative reporters, by definition, usually operate on an adversarial basis, independent of their subjects. Conversely Bob has become a cultivator of power, reflecting the views of people near the top of the executive branch of the American government; his books and other writings now chronicle the actions of that ruling structure. The secrets are thoughts of people at that leadership level, then revealed to the courtiers on the fringes as well as the public via the printed page. When these officials want to express a view or share a confidence, they come to Bob. He is their brand name of choice—a trademarked muckraker. His being the son of a Republican judge, a Yale graduate, a member of a fraternal secret society and a Georgetown resident seemingly places him above most of his muckraking colleagues.

The secret of Deep Throat is that there was no Deep Throat. Deep Throat was a compilation of several sources, Alexander Haig being the most prominent among them. The invention was one of many fabrications, embellishments and literary devices that added spice and commercial value to *All the President's Men*. The William Casey interview reported in *Veil* was simply a convenient and dramatic way to end a book. Both of these very literary gestures have grown from Bob's original ambition to be a novelist when he was at Yale, or, in the case of *All the President's Men*, Carl's long history of embroidering the truth. Was Bob an informant or agent of the Central Intelligence Agency or another covert government group? Probably. One can't say for certain and no one may ever know.

In 1991, the press began to again question the veracity of Bob Woodward's writings. The catalyst was *Silent Coup*, a book by Len Colodny and Robert Gettlin, which largely charged him with having falsified certain events and claims—such as briefing Alexander Haig and also alleging that the U.S. military wanted Richard Nixon out of office. The softening of Nixon's position on relations with the People's Republic of China was one of many reasons proposed by the authors. *The Washington Post* attempted to suppress the book by running a slanted piece featuring denials by two of the author's sources. But both sources were on tape as saying Bob was a briefer to Alexander Haig, a point the newspaper chose not to address. Roger Morris, a source who repeated his allegation that Bob was a briefer, was deleted from the *Post*'s story.

Though Bob called *Silent Coup* "garbage" and Carl called it "a lunatic piece of work," the book unleashed a series of attacks against Bob Woodward. Doug Ireland began an article in the *Village Voice* with "Is Bob Woodward a liar?" The *Columbia Journalism Review* and Robert Sherrill's review in the *Charleston Gazette* ran the same headline: "Did Woodward Lie?" *Mother Jones*, a liberal investigative magazine asked the same question on its cover. *The New Republic* offered a June 1991 piece by Jacob Weisberg, savaging Bob's editor, Alice Mayhew, and saying she never read many of the books assigned to her, farming them out to free-lance editors.[1]

Every byline by Bob Woodward began to be scrutinized by the press. A year later, he would come under fire for writing a front-page *Washington Post* article about the 1992 independent presidential hopeful Ross Perot. Bob reportedly used confidential conversations he had with Perot in 1988 without getting the Texan's permission to quote from them in print. Perot then called Bob a "fruitcake," and Perot's aide called the story "half-assed." Bob's explanation was that since Perot was now a presidential candidate, the rules had changed.

Carl, for the most part, was now thought of as a has-been by many journalists. He continued to pop up regularly on talk shows, decrying gossip and the sorry state of American journalism. He signed a two-year, $100,000-per-annum contract with *Time* in January of 1990, but critics would eventually note his lack of output and point out that the five published stories in his first year at *Time* came at a price of $20,000 an article. One piece in 1990, claiming that East Germans weren't in favor of unification, was considered an embarrassment. There was gossip that Carl would be let go after his first year. In early 1991, Carl reportedly wrote a memo to senior *Time* staffers that said the United Nations' January 15 "get out of Kuwait or else" deadline was a ruse. The real date for the invasion, he claimed, was between February 5 and 11. The invasion, of course, began the evening of January 15. Near the end of his second year, Carl wrote an excellent cover story that said Ronald Reagan and Pope John Paul II had a secret alliance to keep Poland's Solidarity movement alive. It was rumored that Bob had given him the information in order to help him keep his job at *Time*. Because Alexander Haig's name ran twice in the story's first paragraph, there was certainly reason to give credence to the rumors, though they were denied by Bob. *Time* decided not to renew Carl's contract.

A week later, Carl applied for a teaching position at Columbia University's School of Journalism and was denied the job. He then moved from his fashionable East Sixty-second Street address in early 1992 to a loft near Greenwich Village. His life had come nearly full circle—he had lived just blocks away during his one-year stay at the Elizabeth *Daily Journal*. In midyear, he was said to be working on a book on the state of American journalism; some magazines called it a novel.

Carl continued to pursue relationships with high-profile women. There was a long romance with a former daughter-in-law of Katharine Graham's in 1991. She was followed by Faye Wattleton, the former president of Planned Parenthood. The two danced through parties at the 1992 Democratic Party Convention and at a *Playboy* anniversary gala, attracting the cameras of *People* and the tabloids. By 1993, he was reported to be helping her write a book about her years at the birth control agency.

The 1990s may mark an era of tranquillity for Bob Woodward. If so, the credit can go to Elsa Walsh. As Bob wrote to his classmates at Yale when they celebrated the twenty-fifth reunion of the class in 1990, "these have been by far the best and happiest years of my life. We have a house in the country where we go nearly every weekend. (Two marriages in the 1960s and 1970s ended in divorce, victims of my character flaws and work habits.) The stability and somewhat slower pace make life more tranquil, with more reading and a few more walks in the woods, and less time spent working evenings and weekends."

Bob Woodward didn't attend his twenty-fifth Wheaton Community High School reunion. This time there were no phone calls to him and little talk about the boy most likely to succeed. He had been mostly forgotten by his classmates, a far away "name." From time to time, when he would appear on a television news program, a classmate might say, "I went to school with him," before switching channels.

In the fall of 1991 Bob wrote a series of articles with veteran *Post* reporter David Broder about Vice President Dan Quayle. Like all of Bob's other efforts, the series quickly became embroiled in controversy. "Too nice, too soft, too easy," went the media critics' chant on the series when it was released over seven days beginning January 5, 1992.

The criticism was justified. When the authors investigated charges that Quayle had plagiarized work at DePauw University, they interviewed the same two professors who had been called upon many times before, passing up the many classmates and faculty in the vice president's yearbook from whom new information might have been gleaned. One of the professors contacted yawned, "Every time Dan Quayle runs for public office I get called."

Bob reacted to his review with a shrug and a few ready answers. He was used to the drill. He appeared on David Brinkley's Sunday talk show on ABC and said Quayle was "ready" to be president. One year later he wrote an even more flattering portrait of fellow Yalie, and Book and Snake colleague, Les Aspin, Aspin had just been named Secretary of Defense.

And he could afford to be magnanimous. His net worth was now more than $8 million.[2]

He wrote another series of *Post* articles in October 1992 that might yet become a book, this one on the state of the U.S. economy. Bob's sources were said to be "surprised and dismayed" when the series appeared a few weeks before the presidential elections. They complained of being misled. Woodward watchers will look for the transparent hand of former U.S. budget director and good friend Richard Darman in the pages, as well as ex–

treasury secretary Nicholas Brady and former White House chief of staff Samuel Skinner.[3]

Also in October 1992, Alexander Haig weighed in with his memoirs, *Inner Circles*. He devoted an entire chapter to his denial of being Deep Throat and said he never met Bob and Carl until 1974 (Bob has said they met in the spring of 1973). The Haig memoirs were cowritten by Charles McCarry, the former CIA operative whom Bob had named in interviews as his favorite author.[4]

In a room of his Georgetown home hangs an old movie poster for Alfred Hitchcock's *The Man Who Knew Too Much*. Bob has often stood in front of it while speaking to guests. The highlight of the Jimmy Stewart–Doris Day vehicle, had came when Day sang "Whatever will be will be." The movie had been released in 1956, the year Bob's parents' divorce had been finalized. If Bob is aware of that fact, he hasn't said. As the title of the Hitchcock thriller suggests, Bob has always shouldered the burden of his secrets.

While Bob never attended his high school anniversary celebrations, Carl attended his thirtieth high school reunion at a Holiday Inn in the Washington suburb of Bethesda on September 21, 1991. Carl didn't show until ten-thirty that night—fashionably two hours late. His attire included a trendy silk suit combined with socks that were each a different color. The women loved the touch. It made him vulnerable.

He'd been to an earlier pre-reunion party. His date for the night was Nancy Immler, who, at Montgomery Blair High, hadn't given him a second glance. Carl sat at a table of the school's 1961 standouts: Iris Benjamin, a local jazz singer; Lenny Levy, now a southern-California entrepreneur; Ron Oberman, a Columbia Records executive; and Brenda Rosenberg, who had married well. During the party, Carl showed off his still-formidable jitterbug with Bobbi Parzow. There were rumors of a postreunion after-hours party.

Carl wouldn't have wanted the night to end any other way.

APPENDIX A

Greensboro

The author and a research assistant visited Greensboro, North Carolina, in the fall of 1991 and early 1993 seeking out Jewish leaders who were active in either the Greensboro civil rights movement or who were advisers to B'nai B'rith between 1958 and 1960. We also spoke with as many Washington area AZA boys and BBG girls as we could find who traveled to B'nai B'rith conventions at that time. We also interviewed law enforcement officers and train enthusiasts in the Greensboro area. Finally, all the newspaper and other records available of the two daily newspapers in the city were checked for the summers of 1958, 1959, and 1960.

Leah Tannenbaum, a prominent Jewish leader in Greensboro, was given Carl's recollections of his night in Greensboro. She disputed the incident:

"It never took place. I worked in the civil rights movement in Greensboro in the sixties and was involved in getting that train station integrated. I would have heard about the incident Carl Bernstein described if it happened. There was only one Goldstein family in Greensboro at that time and they lived way out. They were not leaders in the Jewish community or bondspeople."

She continued, "The train route described in the book wouldn't have gone that way. It wouldn't have stopped or gone through Chapel Hill. His memory must be fuzzy. Maybe it happened in another town."

Mrs. Tannenbaum, who quizzed members of the Greensboro Jewish community, later wrote to the author, stating, "I have discussed this incident about which he wrote that supposedly happened in Greensboro, North Carolina, in the summer of 'sixty or 'sixty-one and *no one* [her emphasis] in any age group has *any* [her emphasis] memory of such an incident. I have called or seen in person ten or twelve persons who certainly would have been aware of such an incident and no one could enlighten me. I was particularly interested in the response of Mrs. Al Klein. She has been the adviser to BBG girls (and sometimes the AZA chapter also) for many years including those to which he alluded, and she was most definite that she would have known about this incident if it happened here. In fact she was appalled that this was in writing as there is no such record here."

Mrs. Tannenbaum concluded, "The Jewish congregation was certainly not as large at that time and surely one of us would have been aware of this happening."

Mrs. Al Klein, the Greensboro B'nai B'rith leader who was also sent a copy of Carl's account of his spontaneous civil rights, demonstration, wrote this to the author: "I've read Mr. Carl Bernstein's story several times. There are several things I'd question. My family and I and others took that trip from Washington many times. I have before me the old schedule of the *Southern Crescent*, as it was called, not the *Peach Queen* [as Carl referred to it in his book]. It is as follows, quoting from one of the old booklets in my possession: the train left Washington at eight-thirty A.M. It went through the following before coming to Greensboro—Alexandria, Culpeper, Charlottesville, Monroe, Lynchburg, Danville, Greensboro. It never came via Richmond or Chapel Hill. That took another line, coming from Durham to Greensboro to change. The *Peach Queen* is the Seaboard Line, that goes west from Greensboro to Hendersonville, which I took many times since I worked at the [B'nai B'rith] camps and also accompanied groups there. The Seaboard *Peach Queen* went on to Florida.

"I cannot understand why our advisors were not called, or Rabbi Asher, if Jewish help were needed. The Kleins were always notified if a BBYO question came up. I recall many incidents long before 1959–60, as our groups were organized in 1945–46 and both my children were leaders. I think Mr. Bernstein has his information a little twisted.

"I was in touch with a friend who is an attorney who checked the records about 1959–60. There has never been a bondswoman in Greensboro and no one by the name of Goldstein. Please inform Mr. Bernstein that his story needs more research."

Walter Burch, who today is the sheriff of Guilford County, which surrounds Greensboro, concurs that there never has been a bondswoman, Jewish or gentile, in the county. Burch, who was a Greensboro police dispatcher in the summers of 1958, 1959, and 1960, could not remember anything resembling Carl's tale.

Any racial incident that attracted "a large contingent of the Greensboro, North Carolina, police," as Carl put it, would have likely been picked up by one or both of the two Greensboro daily papers, which were chronicling all the news about the imminent civil rights revolution on the front page regularly at that time. The author, who read every page of both Greensboro dailies for June, July and August of 1958 through 1961, found no newspaper accounts of the train station demonstration. Abe D. Jones, an editor at the *Greensboro Daily News and Record*, and a member of the newspaper's staff since 1952, had no recollection of the event.

The distinguished civil rights historian William Chafe, of Duke University, was also contacted. Dr. Chafe, who researched in detail the genesis of the civil rights movement, with particular emphasis on Greensboro, had also never heard of the incident.

Two retired black railway employees were interviewed by the author. Both had worked at the Greensboro depot during that period. Each said that everyone else they'd known who'd been on the night shift had died. One, O. K. Dorsett, who was secretary-treasurer of the Brotherhood of Railway Clerks, said he'd "heard something" but that his hours were only during the day. The other, James R. Fuller, Sr., seventy-nine, worked "thirty-nine years at night for Southern Railroad. It must have happened on a night I had off . . . I heard a whiff of something. [Otherwise] there was no excitement, there was nothing. You know if there'd been more than a whiff, it would've been in the air—it would've been passed along."

Dorsett said it was not uncommon for whites to eat at the seventeen-seat horseshoe-shaped lunch counter when the white side was closed. According to Dorsett, white train crew members ate there often late at night. Caucasians, being the dominant culture of the times, would not have been turned away. A large group of white teenagers, while unusual, would not have been asked to leave, according to Dorsett.

The author, who interviewed several other AZA members who were active with Carl in 1960, could not find anyone who was present with Carl at the civil rights demonstration he wrote about in *Loyalties*. Also, the small room allotted for the seventeen-stool black eating area would have precluded a large "sit-in" demonstration, such as Carl described. He was also puzzled by the small size of the black luncheonette when he visited the former Greensboro train station. *Loyalties* was described by Carl's publisher, Simon and Schuster, on the flap of the dust jacket as "the same kind of meticulous investigation that led reviewers to call *All the President's Men* 'the greatest detective story of the century.' "

APPENDIX B

FOIA/CIA Inquiry

Washington, D.C. 20505

Bernard Yoh
Director of Communications
Accuracy in the Media, Inc.
1275 K Street, NW
Suite 1150
Washington, DC 20005

2 8 JUN 1988

Reference: F87-1239

Dear Mr. Yoh:

This letter concerns your 1 October 1987 Freedom of Information Act (FOIA) request for records pertaining to contacts between the late William Casey, former Director of Central Intelligence, and Bob Woodward, an employee of the Washington Post and author of the book "VEIL: The Secret Wars of the CIA, 1981-1987."

We are enclosing a document which lists all known contacts between Mr. Casey and Mr. Woodard. The contacts are arranged in chronological order, dating from 28 September 1983 to 3 May 1985, and the listing includes particulars about each contact. It has been necessary to redact some information from this document on the basis of FOIA exemptions (b)(3) and (b)(6); an explanation of these exemptions is also enclosed.

For your information, this compilation was created by the Agency when the subject of contacts between Mr. Casey and Mr. Woodward arose in connection with the publication of "VEIL." The compilation is as complete as possible, and is based on all available information. The information was assembled from the DCI's appointment and telephone logs, and from information held by the Office of Public Affairs.

The CIA official responsible for determinations made in the enclosed document is James R. Pittman, Information Review Officer for the Director of Central Intelligence. You have the right to appeal those decisions by addressing your appeal to the CIA Information Review Committee, in my care. Should you choose to do this, please explain the basis of your appeal.

Thank you for the patience you have extended during the time required for our completion of this response.

Sincerely,

John H. Wright
Information and Privacy Coordinator

Enclosures

28 September 1983	Woodward called on DCI at OEOB office.
27 October 1963	Woodward had dinner with DCI at his home to discuss ▮▮▮▮ briefing book.
11 January 1984	DCI hosted breakfast for Mr. Woodward and ▮▮▮ ▮▮▮ of The Washington Post; ▮▮▮▮ George Lauder, ▮▮▮▮▮▮ and ▮ ▮ in the DCI Dining Room, Hqs. to discuss the POST's upcoming series on Middle East terrorism.
12 April 1984	Woodward met with ▮▮▮▮ representatives to discuss ▮▮ prior to Woodward's trip there. George Lauder was present.
13 October 1984	DCI hosted breakfast for Mr. Woodward at his residence. George Lauder was present.
19 November 1984	Woodward met with Sporkin to discuss DCI. George Lauder was present.
12 December 1984	Woodward met with ▮▮▮▮▮ for a briefing ▮▮▮ prior to Woodward's possible visit to ▮▮▮▮▮▮ George Lauder was present.
17 December 1984	Woodward read ▮▮▮ version of CIA study ▮▮▮ at Headquarters.
21 March 1985	Woodward read DCI's autobiographical manuscript at Headquarters.
10 April 1985	Woodward met with Bob Gates to discuss analysis. George Lauder was present.
17 April 1985	Woodward rode on plane from Boston with DCI (Tufts speech).
1 May 1985	Woodward rode on plane from New York with DCI (Metropolitan Club of NYC).
3 May 1985	Woodward met with the DDCI to discuss allegations of conflict between himself and the DCI, as well as ▮▮▮▮ matters. George Lauder was present.

APPENDIX C

Carl Bernstein/Clark Clifford

Partial Transcript of *Larry King Live*, March 30, 1989

John Lofton: Good evening. John Lofton—how are you, sir?

Carl Bernstein: How did you get through? How did you find me? Once again . . .

JL: It's a Communist conspiracy, Carl.

CB: That I have noticed. You must have the secret.

Larry King: Go ahead, John. It's good to hear from you.

JL: Thank you, sir.

LK: Tell the people who you are, John.

JL: I write a column for the *Washington Times*.

LK: John is a well-known conservative columnist.

CB: And we have had many dealings during Watergate when John was defending the president.

LK: What's the question?

JL: But I'm not Deep Throat.

CB: Well, you say so.

JL: A couple of nights ago on National Public Radio, I heard you in an interview talking about your book, and you talked about a conversation you'd had with Clark Clifford, and you said that Clark Clifford told how he and President Truman manufactured a loyalty problem in this country so that Truman could gain reelection. I talked to Clark Clifford on the telephone today and he told me this: "I have never suggested that to Mr. Bernstein or anybody else anything like that."

He doesn't even recall talking to you, and he says he doesn't think that is why President Truman set up that program at all. So what were you talking about when you said Mr. Clifford planned this with Mr. Truman?

CB: Well, I'm right and you should see the notes and the memo of our conversation, and I'm sure that if Clark and I sat down that he would recall it and what he said. His exact words were: "Carl, I don't think there was a real loyalty problem in the country. A problem was being manufactured. As far as J. Edgar Hoover and some people on

226

Capitol Hill were concerned, there was a loyalty problem, but we didn't believe there was one."

And I'm sure Clark Clifford would have no problem recalling those words. But let me go on, John, because it's a fascinating story. The two most astonishing interviews that I have ever had in my life was with the treasurer of the Nixon reelection's committee, Hugh Sloan, when he sat there and told Bob Woodward and myself that John Mitchell, while attorney general of the United States, had controlled the secret fund that paid for the bugging of Watergate and other undercover activities against Nixon's opponents.

And the second astonishing interview in the thirty years I've been in this business was this interview that I described in great detail with Clark Clifford in his office. Mr. Clifford—and to his credit, I think Mr. Clifford was candid—he told me the origin of the loyalty order. He said to me: "Later on, some people were reconstructed." He said he didn't remember the exact mechanism of the loyalty order, but later on some people were reconstructed, and I looked at him and said, Mr. Clifford, can you give me some of their names. And he was silent . . .

JL: I don't want to monopolize the program.

LK: Sure, John.

JL: You say Mr. Clifford would not have any trouble recalling what he said. Well, I talked to him today, he doesn't even remember you interviewing him. But he made the point that even if you interviewed him, he couldn't have told you that because he says he does not believe that and that he, Mr. Clifford, had nothing to do with the loyalty program, that wasn't under his jurisdiction. Thus, he and President Truman couldn't have manufactured anything as you say.

LK: Carl, can we quickly clear up the Clifford matter?

CB: Well, it's fascinating because this whole thing reminds me of what happened when we wrote *The Final Days*. And that terrible scene when Nixon and Kissinger went down on their knees and nobody, including John Lofton, believed it was true. Here is this incredible scene where Clark Clifford makes one of the truly amazing revelations of our time to me, and Mr. Clifford, I'm sure, will remember that he had just returned from the funeral of the Algerian president. He set the scene for me. I was in his office and he said, "My own notion was that there were merely some incidents. My own feeling was there was not a serious loyalty problem." And he went into a long explanation of the history of the loyalty order and how Ramsey Clark had drafted it, how Ramsey's father—

LK: Any idea why he would deny it now?

CB: I think that if Clark called me on the telephone, he and I would straighten this out very quickly. I think that John Lofton has a kind of agenda, not dissimilar to John Lofton's agenda at the time of *The Final Days*. I don't think John even has any trouble with the truth of whatever is in here.

Excerpts from *Loyalties*, Chapter 24

"It was a political problem. [Carl's emphasis.] Truman was going to run in '48, and that was it."
For a minute my father continued to stare at the memo.
"Can you quote him?"
I nodded.
"He says it a few times," I noted. "He won't deny it . . ."

"My own notion was that there were merely some incidents," Clifford had told me. "My own feeling was there was not a serious loyalty problem. I felt the whole thing was being manufactured. We never had a serious discussion about a real loyalty problem."
He had met with the President every day, as his counsel. There had been a daily staff meeting at which the progress of the order (Truman's loyalty order #9835) was periodically discussed.
"I have the sensation that the President didn't attach fundamental importance to the so-called Communist scare. He thought it was a lot of baloney. But political pressures were such that he had to recognize it."

Clark Clifford's Call

Excerpts from Clark M. Clifford's call to the author on January 7, 1993, after reading the **Larry King Live** *transcript and chapter 24 of* **Loyalties***:*

Carl Bernstein's chapter is garbled. Certainly J. Edgar Hoover and Joe McCarthy may have tried to manufacture a "loyalty problem," but not President Truman or myself. That's one of the dumbest things I ever heard of. . . .

It's totally untrue that I said this. . . . It was J. Edgar Hoover who played almost a criminal role in that. He began the Communist scare. President Truman said to me that "I don't think our country is endangered from within, but from Russia . . . but [Carl's chapter] is perfectly dumb. I didn't say that. [President] Truman didn't go along with those who spoke of loyalty problems. My book [*Counsel to the President*] says that.

Mr. Clifford could not remember ever being interviewed by Carl Bernstein but said he had always felt "an obligation to speak to all writers and members of the press."

Excerpt from *Counsel to the President,* Clark Clifford's Memoirs, 1991

In response to a reporter's question—"Mr. President, do you think that the Capitol Hill spy scare is a red herring to divert public attention from inflation?"—he replied, "Yes, I do." . . . Over the next two weeks, reporters repeatedly pressed the President to retract or modify the phrase, but he refused, saying, "I am not going to back down on that because it is a fact, and I will prove it before the campaign is over. . . ."

He continued, in words that I [Clifford] had drafted: "I ought to know something about communism. I have been honored by its bitter enmity and its slanderous statements. . . . That is because I have been fighting communism not merely here where it is a contemptible minority in a land of freedom, but wherever it is a marching and menacing power in the world. The great danger to us does not come from communism in the United States. . . . The Democratic party is for free government and against communism. . . . There is nothing that the communists would like better than to weaken the liberal programs that are our shield against communism. . . ."

[Above excerpt is from Truman's speech in Oklahoma City, September 28, 1948.]

President Truman's reply defused the issue for the rest of the campaign.

CHAPTER NOTES

Chapter 1

1. The Geneva Community Hospital closed on August 31, 1991. A larger, more modern facility had opened outside the city, between Geneva and St. Charles, Illinois.

2. Bill Rathje's daughter, Suzanne, known in Wheaton as the "4-H Queen," and a childhood friend of Bob's, would marry John Block, a former secretary of agriculture and a Reagan cabinet member in the 1980s. Block was from nearby Galesburg, Illinois.

3. Wheaton's population in 1970 was just 32,800; by 1980 it had grown to 43,043. In 1991 the population was given as 46,300.

4. Barbara Simpson (formerly Barbara Wooley) is married to Craig Simpson, another Wheaton Community High School classmate.

5. Although a member of Glen Oak and later of Wheaton's Chicago Golf Club ("the first eighteen-hole course in America"), Al Woodward was never a country-club type according to Wheatonians. He was more at home in the Lions Club and at American Legion meetings where he was both a member and held offices.

6. *Atiba*, a name Sonny Kee began to use later in life, means "understanding." Kee's number, twenty-two, is one of the few ever retired at Wheaton High, such retirement being one of the ultimate honors accorded America's stellar athletes. Also of football interest: Red Grange, the legendary "galloping ghost," was a Wheaton High graduate.

7. The particular McDonald's in question was one of the first ten built in the United States after Ray Kroc began running the fast-food restaurant chain.

8. Kathy Middlekauff lived on West Street in Wheaton, about three and a half blocks from Bob's house on West Prairie Street.

9. Another small trauma occurred when Bob's house on West Prairie caught on fire during high school and the entire family lived in a motel for a week.

Chapter 2

1. The name was changed from Walkowitz when Carl's grandfather immigrated into the United States.

2. Al and Sylvia Bernstein would later have two daughters, Mary and Laura.

3. Besides the daughters of Richard Nixon, various children from branches of the Kennedy family sporadically attended the Pick Temple television show.

4. Ben Stein, Herbert Stein's son, is the well-known financial writer and actor who was featured in the film *Ferris Bueller's Day Off* and the TV series *The Wonder Years*. He was a speechwriter for Richard Nixon during the Nixon administration.

5. Carl, in his 1989 book, *Loyalties*, described Harvey Road as being one mile long, with one hundred houses. Convenient round numbers aside, Harvey Road is less than one-third of a mile long and contains forty-one homes. The Montgomery County Police Department verified the author's measure.

6. WTTG-5 is today part of the Fox television network and its studios are located in upper northwest Washington. The Raleigh Hotel has been torn down and replaced by a glass and concrete box of an office building.

7. According to a B'nai B'rith official in Richmond, Virginia, that would most likely have been Camp Blue Star, owned for years by the Popkin family. It is still used by B'nai B'rith groups from time to time. Carl later described a Camp Blue Star in Pennsylvania, but the author could trace no record of a camp under that name operated by B'nai B'rith in that state.

8. Carl says in *Loyalties* that the train broke down. A much more likely scenario is that the cars going to Hendersonville were uncoupled and then attached to the train going west.

9. *Loyalties*, a careless book, is full of silly errors that show Carl did not check the memory from which he was drawing his material. For instance, Carl wrote of being taken to RKO Keith's movie theater in Washington to see *High Noon* on his ninth birthday. *Peter Pan* was playing at RKO Keith's that day. *High Noon* was the feature at the Dupont Theatre.

10. Keyettes were the distaff side of the Key Club, which is a high school version of the Kiwanis Clubs of America.

11. Goldie Hawn was a sophomore when Carl was a senior. Her hint of thespian promise included parts in *Bye Bye Birdie* and *Li'l Abner*. Also of note, and graduating after Goldie, was Constance Yu-Hwa "Connie" Chung. Although the three may have attended school functions together, neither Carl, Goldie, or Connie were even fleeting high school friends. Chung did, however, gain national fame in 1973 and 1974 as a fledgling TV reporter by staking out Watergate defendants' homes—particularly H. R. Haldeman's—and shouting questions at them as they left or entered.

Chapter 3

1. Bob Woodward was a collector of antique postcards. It can be surmised

that the mysterious Lulu was a turn-of-the-century actress dressed in scanty attire.

2. One of the legends associated with Skull and Bones is that Bonesmen were supposed to leave a room if the phrase *Skull and Bones* was uttered by a nonmember. During his race for president in 1988, George Bush was sometimes heckled on his campaign by groups who yelled the forbidden words. The president-to-be pretended not to hear the dissidents. Bush's father was also a member, as is one of his sons, George W. Bush.

3. Acheson (Yale, 1915), who helped create both the Truman doctrine and the Marshall Plan, was sent to Paris with CIA official Charles "Chip" Bolen to explain the Cuba missile crisis to Charles de Gaulle. During and after World War II, Bolen served as a conduit for Yale men who wished to enter the intelligence community. Cole Porter is an example of the many creative people who have attended Yale. A sampling: Paul Newman, Jodie Foster, Dick Cavett, and Garry Trudeau, creator of *Doonesbury*.

4. The OSS was jokingly referred to as Oh So Secret" by Yale critics. Others, alluding to its recruitment from the elite secret societies, said the intelligence agency's initials stood for "Oh So Social."

5. Bob did his naval ROTC stint at Yale just in time. There were ninety-two naval ROTC men in Bob's 1965 graduating class. Two years later, with America's Vietnam activity at its zenith and the popularity of the war effort plummeting, Yale president Kingman Brewster called ROTC courses "of the trade school variety." The ROTC courses were changed from credit courses to noncredit and were considered extracurricular activities.

Chapter 4

1. Not to be confused with the present Duke Zeibert's. The original was on the ground floor and much more a "joint" than the tony power restaurant it is today.

2. Carl has said that, as dictationist, he took down the details of President John F. Kennedy's assassination on November 22, 1963. Carl remembered that his hands shook and he spelled hospital as "hospotol." The reporter phoning in the story was David Broder, now of the *Washington Post*.

3. The *Elizabeth Daily Journal* ceased publication in 1991.

4. Because of perceived rejection at the *Post*, Carl began peddling human-interest stories at the *Washingtonian* magazine in the late 1960s. A former staffer remembers them as "taxicab stories," although one, on Washington ABM missile sites, earned Carl "about $200."

Chapter 5

1. Bruce Smathers, the senator's son, was a 1965 classmate of Bob's.

2. The other vessels were the U.S.S. *Northampton* and later, the U.S.S. *Saipan*, although the *Saipan* was never fully finished. It was renamed the

Arlington, after the Virginia suburb where the Navy had a major radio communications tower. The *Northampton* alternated alert status with the *Wright.* It also had SIOP teams aboard. Adm. Stansfield Turner, the former director of the CIA, said in his memoir, *Secrecy and Democracy: The C.I.A. in Transition,* that he first met Bob Woodward in 1966. That would have been while Bob was assigned to the *Wright.* But when interviewed by the author, he said it was aboard the *Fox* in Long Beach, California. That would have been in 1968. The admiral said Bob reminded him of their meeting at a TV show in 1977. In his book, he thanked Bob Woodward profusely for being "kind enough to read several drafts and to provide advice on the act of writing books." Stansfield grew up in a suburb of Chicago near Bob's hometown.

3. Lyndon Johnson's presidential diary notes that "the helicopter passed an aircraft carrier with the men standing at attention." It is the author's conclusion from reading Johnson's diary at the Library of Congress in Washington that the president was unaware he was passing a "Presidential Command Ship." But then, it wasn't.

4. The *Wright* was decommissioned on May 27, 1970. The U.S. military had revamped its nuclear implementation system completely to the Pentagon, with the alternate site at Raven Rock, Pennsylvania. These were linked to a command site within Cheyenne Mountain in Colorado and to the Strategic Air Command in Omaha. This was done at the direction of Henry Kissinger, who told Robert McNamara in 1969 that SIOP was "flawed."

5. In *Yale,* on alumni magazine, there were frequent reports of Elihu sons being killed or wounded in Vietnam. This class of '65 alumni report in the periodical in 1967 may have contributed to Bob's misgivings about the war. It was written by Bob's fellow Book and Snake brother Shaun Byrnes, serving aboard the U.S.S. *Turner Joy* in the South China Sea: "I was critically wounded when one of our 5"/54 guns overheated and exploded. My plight only brings to my mind the thought, 'For God, for country, and for Yale.' That was one of the recurring ideas in my mind during those harsh first hours." Byrnes's 1965 class biography describes him as a Russian studies major whose after-college aspirations included an "intelligence" career. Byrnes probably got his wish. In 1990, according to a Yale alumni directory, he was "Deputy, State Department, Moscow, Soviet Union."

6. Kathy Woodward completed her education, getting a Ph.D. Today, as head of twentieth-century studies at the University of Wisconsin at Milwaukee, she is the author of two books and has edited four others. Her works, unlike Bob's, are scholarly, published by the University of Indiana Press in Bloomington.

7. Despite his friendship with Kissinger, Admiral Moorer, according to both the *New York Times* and the *Chicago Tribune,* was concerned about eased relations with mainland China. So much so that he ordered Navy officers to steal and copy documents that Kissinger was carrying to the mainland.

Chapter 6

1. Former naval intelligence chief Adm. Fritz Harflinger later denied letting the Ferre people use the Navy's printing presses. He did not refute the other charges.

2. The Pentagon's spy unit Task Force 157 was disbanded in 1977. Bob Woodward broke the story, which appeared on page one of the *Post*, on May 18th. Included in the story was the name of the cover corporation it operated under, the street address, the number of "free-lance" spies used, and some quotes from Adm. Thomas Moorer. Bob said he learned about Task Force 157 "as a reporter." Jerry Landauer died in 1981 at age forty-nine of a heart attack.

3. Tom Shales is the nationally syndicated television critic for the *Washington Post*.

4. In 1991, Bob Woodward sent Farquhar a twenty-year-old memo he had written relating to the Rap Brown stories. Across the top, he wrote, "Remember this? I do." Besides being a good politician, Bob Woodward is a skillful collector of memos, records and other long-forgotten paperwork. When he worked for the Maryland paper, he kept every issue and would stack them on the floor in his Washington apartment.

5. Wayne Morse also lived at the Watergate, although Bob's local angle for the Montgomery County paper was that he owned a farm in Poolesville, which was in the western part of the county.

Chapter 7

1. In December of 1992, Hersh wrote a revelatory story for *The New Yorker* about the contents of the tapes at the National Archives that contained conversations of Richard Nixon. While most newspapers ran the story on page one or extensively reported it, Bob Woodward personally saw that the news of Hersh's reporting ran as a short news item on page nine of the *Post*.

2. Robert Levey, also known as Bob Levey, today writes a daily column for the *Post* under the latter name.

3. Although Gerstein wasn't mentioned in the movie, his secretary had a decent role. She was played by Polly Holliday who went on to fame as the gum-chewing, wisecracking waitress Flo on the television series *Alice*. Dardis was played by the character actor Ned Beatty. Dardis was fearful he would be played by Mickey Rooney and made to look "a buffoon." Gerstein, whose last case in private practice was defending the actor Pee-wee Herman from indecent-exposure charges, died in 1992.

4. At one point, Bob complained that he was out of soap in his apartment and that he was showering using shampoo. Sussman took fifty cents out of petty cash and sent a copyboy out to purchase three bars of soap and gave them to the young reporter.

5. Deep Throat was named by Howard Simons, the *Post*'s managing editor. *Deep Throat*, a landmark pornographic movie of the early seventies, starred

Linda Lovelace and Harry Reems. Eventually, it reportedly took in about $35 million at the box office on a $40,000 production budget.

6. Page number refers to the Simon and Schuster trade hardback and the 1987 Touchstone paperback. Other editions are paginated differently.

7. Former *Washington Star* drama critic Emerson Beauchamp checked the 1972 city directory after reading the article and also found Bob's apartment to be number 617. He wrote a letter to the editor at the *Post* citing this source, but the letter was not printed. (Bob's other apartment where he allegedly contacted Deep Throat was at 901 Sixth Street, S.W. It is next to Arena Stage, a major regional theater, and across the street from several restaurants and hotels. Taxis are readily available.) Karlyn Barker sat outside Ben Bradlee's office with Bob the morning he was hired, waiting for a "final interview" by the *Post* editor. Barker began working at the newspaper on the same day.

Chapter 8

1. Marinis, now a Houston attorney, told the author he was asked for Watergate information by Bob but refused, citing attorney-client confidentiality. Buzhardt was a key source for Bob in the writing of *The Final Days*.

2. The story of the Ken Clawson Canuck letter was given to Bob and Carl by *Post* reporter Marilyn Berger. It should be noted that Clawson continued to deny authorship of the letter until his death in 1976.

3. When author Jim Hougan appeared on the *Today* show in 1984, he told host Bryant Gumbel that admiral and former CIA deputy chief Bobby Ray Inman was the person most likely to be Deep Throat. Inman called the program and said he wasn't even in Washington during the time of Watergate and couldn't have been a source to Bob. *Today* aired Inman's denial the morning after his call. Hougan dutifully rechecked his sources, determined that Inman had indeed been in Washington during that time and fired off a note to the show. His reaffirmation was never aired. Later, Hougan tracked down the former intelligence chief in Texas and confronted him. Inman admitted that he had been in Washington and then laughed at the success of his trick. Inman's resignation from the CIA in 1982 was another exclusive by Bob Woodward in the *Post*.

4. In 1992, during a twentieth-anniversary program on Watergate, Mike Wallace of CBS said he believed Deep Throat was L. Patrick Gray III, former acting FBI director. While Gray is a former naval officer and did live near Bob once, the theory doesn't hold. Bob and Carl's byline file shows seven stories written about Gray between 1973 and 1976, none of them positive. When Gray was trying to get approved as FBI director, Bob and Carl used a quote from Jack Anderson that described him as "a political hatchet man for Richard Nixon." And in 1976 Bob broke a story charging that Gray, while acting as director, authorized burglaries by the bureau in order to prevent terrorism. Gray was forced to respond through his attorney that he "did nothing illegal."

5. Snyder and Obst later became bitter enemies when Obst bolted to

Random House. Ironically, David Obst also represented John Dean for his book *Blind Ambition*. Lynda Obst, David's former wife, produced *This Is My Life*, a film directed by Carl Bernstein's former wife Nora Ephron in 1992.

6. All weather information was checked in both the *Washington Post* and *New York Times* and then cross-checked with the National Oceanic and Atmospheric Administration in Rockville, Maryland, which keeps an hour-by-hour record of precipitation at all three Washington-area airports as well as keeping three-hour temperature readings. McLean, Virginia, and the Hay-Adams Hotel are both less than six miles from National Airport.

7. The ads in the paper were cross-checked against the phone book. All theaters were advertising that day. Also, see "Scaring Off the Sex Films" by Tom Shales on the front page of the Style Section of the *Washington Post* on November 27, 1972.

8. According to G. Gordon Liddy, Bob even got a ribald story Liddy told wrong. On page 238 of *APM*, Bob described Liddy telling a story of a bomb that was accidently dropped on the red-light district of a Mexican border town by the U.S. military. Liddy told the author he said it was a guided missile that had gone astray. "There's a lot of difference between a bomb dropped from an airplane and a guided missile," Liddy said. The Watergate "silence is dollars" figure sometimes referred to Carl and Bob as "tuffy and stuffy."

9. The *Post* was the third choice in the preliminary voting. Bradlee disqualified himself from the Pulitzer jury (he was on the advisory board), and the paper won on a later ballot. Bob was incensed that he and Carl didn't get the prize personally and rushed into Bradlee's office when he first heard the news. Bradlee convinced him that it was better for all that the award go to the paper.

10. All book money numbers are gross figures. Contractual shares of ancillary rights to the publisher and agent's fees would reduce Bob and Carl's net dollar amount.

Chapter 9

1. Charles Colson wrote an interoffice White House memo to Ken Clawson on October 2, 1972, claiming that presidential candidate George McGovern had heard about the remark and said that "based on Katharine Graham's figure, there's no danger of that." After Richard Nixon resigned, a group of *Post* staffers, including Bob and Carl, gifted the *Post* owner with an antique wringer, which she kept on display in her office.

2. The speech was made to the National Film Theatre in London, England, on February 25, 1986.

3. Edward Kennedy, the Democratic senator from Massachusetts, was an extra in the Library of Congress scene.

4. The box office numbers are Motion Picture Association of America statistics.

Chapter 10

1. For a more complete accounting of Carl's and John Paisley's attendance at group sex parties, consult the book *Widows* by Joseph Trento, Susan Trento and William Corson.

2. When Francie Barnard was replaced by a male colleague in Washington and told to show him around, she sued for sexual discrimination. The *Star-Telegram* settled out of court for $20,000.

3. The remnants of the communications center were still there in late 1991.

4. Brenner has been a reporter for *New York, Vanity Fair*, and the *New Yorker* magazines.

5. In 1989, Bob and Carl had a change of heart. "It wasn't essential," Bob told *TV Guide*, "and I think the older Bernstein and the older Woodward would not have included that."

6. Kissinger's interview was thirty minutes long, with witnesses present. Carl and Bob jointly interviewed Kissinger on a "not for attribution" promise. Bob Woodward telephoned Ollie Atkins to ask for an interview, but when Bob found out the photographer lived in the Virginia suburbs, he decided to do it by telephone. Carl interviewed his boyhood friend Ben Stein. Stephen Bull told the author he had never met or talked with Bob or Carl, but was interviewed for the book by Scott Armstrong.

7. In December of 1975, less than six months after he allegedly wouldn't grant Bob an interview, he talked to Bob, helping to give him and Carl an exclusive. Speaking to Bob by phone from Belgium, he confirmed he had spoken to Gerald Ford prior to Nixon's resignation about a pardon for the president. Bob and Carl, in a front-page story on December 18, 1975, quoted unnamed sources in reporting Haig received assurances from Ford that Nixon would be pardoned after Ford took office. During his frequent trips back to Washington, Haig stayed at the Jefferson, a small exclusive hotel next to the *Washington Post*.

Chapter 11

1. The court later awarded her $1,500 per month.

2. Robert Liotta, a divorce attorney who has represented many journalists, also represented Carl in his divorce from Nora Ephron. Other divorce clients have included Kitty Kelley and former CBS-television legal correspondent Fred Graham.

3. Liz Smith's column was subscribed to, but not printed by, the *Washington Post*. "I used to say they bought it for Ben and Sally to read," the columnist joked, referring to the *Post* editor and his wife. Carl Bernstein has made Liz Smith part of his media-interview repertoire for the past decade, railing against her salary. According to Carl, "Liz Smith is worth six Pulitzer Prize winners to *Newsday* or the *New York Daily News*. Well, this is an absurd situation."

Chapter 12

1. Scott Armstrong told the author that they each took *five* justices (adding a deceased or retired justice to each writer's scope of investigation).

2. *The Brethren* was 444 pages, not including its index.

3. Kester later would become the lead counsel for the *Washington Post*, a position he still held in 1993.

Chapter 13

1. Most colleges won't release transcripts of grades. But many will verify years of attendance. The student can always get a transcript to show to an employer. The *Post* now checks a prospective staff member's education.

2. Later Janet told one friend that she left Toledo because of a break-up with a boyfriend. Janet claimed he had started to date a blonde. Her boyfriend's name, Janet said, was Jimmy.

3. In December of 1979, Janet began to share an apartment with Elsa Walsh, which, coincidentally, was in Carl Bernstein's apartment building, the Ontario. Janet would tell some people that Carl Bernstein had offered her a job at ABC. Bob Woodward would later marry Elsa Walsh, his third wife, in 1989. But he didn't start living with her until after the Janet Cooke scandal.

4. When the story ran, Howard Simons insisted Janet sleep in a place other than her apartment for two days, fearing for her safety.

5. Hinckley, on March 30, 1981, shot Ronald Reagan in front of the Washington Hilton hotel. Hinckley said he did it to impress Jodie Foster, with whom he was infatuated.

Chapter 14

1. Asner had played the head of a fictional TV newsroom in the TV series *The Mary Tyler Moore Show*. Later he played the editor of a newspaper in another series, *Lou Grant*. Robert Walden, an actor on the second show, patterned his role as a reporter after Carl Bernstein. Ironically, he had played Donald Segretti in the film *All the President's Men*.

2. Watson took with him a small entourage of assistants. One, with ABC for less than a year, was Katherine Couric, a recent graduate from the University of Virginia. At CNN, she got enough on-air exposure to put her on a fast track, eventually rising to her present position as anchor on the *Today* show. Watson returned to ABC after one year at CNN and again became head of its Washington bureau in 1985.

3. While Carl was at ABC, Frank Reynolds died. Carl "pitched a fit," according to one observer, because he wasn't allowed on the "first bus" of two that were taking ABC employees to the newsman's funeral service.

4. At one point, Carl reportedly suggested deposing Paramount Pictures chief Barry Diller, but was talked out of it.

5. Actor Mandy Patinkin was originally signed to play Mark/Carl and conferred with Carl Bernstein on how he should play him. He was later scratched due to lack of "star power."

Chapter 15

1. Carl, in a deposition, said his recollection was .09, but written police records show .11.

2. Carl was required to attend a six-session alcohol awareness program as a result of his arrest.

3. Musgrave's attorneys told the court they had thirty-nine witnesses ready to testify, including fifteen medical doctors. To alleviate the pain in his lower back, Musgrave purchased a $4,145 Craftmatic bed, but did not make any payments beyond the initial deposit. A default judgment was entered against him by Household Finance Corporation on February 8, 1985.

4. Musgrave filed a second suit for injuries received in another auto accident when he was "rear-ended" on September 6, 1987. His suit against Carl and ABC Television had been settled four months earlier in May of 1987 and the results sealed. Dr. Musgrave was reported to have "emerged smiling."

5. Musgrave's attorneys were going to contend that Carl was under the influence of Xanax, a tranquilizer, which is said to accelerate the effects of alcohol.

6. In an unusual arrangement, Bob and Carl agreed to supply "tips" to Sam Dash, chief counsel for the Senate Watergate Committee. Supposedly, they were to get nothing in return for supplying the committee with information.

Chapter 16

1. While Carl Bernstein never wrote for the program, he was linked romantically with its female star Betty Thomas.

2. Bob's salary at the *Post* was $45,000 in 1982.

3. William Tavoulareas wrote a 1986 book about his *Post* battle, *Fighting Back*. The *Post* got an advance copy of the manuscript from Simon and Schuster (Bob's publisher) and protested. Simon and Schuster refused to halt publication.

4. While Bob was always a substitute, John Belushi was a terrific football player. He was "all-state, honorable mention," captain of the team and homecoming king. His ambition when he graduated from high school was to become, eventually, a football coach.

5. Judy Belushi's remembrance of her husband, *Samurai Widow*, was published in 1990. Because Bob Woodward did not return records and documents that she had lent him, Judy Belushi said she was forced to refer to *Wired* to check her recollection of dates and times. Her memoir was first titled *Don't Look Back in Anger*.

Chapter 17

1. Murphy, when contacted by the author, was adamant that Bob had used "the press-pass phrase," which was run in the *Miami Herald* and other Knight-Ridder papers. He said Bob had never asked for a retraction or correction.

2. Perhaps it is nit-picking to note that neither Martin nor the *Times* revealed that he was a 1965 Yale English major like Bob or that Martin's near parallel career includes journalism stints at *Newsweek* and CBS television. Martin's naval duty after Yale found him aboard a ship in the Gulf of Tonkin in 1968 near the *Fox*. Certainly Martin, in an interview with the author, was convincing in saying it was a coincidence, that he never knew Bob at Yale and didn't become aware that he was a classmate until years later.

Chapter 18

1. In an eccentric casting move designed to grab publicity, Carl Bernstein was asked by the film's producers to portray Jack Nicholson. In one of his best decisions of the 1980s, Carl declined the role.

2. At that time AT&T's advertising tag line to encourage long-distance calling was "reach out and touch someone."

3. Elsa Walsh became involved in a controversy two weeks later when the drug lord's attorney signed her into a jail as a lawyer instead of a reporter in order for her to get an exclusive interview. As she left the prison, she scratched out *attorney* and wrote *reporter*. Elsa would not have been allowed in as a reporter. She faced no sanctions; the attorney was censured.

Chapter 19

1. Bob dedicated *The Commanders* to Snyder and Ben Bradlee.

2. When he was stationed in San Diego in the late 1960s, Bob spent several weekends in Las Vegas gambling. He plays high-stakes poker today regularly with a group of reporters and politicians. In one such 1980s game, television newsman David Brinkley reportedly lost $2,000 in less than an hour.

3. Although it was reported in several newspapers that Alexander Haig received $2.5 million, informed sources said it was closer to $600,000.

Chapter 20

1. After Jacob Weisberg's critical essay, *Post* writers (including Bob Woodward) who had been edited by Alice Mayhew took part in a letter-writing campaign to *The New Republic*. Gossip columnists took delight in publishing Sally Quinn's wistful lament, which began, "Just who is this Jacob Weisberg anyway?"

2. Simon and Schuster released the Bob Woodward and David Broder forty-thousand-word series as a book in 1992. It did not become a bestseller,

ending Bob's string of six straight number one bestselling books, although perhaps it should not be counted.

3. Like Bob, Sam Skinner grew up in Wheaton, Illinois. Bob purchased his first pair of ice skates from the Skinner family's sporting goods store.

4. A sample of Mr. McCarry's prose (*Second Sight*, 1991): "If life were baseball, I'd gladly swap every agent the Outfit now has in the field for the entire staff of the *Washington Post* and throw in a hundred future draft choices from Yale and Princeton."

A NOTE ON SOURCES

The author began contacting and interviewing people for this book in March of 1991. Many were interviewed several times, some during periods as long as two hours.

This book, like most biographies, relies on many types of sources, not just interviews. Other sources include letters; more than a thousand newspaper, newsletter and magazine articles; books; court proceedings and police records; high school and college yearbooks; transcripts of radio and television programs; inquiries made under the Freedom of Information Act and confidential information supplied by individuals.

In researching this biography, the author and a researcher visited Wheaton, Illinois; Greensboro, North Carolina; New Haven, Connecticut; Norfolk, Virginia; New York City, New York; Silver Spring, Maryland, and Washington, D.C.

The author is grateful for the many courtesies and resources available in these libraries: the Library of Congress and the Washingtonia collection of the Martin Luther King library, Washington, D.C.; Rockville Public Library, Montgomery County, Maryland; Wheaton and Geneva (Illinois) public libraries; Sterling Library at Yale University, New Haven, Connecticut; Norfolk Public Library, Norfolk, Virginia; the Greensboro library, Greensboro, North Carolina; and the New York City Public Library, New York.

As in any biography, conversations recounted by subjects that took place many years ago may not be verbatim; however, the essence of that conversation is accurately communicated to the reader by the author. If the author has described the weather a certain way, the reader can be sure the author checked climate conditions in as many sources as were available. If the interior or exterior of a building is described, the reader can be assured the author was there or had it described in detail by someone who was there.

The author's normal interviewing method was to take notes as unobtrusively as possible. Whenever possible after the interview the notes would be immediately transcribed and entered into a computer. The author also kept a journal in which he detailed many of the events that related to the writing of this book.

BIBLIOGRAPHY

Note: Although all books that are relevant to *Deep Truth* are listed, all newspaper and magazine articles, columns, reviews, etc., are not. That is because thousands were consulted. Thus, only primary sources are named here.

In researching this biography, every bylined article by Carl Bernstein while he worked at the *Washington Post* between 1966 and 1976 was read, as were all of Bob Woodward's bylined articles between 1971 and 1992. The author and an assistant also scanned every page of *Time, Newsweek* and *U.S. News and World Report* between June of 1972 and 1992. Every issue between June 17, 1972, and December 31, 1976, of the *Washington Post* was read (on microfilm). Every issue of the *Yale Alumni Monthly* between 1966 and 1989 was also consulted.

Books

Agee, Philip. *Inside the Company.* New York: Stonehill, 1975.

Apple, Jr., R. W. *The White House Transcripts.* New York: Bantam Books, 1974.

Bates, Stephen. *If No News, Send Rumors.* New York: Henry Holt, 1989.

Belushi, Judith Jacklin. *Samurai Widow.* New York: Carroll & Graf Publishers, 1990.

Ben-Veniste, Richard, and George Frampton, Jr. *Stonewall.* New York: Simon and Schuster, 1977.

Bernstein, Carl. *Loyalties.* New York: Simon and Schuster, 1989.

Bernstein, Carl, and Bob Woodward. *All the President's Men.* New York: Simon and Schuster, 1974.

Bok, Sissela. *Lying: Moral Choice in Public and Private Life.* New York: Pantheon, 1978.

Bray, Howard. *The Pillars of the Post.* New York: W. W. Norton & Co., 1980.

Breckinridge, Scott. *The C.I.A. and the Intelligence Community.* Boulder, Colo.: Westview Press, 1986.

Cheshire, Maxine, and John Greenya. *Maxine Cheshire Reporter.* Boston: Houghton Mifflin, 1978.

Christenson, Terry. *Reel Politics.* New York: Basil Blackwell, 1987.

Colodny, Len and Robert Gettlin. *Silent Coup.* New York: St. Martin's, 1991.

Corson, William R., and Susan B. and Joseph J. Trento. *Widows.* New York: Crown Publishers, 1989.

Cose, Ellis. *The Press.* New York: William Morrow and Company, 1989.

Crouse, Timothy. *The Boys on the Bus*. New York: Random House, 1972.

Dash, Samuel. *Chief Counsel*. New York: Random House, 1976.

Davis, Deborah. *Katharine the Great*. Bethesda, Md.: National Press, 1979.

Downie, Jr., Leonard. *The New Muckrakers*. Washington, D.C.: The New Republic Book Company, 1976.

Downs, Robert. *Books That Changed America*. New York: Macmillan, 1970.

Doyle, James. *Not Above the Law, The Battles of Watergate Prosecutors Cox and Jaworski*. New York: William Morrow and Company, 1977.

Ephron, Nora. *Crazy Salad*. New York: Alfred A. Knopf, 1975.

_____. *Heartburn*. New York: Alfred A. Knopf, 1983.

_____. *Scribble Scribble*. New York: Alfred A. Knopf, 1978.

Goldman, William. *Adventures in the Screen Trade*. New York: Warner Books, 1983.

Goulden, Joseph. *The Death Merchant*. New York: Simon and Schuster, 1984.

Haig, Alexander M., with Charles McCarry. *Inner Circles*. New York: Warner Books, 1992.

Haldeman, H. R., with Joseph DiMona. *The Ends of Power*. New York: Times Books, 1978.

Halperin, Morton H. *Nuclear Fallacy*. Cambridge, Mass.: Ballinger Publishing, 1987.

Herken, Gregg. *Counsels of War*. New York: Alfred A. Knopf, 1985.

Holt, Patricia. *The Bug in the Martini Olive and Other True Cases from the Files of Hal Lipset, Private Eye*. Boston: Little, Brown and Company, 1991.

Hoyt, Ken, and Frances Spatz Leighton. *Drunk Before Noon*. Englewood Cliffs, N.J.: Prentice Hall, 1979.

Isaacson, Walter, and Evan Thomas. *The Wise Men: Six Friends and the World They Made*. New York: Simon and Schuster, 1986.

Lasky, Victor. *It Didn't Start with Watergate*. New York: The Dial Press, 1977.

Liddy, G. Gordon. *Will*. New York: St. Martin's Paperbacks, 1991.

Maas, Peter. *Manhunt*. New York: Random House, 1986.

Magruder, Jeb Stuart. *An American Life*. New York: Atheneum, 1974.

Mankiewicz, Frank. *Perfectly Clear*. New York: Quadrangle, The New York Times Book Company, 1973.

_____. *U.S. v. Richard M. Nixon: The Final Crisis*. New York: Ballantine Books, 1975.

McCarry, Charles. *Second Sight*. New York: Dutton, 1991.

McClendon, Sarah. *My Eight Presidents*. New York: Wyden Books, 1978.

McLendon, Winzola. *Martha, the Life of Martha Mitchell*. New York: Ballantine Books, 1980.

Meese III, Edwin. *With Reagan*. Washington, D.C.: Regnery Gateway, 1992.

Mencher, Melvin. *News Reporting and Writing*. Dubuque, Ia.: Wm. C. Brown, 1991.

Mollenhoff, Clark. *The Man Who Pardoned Nixon*. New York: St. Martin's Press, 1976.

Moore, John. *Jane's American Fighting Ships of the 20th Century*. New York: Mallard Press, 1991.

Moore, Robin. *The Washington Connection*. New York: Condor, 1977.

Morris, Roger, *Haig: The General's Progress*. New York: Playboy Press, 1982.

Newhouse, John. *War and Peace in the Nuclear Age*. New York: Alfred A. Knopf, 1989.

O'Toole, G. J. A. *Honorable Treachery*. New York: Atlantic Monthly Press, 1991.

Persico, Joseph E. *Casey*. New York: Viking Penguin, 1990.

Price, Raymond. *With Nixon*. New York: Viking, 1977.

Pringle, Peter, and William Arkin. *S.I.O.P.: The Secret U.S. Plan for Nuclear War*. New York: W. W. Norton, 1983.

Quinn, Sally. *We're Going to Make You a Star*. New York: Simon and Schuster, 1975.

Ranelagh, John. *The Agency*. New York: Simon and Schuster, 1986.

Reagan, Nancy. *My Turn*. New York: Random House, 1989.

Roberts, Chalmers M. *The Washington Post: The First 100 Years*. Boston: Houghton Mifflin, 1977.

Safire, William. *Safire's Washington*. New York: Times Books, 1980.

Schwed, Peter. *Turning the Pages*. New York: Macmillan, 1984.

Slansky, Paul. *The Clothes Have No Emperor*. New York: Fireside, 1989.

Sussman, Barry. *The Great Cover-Up: Nixon and the Scandal of Watergate*. New York: Thomas Y. Crowell, 1974.

Thomas, Evan. *The Man to See*. New York: Simon and Schuster, 1991.

Turner, Stansfield. *Secrecy and Democracy: The CIA in Transition*. Boston: Houghton Mifflin, 1985.

Volkman, Ernest. *Warriors of the Night*. New York: William Morrow and Company, 1985.

Washington Post. *The Fall of a President*. New York: Dell Publishing Co., 1974.

———. *The Presidential Transcripts*. New York: Dell Publishing Co., 1974.

Weinberg, Arthur and Lila. *The Muckrakers*. New York: Simon and Schuster, 1961.

Weinberg, Steve. *Trade Secrets of Washington Journalists*. Washington: Acropolis Books Ltd., 1981.

White, Theodore H. *Breach of Faith*. New York: Atheneum Publisher's, Reader's Digest Press, 1975.

Williams, Juan. *Eyes on the Prize: America's Civil Rights Years, 1954–1965*. New York: Viking Penguin, 1987.

Winks, Robin W. *Cloak & Gown*. New York: William Morrow and Company, 1987.

Woodward, Bob. *The Commanders*. New York: Simon and Schuster, 1991.

———. *Veil: The Secret Wars of the CIA 1981–1987*. New York: Simon and Schuster, 1987.

———. *Wired*. New York: Simon and Schuster, 1984.

Woodward, Bob, and Scott Armstrong. *The Brethren*. New York: Simon and Schuster, 1979.

Woodward, Bob, and Carl Bernstein. *The Final Days*. New York: Simon and Schuster, 1976.

Woodward, Bob, and David Broder. *The Man Who Would Be President: Dan Quayle.* New York: Simon and Schuster, 1992.

Woodward, Kathleen. *Aging and Its Discontents.* Bloomington and Indianapolis: Indiana University Press, 1991.

Periodicals and Newspapers

"*All the President's Men* Brings Central DuPage Hospital $20,000." *Wheaton Journal* (14 Apr. 1976).

"Carl Bernstein Goes to Court." *Washingtonian* (Apr. 1987).

"Covering Watergate: Success and Backlash." *Time* (8 July 1974).

"Did Woodward Cross the Line?" *Washingtonian* (July 1984).

"Does Al Need a Plumber?" *Washingtonian* (Apr. 1982).

"The Dynamic Duo." *Newsweek* (30 Oct. 1972).

"The Furor Over the Book." *Newsweek* (12 Apr. 1976).

"Further Notes on Nixon's Downfall." *Time* (5 Apr. 1976).

"A Gallery of the Guilty." *Time* (13 Jan. 1975).

"Haig's Departure Should Plug a Lot of Leaks." *Washingtonian* (Aug. 1982).

"Hell Hath No Fury Like Nora." *Washingtonian* (Mar. 1983).

"The Honorable Tradition of Deep Throat Reporting." *Maclean's* (9 June 1980).

"How *Washington Post* and the Pulitzer Board Were Duped." *Wall Street Journal* (17 Apr. 1981).

"Instant Replay on Nixon." *Time* (12 Apr. 1976).

"Judge Refuses to Halt Belushi Book." *Publisher's Weekly* (15 June 1984).

"More on Deep Throat." *Washingtonian* (Dec. 1975).

"Operation Watergate." *Newsweek* (3 July 1972).

"A Rap With . . . All the President's Men." *Senior Scholastic* (13 Jan. 1976).

"Scandal Sleuth Voted for Nixon." *Chicago Tribune* (20 June 1974).

"Supersnoop." *Time* (6 Jan. 1975).

"The Supersnoopers on the Road." *People* (28 July 1974).

"Watergate on Film." *Time* (29 Mar. 1976).

" 'Woodstein' Meets 'Deep Throat.' " *Time* (22 Apr. 1974).

"Woodstein's Retreat." *Time* (30 Dec. 1974).

"Woodward Interview." *L'Express* (16 Oct. 1988).

Abrams, Garry. "Just Another Star Turn." *Los Angeles Times* (17 Feb. 1989).

Alpern, David. "Now It's 'Deep Book.' " *Time* (27 Feb. 1978).

———. "The Dark Side of the Clown." *Newsweek* (24 May 1984).

———. "The Man Who Wasn't There." *Newsweek* (5 Oct. 1987).

Armstrong, Scott, and Bob Woodward. "The Evidence of *The Brethren:* An Exchange." *New York Review of Books* (12 June 1980).

Bachrach, Judy. "Politicians Are the Lousiest Lovers." *Washington* (Dec. 1981).

Balamaci, Marilyn, "Behind Our Lines." *People* (20 May 1991).

Belushi, Judith Jacklin. "A Widow's Dismay." *People* (11 June 1984).

Benjamin, Milton. "On His Own." *Washington Post.* (26 June 1982).

Bennetts, Leslie. "Nora's Arc." *Vanity Fair* (Feb. 1992).

Bernstein, Carl. "The C.I.A. and the Media." *Rolling Stone* (20 Oct. 1977).

———. "The Holy Alliance." *Time* (24 Feb. 1992).

———. "The Idiot Culture." *The New Republic* (8 June 1992).

———. "Yes, Kids, There Is Life After High School." *Washington Post* (3 June 1979).

Berry, John. "History on the Run." *Library Journal* (1 May 1976).

Beveridge, George. "Woodstein on Criticism of 'Final Days.' " *Washington Star* (11 Apr. 1976).

Bonafede, Dom. "Dancing on the Grave?" *Washingtonian* (May 1976).

Branch, Taylor. "Gagging on Deep Throat." *Esquire* (Nov. 1976).

Brill, Steven. "Back on the Beat with Woodward and Bernstein." *Esquire* (Dec. 1983).

Cameron, Julie. "A Portrait of the Watergate Reporters as a Young, Rich, Sexy, Glamorous Star." *Washingtonian* (May 1974).

Carmody, Diedre. "Nixon Book Stirs Furor." New York Times News Service (4 Apr. 1976).

Carroll, Jerry. "Looking for a New Story." *San Francisco Chronicle* (28 June 1974).

Claffey, Charles. "Going Forward by Going Back." *Boston Globe* (12 Apr. 1989).

Clifford, Garry. "Woodward and Armstrong Show Little Brotherly Love." *People* (21 Jan. 1980).

Cocks, Jay. "Overdosing on Bad Dreams." *Time* (11 June 1984).

Cohen, Richard. "Being Bernstein's Buddy." *Washington Post* (28 Mar. 1976).

Conconi, Chuck. "Divorce With a Heartburn Clause." *Washington Post* (28 June 1985).

Cooke, Janet. "Jimmy's World." *Washington Post* (28 Sept. 1980).

———. "Memories of a Violent Marriage." *Toledo Blade* (11 Mar. 1979).

———. "Stuffy Image Bothers Opera Booster." *Toledo Blade* (1 Oct. 1979).

Cuniberti, Betty. "Woodward's High-Wire Act." *Los Angeles Times* (2 Oct. 1987).

Dahlin, Richard. "The Final Days." *Publisher's Weekly* (26 Apr. 1976).

DeParle, Jason. "From Low-Level Aides to Power Wielders." *New York Times* (7 Feb. 1992).

Doyle, James, and Ronald Sarro. "Hunt, While Aiding Colson . . ." *Washington Star* (23 June 1972).

Easton, Nina, and Jack Mathews. "Another Chapter in the Strange Odyssey of 'Wired.' " *Los Angeles Times* (11 Apr. 1989).

Elder, Sharon. "All the Journalist's Men." *Yale* (May 1988).

Ephron, Nora. "Having a Baby After 35." *New York Times Magazine* (26 Nov. 1978).

Epstein, Edward Jay. "Did the Press Uncover Watergate?" *Commentary* (July 1976).

Fischer, Mary. "Bob Woodward Trashed." *People* (23 July 1984).

Goldman, John. "Fraudulent Pulitzer Winner Faced Opposition." *Los Angeles Times* (15 Apr. 1981).

Gorey, Hays. "Woodward on the Record—Sort Of." *Time* (3 May 1976).

Green, Bill. "Janet's World." *Washington Post* (19 Apr. 1981).

Greenfield, Jeff. "The Yale Plot to Run America." *M* (May 1992).

Grossberger, Lewis. "The Pulitzer Prize Hoax." *Newsweek* (27 Apr. 1981).

Guzior, Betsey. "Vietnam Wall Comes to DuPage." *Wheaton Journal* (16 Aug. 1991).

Hall, Carla. "Avon Buys 'Brethren.' " *Washington Post* (21 Dec. 1979).

———. "Scribes du Jour." *Washington Post* (6 Feb. 1980).

Harrington, Walt. "He Went From Watergate to Heartburn." *Washington Post Magazine* (19 Mar. 1989).

Hedges, Michael. " 'Silent Coup' Authors Cite Vendetta." *Washington Times* (25 Nov. 1991).

Hirschberg, Lynn. "The Controversy Over *Wired.*" *Rolling Stone* (27 Sept. 1984).

Hougan, Jim. "Peeking Under Bob Woodward's Veil." *City Paper* (30 Oct. 1987).

Huey, John. "It Was Basic Reporting." *Atlanta Constitution* (16 July 1974).

Ireland, Doug. "Knock on Woodward." *The Village Voice* (4 June 1991).

Janeway, Michael. "Woodward & Bernstein's Long Goodbye." *The Atlantic* (June 1976).

Johnson, Haynes. "Entering a Week of Watergate Revisited." *Washington Post* (27 Mar. 1976).

Kaplan, Paul. "The Claxa Caper." *Washingtonian* (July 1976).

Kaylin, Lucy. "The Ironman Resteth." *GQ* (Jan. 1991).

Kester, John. "Breaking Confidences." *Washingtonian* (Feb. 1980).

Kowet, Don. "Bob Woodward Reconsidered." *Washington Times* (15 June 1992).

———. "Post's Smear of Tower." *Washington Times* (7 Mar. 1989).

Landauer, Jerry. "Politicos in Blue: The Navy in Puerto Rico." *Wall Street Journal* (3 Nov. 1972).

Langdon, Dolly. "Can Carl Bernstein Handle Deep Troth." *People* (14 Jan. 1980).

———. "The Search for John Belushi." *People* (11 June 1984).

Lasky, Victor. "The Woodstein Ripoff." *A.I.M. Report* (Oct. 1976).

———. "Woodward Unveiled." *A.I.M. Report* (May 1988).

Lavin, Cheryl. "Falling Star." *Chicago Tribune Magazine* (23 May 1982).

Leaky, Michael. "The Nixon Drama." *TV Guide* (28 Oct. 1989).

Lee, Richard. "Carl Bernstein: Life After Watergate." *Washingtonian* (July 1981).

———. "If Bob Woodward had been editor of the *Post* during Watergate, it would have never been reported." *Washingtonian* (July 1980).

———. "The Return of Sally Quinn." *Washingtonian* (Aug. 1986).

Lerner, Max. "Writing 'Hot History.' " *Saturday Review* (29 May 1976).

Lewis, Alfred. "5 Held in Plot to Bug." *Washington Post* (18 June 1972).

Lewis, Anthony. "Supreme Court Confidential." *New York Review of Books* (7 Feb. 1980).

Limpert, Jack. "Deep Into Deep Throat." *Washingtonian* (Aug. 1974).

_____. "Deep Throat: If It Isn't Tricia It Must Be." *Washingtonian* (June 1974).

Lukas, J. Anthony. "Playboy Interview: Bob Woodward." *Playboy* (May 1989).

Lyman, Rick. " 'Pulp Trash' Says Aykroyd." *Philadelphia Inquirer* (7 June 1984).

Mann, Charles. "The Book of Carl." *Fame* (Mar. 1989).

Mann, James. "Deep Throat: An Institutional Analysis." *Atlantic Monthly* (May 1992).

Mano, D. Keith. "David Obst, Super Agent." *Esquire* (Nov. 1976).

Maraniss, David. "*Post* Reporter's Pulitzer Prize Is Withdrawn." *Washington Post* (16 Apr. 1981).

Matusow, Barbara. "He's Not Bradlee." *Washingtonian* (July 1988).

_____. "Woodward Strikes Again." *Washingtonian* (Sept. 1987).

Maxa, Rudy. "The Book on Bradlee." *Washingtonian* (May 1987).

_____. "Watergate's Bad Boy." *Washingtonian* (Jan. 1984).

Maxa, Rudy, and Laura Elliott. "The Journalism Establishment." *Washingtonian* (Dec. 1983).

McGrath, Ellie. "A Fraud in the Pulitzers." *Time* (27 Apr. 1981).

Murphy, Ryan P. "Lifting the Veil." *Miami Herald* (27 Sept. 1992).

Nobile, Philip. "Carl Bernstein Learns the ABC's of TV News." *New York* (26 May 1980).

Pack, Robert. "Inside the *Post*." *Washingtonian* (Dec. 1982).

Perry, James. "CBS Tries to Hire Bob Woodward." *Wall Street Journal* (5 Apr. 1982).

Pooley, Eric. "This Boy's Life." *New York* (13 Feb. 1989).

Powers, Charles. "Opposites Who Attracted the Pulitzer Prize." *Los Angeles Times* (28 June 1974).

Randolph, Eleanor. "Boost Seen for Investigative Journalism." *Washington Post* (6 Oct. 1987).

Reed, Rex. "How the Big Fish Was Caught." *New York Daily News* (4 Apr. 1976).

Sansing, John. "Janet Cooke: Who Is She?" *Washingtonian* (June 1981).

_____. "Woodward Ousted as Head of Metro." *Washingtonian* (Jan. 1982).

Sauer, Mark. "Woodward Has No Apologies." *Wheaton Journal* (17 June 1984).

Schwartz, Tony. "Playboy Interview: Carl Bernstein." *Playboy* (Sept. 1986).

Segers, Frank. "Pix Profanity for Whole Family." *Variety* (3 Mar. 1976).

Seib, Charles. "The Furor Over *The Final Days*." *Washington Post* (7 May 1976).

Seymore, James. "Hollywood Stays in Hollywood." *Washingtonian* (Apr. 1975).

Shafer, Jack. "14 or 15 Reasons Why I Trust Bob Woodward." *City Paper* (24 Apr. 1992).

Shales, Tom. "Scaring Off the Sex Films." *Washington Post* (27 Nov. 1972).

————. "Watching the Media Watch the Stars." *Washington Post* (5 Apr. 1976).

Shales, Tom, Zito, Tom, and Jeannette Smyth. "When Worlds Collide: Lights! Cameras! Egos!" *Washington Post* (11 Apr. 1976).

Shapiro, Martin. "Character Assassination by Attribution." *Wall Street Journal* (12 Dec. 1979).

Sheff, David. "Playboy Interview: Liz Smith." *Playboy* (May 1992).

Sherman, Norman. " 'Who the Hell Was That?' 'He's the Editor of the *Post*.' 'Jesus, I Thought He Was Your Bookie.' " *Washingtonian* (July 1974).

Sherrill, Robert. "Did Woodward Lie?' *Charleston Gazette* (4 Aug. 1991).

Sniffen, Michael. "David and Ed Rip That Book." *New York Post* (3 Apr. 1976).

Solnik, Claude. "From Pulitzer Hoax to Paris Housewife." *Manhattan Spirit* (27 Aug. 1991).

Stanford, Phil. "Watergate Revisited." *Columbia Journalism Review* (Mar.–Apr. 1986).

Thompson, Toby. "Red-Diaper Bernstein." *Vanity Fair* (Mar. 1989).

Tyler, Patrick, and Lewis Simons. " 'Jimmy' Episode Evokes Outrage." *Washington Post* (17 Apr. 1981).

Unger, Craig. "Twisting in the ABC Wind." *New York* (20 Apr. 1981).

Van, Jon. "The Watergate Reporters—No Time to Shop." *Chicago Tribune* (23 June 1974).

Viorst, Judith. "Katharine Graham is a better publisher than her husband, Phil . . ." *Washingtonian* (Sept. 1967).

von Hoffman, Nicholas. "Journalism and the C.I.A." *Washington Post* (5 Oct. 1977).

Weinberg, Steve. "The Kitty Kelley Syndrome." *Columbia Journalism Review* (July–Aug. 1991).

————. "The Secret Sharer." *Mother Jones* (May–June 1992).

————. "Was Nixon Duped? Did Woodward Lie?' *Columbia Journalism Review* (Nov.–Dec. 1991).

White, Jean. "Only Woodward Knew for Sure." *Washington Post* (14 June 1974).

Woodward, Bob. "Haig Reportedly Believes He Was Set Up." *Washington Post* (30 June 1982).

————. "Meetings' Notes Show the Unvarnished Haig." *Washington Post* (18 Feb. 1982).

————. "Pentagon to Abolish Secret Spy Unit." *Washington Post* (18 May 1977).

Radio and Television

"Bob Woodward and Carl Bernstein." NBC Television: *Meet the Press* (18 Apr. 1976).

"Carl Bernstein Interview." CBS Television: *Nightwatch* (4 Apr. 1989).

"Carl Bernstein Interviewed." CBS Television: *Morning News* (28 Mar. 1989).

"Carl Bernstein Interviewed." CNN Cable: *Larry King Live* (30 Mar. 1989).

"Carl Bernstein Profiled." CNBC-TV (23 Mar. 1992).
"An Interview With Carl Bernstein." ABC Television: *Good Morning America* (27 Mar. 1989).
"Interview With Carl Bernstein."WTOP Radio (15 Apr. 1989).
"That (Expletive Deleted) Newspaper." CBS Television: *60 Minutes* (4 Aug. 1974).
"What About Bill Casey?" CBS Television: *60 Minutes* (27 Sept. 1987).
"What's News, What's Not." CNN: *Crossfire* (29 Apr. 1991).
"Woodward and Bernstein: Watergate Revisited." ABC Television: *Nightline* (17 June 1982).
"Woodward or Casey—*Veil*." ABC Television: *Nightline* (1 Oct. 1987).

Feature and Television Films

All the President's Men Warner Brothers, 1976.
The Final Days. ABC Television, 1989.
Heartburn. Paramount Pictures, 1986.
Summer of Judgment. PBS Television, 1983.
Wired. Taurus Entertainment, 1989.

Litigation

Carl Bernstein v. Nora Ephron, Superior Court of the District of Columbia, 1984.
Carol Honsa Bernstein v. Carl M. Bernstein, Superior Court of the District of Columbia, 1972.
District of Columbia v. Carl Bernstein, Superior Court of the District of Columbia, Criminal Division, 1983.
Frances Barnard Woodward v. Robert U. Woodward, Superior Court of the District of Columbia, 1979.
Franklyn Musgrave et al. v. Carl Bernstein et al., Superior Court of the District of Columbia, 1984.
Judith Jacklin Belushi v. Bob Woodward and Simon and Schuster, Superior Court of the District of Columbia, 1984.
Household Finance v. Franklyn Musgrave, Superior Court of the District of Columbia, 1985.
Mildred Lockridge, James Archie, Jr., R. Calvin Lockridge v. The Washington Post, Donald Graham, Benjamin C. Bradlee, Meg Greenfield, Howard Simon [sic], Robert U. Woodward, Milton Coleman, Janet Cooke, Superior Court of the District of Columbia, 1981.
Nora Ephron v. Carl Bernstein, Supreme Court of the State of New York, 1980.

INTERVIEWS

The following are on-the-record interviews of people who consented to having their names revealed in this book. Many did—particularly those in the intelligence field or those currently employed by the *Washington Post* or in the Washington press corps. The interviews are divided into categories, and in a few instances, a name may appear in several areas. A number in parentheses after a name denotes the number of interviews, if more than one, conducted with that person.

Bob's Childhood: Kathleen Woodward (2), Chuck Krueger, Sonny Kee, Albie Harris, Elease Ware, Craig Simpson (2), Tim Fitzsimons, Johnny Knox, Paul Chummers (3), Barbara Wooley Simpson (2), Steve Matson (2). Two were confidential.

Carl's Childhood: Iris Benjamin, Pick Temple, Gene Daumit, Gay Gerson, Rita Callen-Westlieb, Bruce Fingerhut, Philip Berg, Martha Gray, Alan Akman, Allan Goldberg, Jerry Akman, Mike Nahan, Barbara "Bobbi" Parzow, Marty Stein, Linda Saperstein-Baggish, Alan Schlaifer, Sylvia Wubnig, Brenda Rosenberg-Kramer, Ben Stein. Four were confidential.

Bob at Yale: Robin Winks, Richard B. Sewall, Jim Jalenak, Terry P. Ellsworth, Tom Marinis, Kathleen Woodward, Tom Mankiewicz, Jonathan Leader, James Wood, Scott Armstrong. Two were confidential.

Carl at the Washington Star: Jerry O'Leary, Emerson Beauchamp, John Sherwood, Jim Doyle. Three were confidential.

Greensboro, North Carolina: Ken Eisenberg, O. K. Dorsett, Leah Tannenbaum, Min Klein, Walter Burch, Bill Stern, William Chafe and two others confidential.

Bob's Navy Career: Roger Sullivan, David Juarin (2), Frank Corley (Rear Admiral, U.S.N., retired), Bill Brinkmann (Captain, U.S.N.), Glenn Bates (Commander, U.S.N., retired), Richard Copaken, Esq., Frank Romanick (Captain, U.S.N., retired), Jeremy Clark, Thomas Moorer (Admiral, U.S.N., retired), Stansfield Turner (Admiral, U.S.N., retired), Kathleen Woodward, Jim Arrison (Captain, U.S.N., retired), Jack Dempsey. Six were confidential.

Carl in New York: Liz Smith, Gil Spencer, Marie Brenner, Kurt Andersen, Chen Sam. Two were confidential.

Bob at the Sentinel: David C. Bartlett, Roger Farquhar (2), and one confidential.

Present and Former Washington Post *Staffers:* Ron Kessler, Barry Sussman, Ben Cason, John "Jack" Lemmon, Michael Kernan, Tom Sherwood, Barbara Feinman, Scott Armstrong, Chuck Conconi, Steve Nearman, Gary Arnold, Tom Grubisich, Rudy Maxa, David A. Jewell. Three were confidential.

B'nai B'rith: Donna Ostrower, Julie Greenwald.

The Nixon White House: Stephen Bull, Mike Karem, Dewey Clower, Andrew Combe, Jack Brennan, G. Gordon Liddy, Ben Stein. Four were confidential.

Others: Judy Belushi Pisano, Les Kripman, Roger Morris, Bob Gettlin (2), Edward Katz, M.D., Francie Barnard (2), Barbara Matusow, Jack Limpert, Sarah McClendon, Jim Hougan, Robert Fink, Norma Hayman, Len Colodny, Peter Nye, John Kester, Esq., Sophia Casey (2), Ted Pedas, Steve Weinberg, Clark M. Clifford, John Lofton, Bill Murphy, Andy Miller, Ryan Murphy, John Strauchs, Larry Sulc, Robert Feder, M.D., and seven other sources who asked not to be named.

ACKNOWLEDGMENTS

This book could not have been completed without the support of the many people and organizations who helped me find articles and records or who supplied otherwise unobtainable material. In particular, the men and women in the intelligence community who confirmed much of the military information within these covers will always be remembered. As usual, Brenda Nicely Atkins was always on hand for proofing and editing at all hours. And thanks to the following, who contributed greatly in helping this book reach the reader: Accuracy in Media, The Nathan Hale Institute, The Motion Picture Association of America, B'nai B'rith, The National Archives, National Oceanic and Atmospheric Administration, Scott and Stringfellow Investment Corp., the U.S. Naval Museum in Washington, the "Gnats" and the Vienna Toastmasters, who helped more than they'll ever know.

And these people: Florence Sessoms, Gwen and David Swinburne, Bill and Susan Dalton, Renie Freedman, Julie Bedell, Dr. Susan Huck, Ann Tutt, Joseph Goulden, Jack Limpert, Pat Hughes, Joseph Zanetti, Compton S. Jones, Betty Cole Dukert, Shang Patterson, Benno Gerson, Kim Eisler, G. Gordon Liddy, Jacqueline Mashin, Jim and Ginny Gustafson, Robert Nelson, Ph.D., and Susan Williams.

Finally, a big thanks to all the people at Birch Lane Press, particularly my editor, Bruce Shostak, who was with me and there for me, every step along the way.

Index